THE
SELF-SUFFICIENT
HOUSE

THE SELF-SUFFICIENT HOUSE

FRANK COFFEE

HOLT, RINEHART AND WINSTON   🦉   **NEW YORK**

Copyright © 1981 by Frank Coffee
All rights reserved, including the right to
reproduce this book or portions thereof in any form.
Published by Holt, Rinehart and Winston,
383 Madison Avenue, New York, New York 10017.
Published simultaneously in Canada by
Holt, Rinehart and Winston of Canada, Limited.

Library of Congress Cataloging in Publication Data
Coffee, Frank.
    The self-sufficient house.
    Bibliography: p.
    Includes index.
    1. Dwellings—Environmental engineering.
    2. Dwellings—Energy conservation. I. Title.
TH4812.C63   696   80-13434
ISBN Hardcover: 0-03-053611-1
ISBN Paperback: 0-03-059171-6
First Edition

Designer: Amy Hill
Printed in the United States of America

CONTENTS

THREE
HEATING AND COOLING   55

FOUR
GENERATING YOUR OWN ELECTRICITY   143

THE
SELF-SUFFICIENT
HOUSE

INTRODUCTION

If you're looking for a guide to "agrarian independence," you've picked up the wrong book. You won't find anything in these pages about living off the land. Nor does this volume advocate a retreat to candle power and the pit privy. We respect the pioneer spirit, but rather than repudiating technology, our vision of self-sufficiency embraces all those ecologically acceptable alternative systems of water supply, waste disposal, heating, cooling, and generating electricity that, out of choice or necessity, can make a house not only energy efficient but protractedly autonomous—while still allowing all the usual creature comforts.

The operative word here is *house.* Whether a suburban or rural residence, a primary or vacation home, there's much that can be done to make that house largely self-sufficient—from incorporating passive solar design and superior insulation to installing a wood stove and harnessing the wind. The aim of this book is to provide you with the essential knowledge of those systems that can get you out from under the psychological and economic pressures of an uncertain energy supply and spiraling utility charges, which are becoming a threat to home ownership.

Many of the alternative systems presented, such as wastewater recycling and fuel cells, represent advanced technologies. But we also consider such basic systems of autonomous living as septic tanks and cisterns. If you are building a new home instead of retrofitting an older one, and in a rural area rather than close to the city, so much the better.

For most would-be homeowners, it's no longer just the problem of scraping together the mortgage payments, but meeting the escalating costs of operating the house that causes sleepless nights. The average homeowner's combined oil, gas, and electric bill doubled between 1973 and 1979 and now exceeds $3,000 per year. Self-sufficiency can put a lid on the cost of utilities and make you feel you have some control over your destiny.

Where power from a utility is not accessible (in rural areas it can cost up to $10,000 per mile to have electricity brought in) or where water is in short supply, a measure of self-sufficiency in the form of wind power or water recycling can make the difference between building or not building. It can open up tracts of land for construction where the extension of sewer lines is not economically feasible or where soil with poor permeability makes a conventional septic tank and absorption field unacceptable.

Developed land, with access to electric power and sometimes to water and sewer mains, has become depressingly expensive. But if you build for self-sufficiency, you can laugh at the developers as well as at the utility companies. While the initial costs of self-sufficiency, for a wind energy conversion system, say, or a private water supply system, are not cheap, the trade-offs increasingly favor self-sufficiency.

There are many "perfect" locations that are going begging because the nearest power line is several miles away or the land has been classified as unacceptable for septic systems. For the same price you might pay for a quarter-acre or less in suburbia, you might find a 10-acre tract in an outlying area because, for one or more of the reasons just cited, the developers aren't interested in it. In the same Virginia county, we've seen sewered sites listed at $18,000 per acre, nonsewered sites listed at $9,000 per acre, and otherwise comparable nonsewered, nonpercable-soil sites listed at just over $2,000 per acre. You can buy a lot of self-sufficiency for $16,000!

We're not suggesting that a totally autonomous house is for everyone, nor would it always be desirable where centralized servicing is available. If an umbilical can be stretched to a power grid or gas supply line at reasonable cost, the convenience of a central system may be preferable to an alternative on-site system—even one that insulates you from an uncertain energy future. Nothing beats the convenience of an unlimited source of electricity or piped-in natural gas—and, as will be seen, there are plenty of ways you can cut down on the heating and cooling loads through foresight at the early planning stages to keep within an energy budget. But several states have barred new natural-gas tap-ins. And self-sufficiency is being forced upon other homeowners by the spread of county-imposed moratoriums on sewer and water-service hookups.

Maybe you have access to electricity, but not to a sewer main. Or you would like to shut off the oil burner and turn to wood heating, but don't know whether you would be better off with a wood stove or a multi-fuel furnace. You may not even know that there are furnaces that can switch from one fuel to another—from oil to wood, for example. You might be plagued by a balky septic system and want to know how you can upgrade it. Or you might want to learn more about solar heating and be less confused by the conflicting claims that are being made for it. If so, you've picked up the *right* book.

Not every alternative presented in these pages represents an economical trade-off. You may discover, however, the one system that makes it possible for you to build on a particular piece of land and escape from the city or from a characterless subdivision of ticky-tacky houses.

You'll find that we're not overly enthusiastic about some of the energy alternatives that others are applauding. We would like to see active solar heating downplayed in favor of passive solar heating. New government studies show that passive solar design provides more useful solar energy than flat-plate collector systems and is more cost effective and less complex. There's a whole series of energy-saving steps that should be given a higher priority than active solar space heating.

We give no coverage to the generation of methane gas to fire a stove, water heater, or furnace. A methane digester needs manure and other organic wastes in quantities that are available only on farms with horses or cows and other animals—and, a daily muck-handling routine you probably wouldn't care to be saddled with. Most of the methane digesters of which we have personal knowledge haven't worked very well, and the reliability of digesters has not yet been proved.

We have also consciously avoided the "beer can" approach to self-sufficiency. If you want to read about rooftop solar collectors made from recycled beer and soda cans, or Savonius-type wind machines made from oil drums, you'll have to go to other sources, such as *The Mother Earth News* and *Alternative Sources of Energy*. We don't mean to downgrade those two estimable publications, but our approach here has been to go largely with off-the-shelf hardware rather than to take the total do-it-yourself route. We not only mention specific products but provide the address of the manufacturer in the Product Source List beginning on page 193.

For continuing topical coverage of the hardware of self-sufficiency, *Popular Science* does the best job of any of the many energy- and construction-related publications we read regularly. Another magazine that gives excellent, though less frequent, coverage in such areas of self-sufficiency as waste treatment and wood heating is Blair & Ketchum's *Country Journal*. Though it is oriented toward a New England audience, we can recommend it to readers everywhere, without reservation.

Regulations and standards for everything from developing a water supply system to installing a solar water heater may differ from one jurisdiction to the next. In some counties you may encounter building and/or zoning codes that do not recognize the desirability of a change to such "radical" housing designs as geodesic domes and earth-sheltered structures, however energy efficient they may be. Nor do existing sanitary codes always accommodate the newer, nonpolluting methods of on-site sewage treatment, such as aerobic equipment. But with the sheer numbers of families who are seeking a lifestyle of greater self-sufficiency and want to avoid dependence upon a thin line of oil tankers from mostly unfriendly countries, the momentum for change is everywhere.

One of the best examples of what this book is about is the Ouroboros South Project, an ongoing learning experiment in autonomous living and low-impact technology conceived and built by the Environmental Design class of Dennis Holloway, an associate professor of architecture at the University of Minnesota. The house, built on university property near Rosemount, Minnesota, is a full-scale working dwelling, and one of the first to combine energy-conserving experiments with "gentle" architecture. Ouroboros (pronounced ōr-ō-bōr-ōs) was a mythical serpent that survived and regenerated itself by eating its own tail, thereby achieving a state of complete self-sufficiency.

The three-level, 2,000-square-foot house is essentially a post-and-beam salt-box design, with 50 percent of the south-facing wall glassed to capture the heat of the sun during the winter months. A trapezoid-shaped roof slopes to the rear, minimizing the impact of the prevailing north winds. Earth berms on the north, east, and west walls, plus a sod-covered roof, pre-

An ongoing project of the
School of Architecture of
the University of Minnesota,
the Ouroboros house is
designed to be totally self-
sufficient, with no
umbilicals to the usual
public utilities. *R. Scott Geddy
and Tom Foley, Ouroboros South
Project*

Earth-berming on three sides and a sod cover on the low-angled, trapezoid-shaped roof minimize the effect of the prevailing winter winds. Windows up near the roofline provide natural
ventilation in the warmer months. *R. Scott Geddy and Tom Foley, Ouroboros South Project*

The south face of the Ouroboros house includes large windows and an attached greenhouse for passive solar heating. Water-filled drums in the greenhouse absorb solar heat during the day and reradiate it to the greenhouse at night. *R. Scott Geddy and Tom Foley, Ouroboros South Project*

vent excessive heat loss in winter or heat gain in summer. In the winter, the low-angled roof collects snow atop the sod for added insulation. A row of trees to the northwest of the house breaks the force of the prevailing winter winds.

Fiberglas insulation is used throughout the house above grade, with up to 9½ inches of insulation in the roof and walls. Below grade, a combination of polystyrene and Fiberglas is used. A greenhouse, with 300 square feet of floor area, abuts the southeast face of the house. It is capable of heating up to 100° F. by direct solar gain in the dead of winter and passing heat to the interior of the house. Liquid-type solar collectors cover the south-facing roof and gather heat for space heating and domestic hot water.

Electricity is provided by a wind generator with a peak output of 3 kw at a wind speed of 25 mph. Any excess electricity is dumped via resistive heating into the heat-storage tanks used by the solar collectors. The two systems, solar and wind, complement each other, particularly since periods of high wind usually occur during

cloudy weather. A wood stove provides auxiliary heating.

Natural air conditioning is built into the house. Vents just below the north roofline are opened to draw cool air in at night during the warmer months and exhaust accumulated heat from inside the house through vents in the south wall. Roof overhangs shield the large expanse of south-facing glass and other windows from the direct summer sun.

The autonomous features also include a dry composting toilet, which minimizes domestic water usage and produces fertilizer for the greenhouse and garden by breaking down human and kitchen wastes through aerobic action. Further water saving is achieved through the use of flow-restricting devices on the faucets and showerhead.

Another house from which you might draw inspiration is an experimental unit built by the National Aeronautics and Space Administration (NASA) at the Langley Research Center in Hampton, Virginia. Applying spinoffs from the space program to the down-to-earth

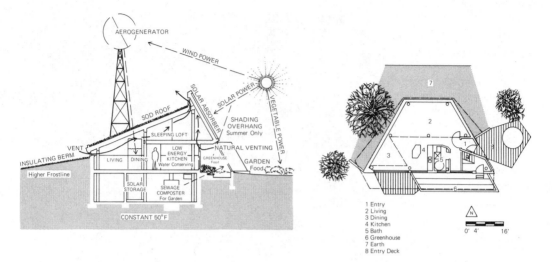

Elevation and floor plan of the Ouroboros House. *Ouroboros South Project, University of Minnesota*

The NASA Tech House is not autonomous, but it boasts solar and other energy efficiencies that reduce by two-thirds its electrical demand over conventional houses with the same floor area; plus a water-recycling system and flow-restricting devices that cut fresh water needs in half. *National Aeronautics and Space Administration*

problems of energy-efficient residential design, the NASA Technology Utilization House, or Tech House, consumes only about one-third the electricity and one-half the water of a comparably sized conventional house occupied by a family of four. It incorporates solar heating, a groundwater-assisted heat pump (which also provides central air conditioning), an energy-engineered fireplace, area temperature controls, roll-down thermal shutters, fire-resistant construction, a wastewater recycler, emergency lighting that runs off a battery charged by solar cells, three bedrooms, two bathrooms, and an attached garage into a design that could be built commercially for approximately $55,000 (in 1979 dollars) on an existing lot.

Tech House is a single-level structure of contemporary design, comprised of two square modules connected by a flat-roofed, skylighted foyer flanked at the front and rear by double-doored entry vestibules, which act as airlocks to prevent the escape of large amounts of heated or cooled air when people enter or leave the house. Each module features a distinctive pitched roofline to maximize exposure of roof-mounted solar collectors to the sun's rays.

Any homebuilder would do well to apply the sort of planning that went into Tech House. One of the first steps was to determine the house's energy-consumption requirements and how they could be reduced. Before ground was broken, different systems and products, from doors and insulating materials to commodes and solar collectors, were analyzed to determine which would be the most energy efficient and cost effective. A system or product was considered cost effective if its added initial cost plus 10 percent interest per year could be returned to the buyer

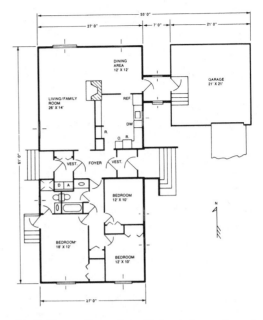

Tech House floor plan. *National Aeronautics and Space Administration*

through energy or other savings over its service life expectancy. NASA's Tech House team estimated that over a twenty-year period the equipment and materials in Tech House, properly installed, could bring about reductions in utility charges for heating, cooling, and water that would exceed their cost by some $23,000 at today's rates.

It should be pointed out that energy-conserving homes are most efficient when carefully designed to fit specific sites with their particular characteristics and natural resources, including orientation to the sun and prevailing winds. Obviously, if you live in the woods and and don't have an unobstructed southern exposure, solar power is out. But then, you have access to wood, one of the most economical alternate-energy resources. In a mountainous area, you may also have access to a tumbling stream that could be tapped for a small-scale hydroelectric system to provide all the electricity (the most versatile energy form) you need for heating and other purposes. In an exposed, hilly area, you might want to consider an earth-sheltered house.

One of the best examples of a house designed to provide liberation from rising utility costs in a mountainous area is Crowell House, in the Green Mountains of Vermont. This is a small house set into the side of a large hill, with 18 inches of earth covering the roof. Only the south face of the house is exposed. Heat is captured in the fall, winter, and spring by direct solar gain. The low-arcing sun strikes an interior rear wall of concrete, which is insulated from the earth behind it, and solar heat is absorbed in its mass. At night the heat is reradiated to the living space. During sunless periods in the coldest months, the temperature of the concrete wall never drops below 50° F., the temperature of the earth below the frost line. Two wood-burning stoves are available for auxiliary heating. Water is supplied, without pumps, from hillside springs. Electricity for lighting and refrigeration is provided by wind power, an abundant local resource.

Another excellent example of self-sufficiency in a harsh winter environment is located in the northeast corner of Minnesota, on Sawbill Lake. Frank and Mary Ellen Hansen and their son Carl, the owners and operators of Sawbill Canoe Outfitters, have made a concerted effort at self-sufficiency in an environmentally delicate area. Their house is a 50-foot-diameter geodesic dome, erected by the Hansens and The Big Outdoors People (one of the major dome kit manufacturers and builders), with over 2,800 square feet of usable floor area on two levels. With the dome's decrease in the ratio of floor space to exterior surface area, and by improved air circulation through the elimination of corners with dead-air space, the dome is at least 35 percent more efficient to heat and cool than a conventional structure of equal floor area.

The house is far from power lines, so electricity is provided by a 2,000-watt Dunlite wind generator, backed up by a 3-kw diesel-fueled generator. The problem of waste handling is met with a Clivus Multrum composting toilet. The primary fuel source for heating the Hansen residence is wood, burned in a Jøtul radiant stove and a Monogram heat circulator. The water supply system includes a 900-gallon storage tank to minimize energy-inefficient short cyclings of the pump while providing stable water pressure. A low-flow showerhead reduces the amount of water heated and used.

Self-sufficiency is its own reward. But keep in mind, too, that there is a tax credit of up to $4,000 for homebuilders and homeowners who install an alternate-energy device that taps a "renewable energy source." This includes solar, geothermal, and wind energy conversion systems. Adopted under the National Energy Act of 1978, the tax credit applies to systems installed after April 19, 1977, in both newly constructed and older homes, and extends through December 31, 1985. Application is to a primary residence only, not a vacation home.

For devices that use a renewable energy source, the tax credit, initially 30 percent of the first $2,000, plus 20 percent of the next $8,000 spent on the implementing hardware and its installation, was liberalized in 1980 to 40 percent of the first $10,000. This means that if you install a wind energy conversion system, and it costs you $6,500 total, you have a tax credit of $2,600 coming to you. Do not confuse a tax credit with a tax deduction. A credit is much better than a deduction.

It comes off the top and is subtracted dollar for dollar from the tax liability. The net cost of the wind system, therefore, is only $3,900.

Unused credits may be carried forward until 1987 and should be claimed on IRS Form 5695. IRS publication 903, *Energy Credits for Individuals,* spells out the details. Wood stoves and passive heating systems that are structurally part of the house are excluded from coverage. Amendments that would bring them within the provisions of the tax law have been proposed, however. If you have any doubts, check with your local IRS office to see whether or not the alternate-energy installation you may be considering is covered.

There's another tax credit for energy conservation achieved through adding insulation, installing storm doors and windows, putting in an automatic clock thermostat, and substituting a more efficient burner for gas- and oil-fueled heating systems. This tax credit, 15 percent of the first $2,000 of qualifying energy-con-servation expenditures for a maximum tax credit of $300, applies only to houses that were substantially completed before April 20, 1977.

Most states also have introduced energy-related tax breaks, from sales tax exemptions on the hardware to property tax relief for homeowners who install solar and other alternate-energy systems. Be sure to check them out at tax time. The National Solar Heating and Cooling Information Center, Box 1607, Rockville, Maryland 20850, will provide you with a rundown of state and local financial incentives that can ease your conversion to solar or other alternate-energy systems.

Don't hold us or the manufacturers to the prices quoted in this book. We have strived to be as accurate and up to date as possible, but with inflation pummeling the dollar, there are bound to be changes between the time of the writing of this book and your reading it. Such changes, however, should only emphasize the need to secure a more self-sufficient future.

ONE

PRIVATE WATER
SUPPLY SYSTEMS

GROUNDWATER

Of all the fresh water in the world, less than 3 percent of it, excluding polar ice, is found on the surface of the earth—in the form of ponds, lakes, rivers, and the like. The rest—better than 97 percent—is groundwater, found in saturated strata of largely sedimentary rock at varying depths beneath the earth's surface.

Most groundwater, having been filtered by the underground formations through which it passes, is chemically and bacteriologically safer than surface water today. It is the preferred source of supply for domestic uses when installing a private water system beyond the reaches of a city water main. There are other alternatives, which will be discussed, but in most cases a private water supply system will mean a well, pump, pressure/storage tank, and the accessories needed to operate the system automatically.

Beyond the public mains—and, in many localities, as a supplement to beat water shortages—the private water system is as essential to 1980s' lifestyles as it was when homesteading was the fashion.

It also is often more economical today to install and maintain a private water supply system than it is to pay the accelerating piping and operating costs of a central system, such as one offered by a rural water district.

In a region of adequate rainfall and favorable geology, locating groundwater is no great challenge. There is *some* water beneath the earth's surface almost everywhere—hence the "success" of so many water dowsers. Left unanswered by the man with the forked stick, however, are such all-important questions as: How much water? At what depth? How free is it to come into a well? Can it come in fast enough to make the well useful for a continuing water supply? What about its quality?

Contrary to what most dowsers (also known as diviners and water witches) would have you believe, groundwater does not commonly occur in veins, domes, or underground rivers. Groundwater is the water that, under the pull of gravity, seeps downward below the root zone and fills the pores, joints, and crevices in underground rock. In the language of the

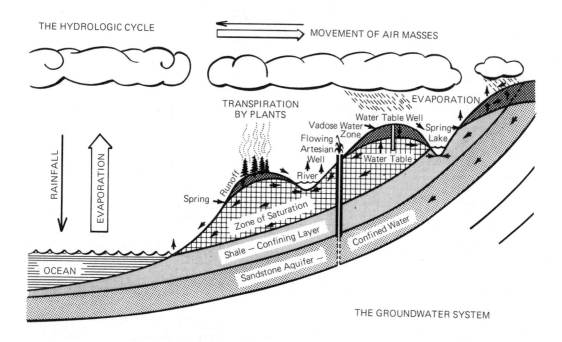

THE HYDROLOGIC CYCLE

MOVEMENT OF AIR MASSES

TRANSPIRATION BY PLANTS

EVAPORATION

Water Table Well

Vadose Water Zone

Flowing Artesian Well

Spring Lake

Water Table

River

RAINFALL

EVAPORATION

Spring

Runoff

Zone of Saturation

Shale — Confining Layer

Confined Water

Sandstone Aquifer —

OCEAN

THE GROUNDWATER SYSTEM

This diagram of the hydrologic cycle illustrates how water occurs in nature. There is a continuous exchange or circulation of water between the earth and the atmosphere. Groundwater, the source for wells and springs, is the water that, under the pull of gravity, fills the pores and crevices in underground rocks. The top of the zone of saturation—the zone in which all the rocks are saturated with water—is called the water table. *Source:* Water Supply Sources for the Farmstead and Rural Home

hydrologist, *rock* refers to loose, unconsolidated sediment as well as hard, consolidated formations.

The top of this zone of saturation—the zone in which all the rocks are saturated with water—is called the water table. The water table isn't flat. In general, it follows the contour of the land. It is at a higher elevation under hills than beneath valleys. It may be near the surface or many hundreds of feet below it. It may rise during rainy spells and drop during droughts.

Groundwater isn't static. It moves slowly but constantly—at rates varying from a few feet per year to a few feet per day—toward voids and points of lower elevation, and may surface in springs, lakes, streams, rivers, or oceans. It is replenished by precipitation and irrigation, which per-

colate down through the soil, and it is variable in both amount and quality.

The stratum in the earth where a usable supply of water occurs is called an aquifer, and it may cover hundreds of square miles. But as a rule, most aquifers are only of local extent—and, conveniently, over 90 percent of all groundwater is held in water-bearing formations within 200 feet of the surface. Beneath all aquifers, at varying depths, there is an impervious base of watertight rock, great pressures having closed up the cracks and pores. When you consider the diameter of our planet (7,918 miles), groundwater and the rock that holds it is little more than a splotchy film on the face of the earth.

There are a number of visual clues that can be helpful in locating aquifers. Any area where water shows up at the surface—in springs, seeps, swamps, or lakes—has to have some groundwater, though not necessarily in large quantity or of usable quality. In semiarid regions, certain species of "water-loving" plants give the tip-off that there is groundwater at relatively shallow depths. But according to *A Primer on Ground Water* (U.S. Geological Survey), it's the rocks common to the area that provide the most valuable clues. Coarse, porous sandstone, cavernous limestone, and broken lava rock are productive water carriers. In unconsolidated rock formations, such as clean, coarse sand and gravel, the porosity may be as high as 30 or 40 percent. On the other hand, clay or "tight" rock with tiny pores or only a few hairline cracks, such as shale or crystalline rock—the term used for the great variety of hard rocks that make up the bulk of the earth's crust—may give up its water so slowly that several days would be required for a new well to fill up to the level of the water table. Obviously, rock formations whose porosity is minimal make poor reservoirs.

Finding the right location and putting down a well that produces a good, steady supply of extractable water, year in and year out, is a problem, then, for experts. First, a hydrologist should be consulted. He can tell you what your prospects are. Then, a competent well driller is needed to sink the well.

State universities include hydrologists on their staffs and can provide information, including survey maps, on local groundwater conditions. The Science and Education Administration, which was formed in January 1978 by merging four U.S. Department of Agriculture agencies—the Agricultural Research Service, Cooperative State Research Service, Extension Service, and National Agricultural

Library—can be very helpful, as can the U.S. Geological Survey, a branch of the Department of the Interior. Information about local groundwater conditions may be found in the offices that the U.S. Geological Survey's Water Resources Division maintains in all fifty states.

While the water table is likely to be nearest the surface at the lowest point on your property, a well should be located at the highest practicable point. The shallower the well, the greater the risk of the water being, or becoming, contaminated. Under the HUD-FHA Minimum Property Standards for One and Two Living Units, a source of supply that comes from "any formation which may be polluted or contaminated or is fissured or creviced or which is less than 20 feet below the natural ground surface" is not acceptable.

A well should be situated away from and upstream of any known or possible sources of surface and near-surface contamination. Codes usually call for the well to be at least 10 feet away from property lines, 50 feet from septic tanks, and 100 feet from absorption fields and seepage pits. In all cases, the well casing should extend above the ground, and the well site should be built up where necessary so that surface water will drain away from the well in all directions. Locating a well within the foundation walls of a dwelling is acceptable only in arctic and subarctic regions.

TYPES OF WELLS

There are four common types of wells, classified according to the method used to create them: dug, bored, driven, and drilled. The type of well installed will depend on such considerations as ground formations, the desired yield, the depth to

TABLE ONE

CHARACTERISTICS OF VARIOUS TYPES OF WELLS

| Characteristics | Dug | Bored | Driven | DRILLED | |
				Percussion	Rotary
Range of practical depths	0–50 feet	0–100 feet	0–50 feet	0–1,000 feet	0–1,000 feet
Diameter	3–20 feet	2–30 inches	1¼–2 inches	4–18 inches	4–24 inches
Type of geologic formation:					
Clay	Yes	Yes	Yes	Yes	Yes
Silt	Yes	Yes	Yes	Yes	Yes
Sand	Yes	Yes	Yes	Yes	Yes
Gravel	Yes	Yes	Yes, if fine gravel	Yes	Yes
Cemented gravel	Yes	No	No	Yes	Yes
Boulders	Yes	Yes, if less than well diameter	No	Yes, when in firm bedding	Difficult
Sandstone	Yes, if soft and/or fractured	Yes, if soft and/or fractured	Thin layers only	Yes	Yes
Limestone			No	Yes	Yes
Dense igneous rock	No	No	No	Yes	Yes

Source: Manual of Individual Water Supply Systems

the water table, characteristics of the aquifer, and construction costs. Contrary to popular belief, doubling the diameter of a well increases its yield by only about 10 percent. All but drilled wells are limited to loose, unconsolidated formations containing few large rocks, and they rarely exceed 50 feet in depth.

Those old-fashioned "wishing" wells, complete with cupola and a bucket hauled up by turning a crank, were dug wells. Generally excavated with pick and shovel, and not very deep, dug wells typically measure 5 to 6 feet in diameter and must be lined, or *curbed* with stones, bricks, or concrete well rings to keep the sides from collapsing. Dewatering such a well while digging takes more than a little skill and experience.

Since they can absorb near-surface drainage, dug wells often become health hazards and are not recommended today. Even where there is little danger of pollution, dug wells are not particularly good providers. Because of their shallow pene-

tration into the zone of saturation, most dug wells for private water supplies are capable of yielding only 1 to 2 gallons per minute when pumped steadily. Many fail during dry periods when the water table drops.

Bored wells are a lot like dug wells, but they are constructed by boring a hole with an earth auger. If bored by hand, they generally are between 2 and 8 inches in diameter and not more than 40 feet deep. Machine-bored wells may be as large as 30 inches in diameter and up to 100 feet deep. Bored wells are cased with vitrified draintile or steel pipe, usually to a point below the pumping level, and unless the space between the bore wall and the case is sealed with cement grout to a depth of at least 20 feet below ground level, they too can become contaminated. The pump pipe hangs down inside the casing, terminating below the water's maximum drawdown (the difference between the normal water level and the level after a period of pumping).

Driven wells can be the quickest and cheapest of all wells to install. Generally between $1\frac{1}{4}$ and 2 inches in diameter, they are constructed by driving tightly coupled pipe sections, with a drive-well point and screen on the business end, down into the ground until the point pokes into the aquifer. In areas where the aquifer is composed of relatively coarse sand, a driven well, which is pounded into the ground with a maul or pile driver, is the simplest means of obtaining limited quantities of water. In fine sand or sandy clay formations, the yield may be less than 5 gallons per minute. If more water is needed, up to four driven wells, at least 8 feet apart, can be connected by surface or subsurface piping and worked by a single pump. Driven wells seldom go deeper than 30 feet.

Machine-drilled wells are the answer when the water table is more than 50 feet down and a large volume of water is needed. Drilled wells, for household water supplies usually measure from 4 to 6 inches in diameter. Their construction requires expensive equipment that can drill to depths as great as 1,000 feet, even through consolidated rock formations, utilizing either percussion or rotary drilling tools. Percussion, also known as cable-tool work, employs a heavy, chisel-shaped drilling tool that is lifted and dropped repeatedly from a truck-mounted tower to punch deeper and deeper until water is reached. In rotary drilling, a drilling bit fixed to the lower end of a steel drill pipe is rotated to form the well. Additional sections of drill stem are screwed on as the bit chews deeper. Casing is installed as the drilling proceeds in cable-tool work. With rotary drilling, the casing, either plastic or steel, is set after full depth has been reached. A well screen is normally attached to the bottom of the casing to keep out sand and gravel yet still permit a good flow of water.

When a drilled well reaches into an aquifer that is confined between two layers of "impermeable" rock, the groundwater is likely to be under sufficient hydrostatic pressure to make it rise above the top of the aquifer. This would be an artesian well. In some instances, the water will rise high enough to flow from the well spontaneously. Flowing wells are most common in valleys and coastal areas.

Regardless of whether you dig, bore, drive, or drill, the well *must* be protected from possible contamination. Bacteriological contamination from surface sources can extend 20 feet down in soils with a high degree of permeability. In creviced rock, the zone of surface contamination can go deeper still. This is why the well casing must be durable and watertight, with the sections carefully joined. The space between the well casing and the bore should be filled with cement grout to a point below the zone of contamination, so that surface water cannot seep down the outside of the casing. Watertight seals at the pump mounting or the point at which the well discharge line connects to the water supply system should be installed. A sloping cement platform that extends several feet in all directions from the well to shed surface wash is recommended.

To remove drilling mud from the hole, the well is flushed with fresh water and then pumped or bailed out. Well drillers also employ a process called surging. This involves moving a piston or plunger up and down in the water to extract silt and grit from the water-bearing rock surrounding the well screen. It's all part of developing the well for maximum yield of water with minimum drawdown. The process retards the clogging of screens and pumps and facilitates the flow of water into the well.

If you want to drill your own well, you might contact the DeepRock Manufacturing Company, Opelika, Alabama 36801. This company sells a portable drilling rig, powered by a 3-hp gasoline engine; several do-it-yourselfers we know have had success with it in putting down wells for 2-inch-diameter casing to depths from 40 to 100 feet or so. The equipment can also be used for drilling horizontally into the side of a hill to create an artificial spring. With commercial well drillers charging from $6 to $25 per foot, depending on the going and the diameter of the well, you might be ahead of the game with one of these rigs.

SELECTING THE PROPER PUMP

The well yield should be determined before you buy the pump. Again, this calls for specialized know-how. To test the capacity of a well, the water level should be measured, and the well then pumped at a steady rate. The water level will drop quickly at first, then more slowly, as the rate at which water enters the well approaches the pumping rate. After the well has been developed, a test of at least four hours' duration is required to determine the yield and maximum drawdown of the well. Pump capacity should *never* exceed the yield.

The discharge rate, in gallons per minute, is determined by a measuring device attached to the discharge test pipe. A sustained flow of 5 gallons per minute is the minimum recommended under FHA Minimum Property Standards. The Water Systems Council offers a simple formula for determining what the capacity of a

water-system pump should be for any household. The capacity of the system in gallons per minute should equal the number of water-using fixtures in the home but should not be less than the peak demand for the largest single fixture. A typical one-bathroom house, for example, with one toilet, one lavatory (hot and cold faucets count as one), one bathtub (or shower), a kitchen sink, a dishwasher, an automatic clothes washer, and an outside hose bibb, would demand 7 gallons per minute. The well should be provided with a pump capable of delivering this volume of water under normal operating pressure within the living unit.

You're not likely to use seven gallons per minute throughout the day (a good rule of thumb might be 75 gallons per person per day, excluding allowance for lawn watering and other outdoor needs). But the pump must be capable of delivering water at, in this case, an average sustained peak use rate of 420 gallons per hour to avoid a reduction in flow to an annoying trickle if, say, a bath is being drawn or the dishwasher's in action and the toilet has just been flushed. To operate major appliances, such as dishwashers, and to provide fire-fighting protection, a constant pressure of 30 to 50 pounds is needed. If carefully selected, a pump to meet these demands need only work the equivalent in intermittent service of one to two hours a day.

Well-drilling contractors and pump suppliers have sheaves of tables that show what size (horsepower) pump and diameter piping are needed to match the volume of water required according to the distance it must be lifted and delivered to all fixtures within the living unit under normal operating pressure. Most well-drilling contractors sell, install, and service pumps, and they can advise and supply

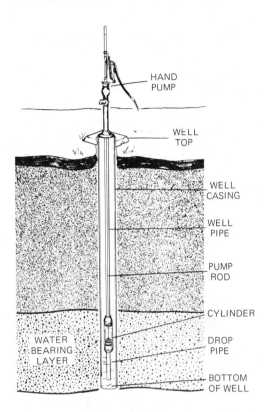

The old-fashioned way: A few companies, such as Dempster Industries, still offer cast-iron force pumps; Dempster pumps can be adapted for wells of any depth. *Dempster Industries, Inc.*

ceptable water level. In theory, under standard atmospheric conditions, it should be possible to lift water 34 feet with a reciprocating or piston pump, which is the most common positive-displacement pump. These pumps draw water by creating a vacuum at their inlet, allowing atmospheric pressure to push water into the suction pipe and up to the pump. But friction, introduced by valves, bends, and the water moving up the drop pipe, reduces the *practical* lifting capability of these simple pumps to roughly 22 to 25 feet.

Shallow-well pumps, which include low-horsepower, one-stage jet pumps, are recommended only where the total lift is 20 feet or less. If the water supply inlet is more than 20 feet below the pump—keeping in mind that some pumps, jets in particular, *can* be offset and installed below ground level—a deep-well pump is recommended.

Single- and multi-stage jet pumps, which raise water by suction and include a foot valve to prevent backflow and excessive vacuum loss, are very useful for

you with a complete water system.

Although long-handled lift pumps are still carried in the Sears catalog and windmills (see pages 161–163) can be useful where you need larger quantities of water for livestock and irrigation, most wells designed solely to meet household water needs, our concern here, are now operated with electric pumps. Where electricity is not available or is subject to outages, gasoline-driven pumps are an alternative.

Basically, there are shallow wells and deep wells, and three types of pumps—positive-displacement, jet (ejector), and centrifugal (including submersible). Shallow wells include all wells with a depth of 25 feet or less from pump to lowest ac-

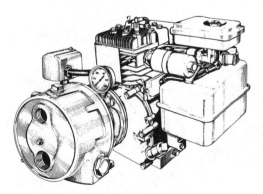

Engine-driven pumps are an alternative for installations where electricity is either unavailable or undependable. The unit shown here is a 1.4-hp Jacuzzi convertible jet pump; it can be used with shallow or deep wells. *Jacuzzi Bros., Inc.*

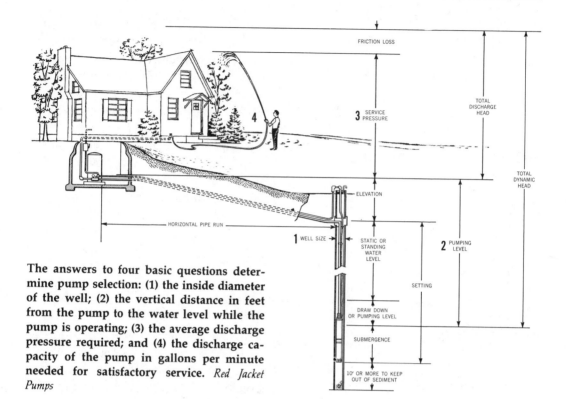

FRICTION LOSS

TOTAL DISCHARGE HEAD

3 SERVICE PRESSURE

TOTAL DYNAMIC HEAD

ELEVATION

HORIZONTAL PIPE RUN

1 WELL SIZE

STATIC OR STANDING WATER LEVEL

2 PUMPING LEVEL

SETTING

DRAW DOWN OR PUMPING LEVEL

SUBMERGENCE

10' OR MORE TO KEEP OUT OF SEDIMENT

The answers to four basic questions determine pump selection: (1) the inside diameter of the well; (2) the vertical distance in feet from the pump to the water level while the pump is operating; (3) the average discharge pressure required; and (4) the discharge capacity of the pump in gallons per minute needed for satisfactory service. *Red Jacket Pumps*

Jet pumps are simple, compactly designed units, which can be located away from the well to eliminate the need for a special pump house or pit. For deep-well installations, they can be used with well casings as small as 2 inches in diameter; shallow-well installations can use suction piping as small as 1 inch in diameter. *Red Jacket Pumps*

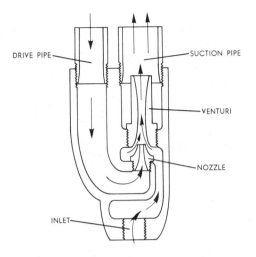

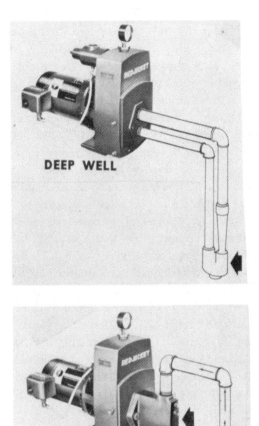

DEEP WELL

SHALLOW WELL

How a jet pump works: Water picked up by the jet in the well is discharged by the pump with a portion of it recirculating through the injector to enable the jet to function. When the vertical distance between the pump and the water level in the well is more than 25 feet, the injector is placed below the water level in the well. Where the vertical distance is less than 25 feet, the injector is mounted on the pump, with passages in the pump-case casting serving the functions of the pressure and suction pipes used with deep-well jet pumps. *Red Jacket Pumps*

small-diameter wells, but they become uneconomical to operate at depths of more than 80 or 90 feet because of the great increase in power requirements. Utilizing a deep-well jet pump to deliver the same volume of water and pressure, you would have to roughly double your horsepower for every 30 to 40 feet.

With submersible pumps, which are long, slender, and cylindrical, the entire pump, motor and all, is attached to the well pipe and placed in the casing below the maximum drawdown of the well. Submersible pumps, which transform kinetic energy into pressure via a rapidly rotating impeller, are capable of forcing or pushing water from very deep wells but can be used only when the well's inside diameter is 4 inches or more. Submersible pump motor housings are watertight; an insulated cable connects the pump motor, attached to the pump directly below the water-intake screen, to a surface source of electricity.

Submersible pumps can handle larger amounts of water from a deep well at lower operating costs than other electrical pumps. Where a 0.5-hp submersible pump with a 1-inch discharge can pump 9.1 gallons per minute from a depth of 100 feet, it takes a 1.5-hp jet package to do the same job.

The pump and water system should be large enough not only for present needs but also for expected future needs, whether they include additions to the family, additions to the house, or both. You can't anticipate long-term changes in the depth of the water table, but jet pumps that can easily be converted from shallow- to deep-well applications are available. Something else to look for in a submersible pump is a built-in surge arrestor. Thousands of unprotected submersible pumps are knocked out by lightning each year.

The old-fashioned force pump had to be mounted directly over the well, but jet pumps can be located at the well or some distance from it—in a heated pump house, utility room, or the basement of the house. In all cases, surface pumps should be located where they will be protected from the elements and extremes of temperature.

Below-grade well pits for pump installation are subject to state and local codes and are not generally recommended. It's difficult to provide proper drainage from a well pit, and many cases of well pollution have been traced to the flooding of pits. Instead of a pit, a common practice with jet (and submersible) pump systems is to use a pitless adapter, which allows termination of the casing aboveground and connection of the discharge pipe below the frost line. The lateral run to the house should be protected by sealed casing pipe or concrete pipe with a minimum diameter of 4 inches.

PRESSURE/STORAGE TANKS

Several pump manufacturers offer regulating valves or other pressurizing devices that allow demand water systems to oper-

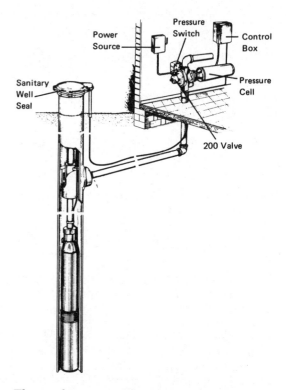

The modern way: The Jacuzzi AquaGenie 200 installation, with 4-inch-diameter submersible pump. The AquaGenie was the first constant-pressure individual water system. *Jacuzzi Bros., Inc.*

ate without a large storage tank. Jacuzzi's AquaGenie and Red Jacket's HydroServant are adaptable to both jet and submersible pumps, and they maintain constant household water pressure even when there is no demand for water. When demand occurs, a sensitive pressure switch activates the pump and maintains both pressure and volume as long as desired (the same process that occurs with city water). Most private water systems, however, include a storage device in the form of a hydropneumatic tank, which supplies water to all outlets at a fairly uniform pressure and provides water, at least for a while, if the pump quits or the power fails.

Hydropneumatic tanks, more commonly referred to as pressure tanks, are pre-charged with air. As the tank partly fills, the air above the rising water is compressed. When a fixed pressure is reached, a pressure switch opens the electrical circuit and the pump stops automatically. After a certain amount of water—called the usable tank volume, draw-off capacity, or drawdown—has been withdrawn, the air cushion expands and the drop in pressure causes the pump to start up again.

Recommended volume for a conventional hydropneumatic tank is approximately seven times the pump capacity in gallons per minute (gpm). A 42-gallon tank (the most common size) would be in order with a 6-gpm pump. This size tank allows you to use about 8 gallons of water between the stopping and starting of the pump. The second most common tank size is 82 gallons, for pump capacities be-

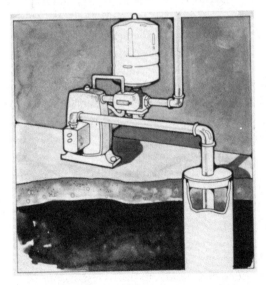

Red Jacket's HydroServant I, with capacities to 20 gallons per minute, assures constant water pressure, just like city water. The compact unit, which replaces the conventional pressure/storage tank, is adaptable to submersible and jet pumps and can be installed anywhere in the service line. *Red Jacket Pumps*

tween 6 gpm and 12 gpm. A 120-gallon tank is recommended for pump capacities from 12 gpm to 17 gpm.

Conventional pressure tanks do not physically separate the air from the water stored in the tank. Under these conditions, the pressurized air is gradually absorbed by the water and the air cushion grows smaller and smaller. With little air left, the tank reaches a "waterlogged" state, characterized by rapid starts and stops of the pump motor. Using a tire pump to recharge the tank is exhausting, and the alternative is to invest in an air charger. Today, however, you also have the option of tanks that come with disc-type floats, water- or air-storage bags made of heavy-gauge vinyl, diaphragms, and other devices that keep the air and water separated.

Diaphragm and bladder-type tanks with positive separation of air and water are more compact than conventional tanks of comparable drawdown capacity. With these tanks, and where the source of water is reliable, storage becomes unimportant. The crucial thing here is that the tank be sized to let the pump cycle at a rate which suits the motor and other electrical components. Sears's 19-gallon Captive Air tank, for example, with up to 6.3-gallon drawdown, meets FHA requirements to replace 42-gallon conventional tanks.

With or without positive separation of air and water, larger tanks may be needed with wells of low capacity, smaller-size pumps, and longer pumping times. Wells yielding as little as 1 to 2 gpm, while not ideal, can thus be made to serve a sizable household. The pumping must be almost continuous, though, and the tank would have to be of sufficient capacity to meet peak demands. The capacity of the tank plus the amount delivered by two hours of pumping should be at least equal to the daily water requirement.

A two-pump system could also be used here, with the first-stage well pump, rated for continuous duty, discharging into a covered, atmospheric tank with a float-switch control. The second pump would draw water from this larger tank and feed it into a conventional-size hydropneumatic tank as required.

The pressure tank can be located almost anywhere in the service line—in a utility room or the basement, or close to the well. With surface pumps, the pump, tank, and water treatment devices usually are located in the same general area. Depending on local or state codes, tanks are sometimes buried next to the well, freeing space in the house for other purposes. But remember that when something in the system goes wrong, whether a clogged well screen or a malfunctioning switch, the easier it is to get at the source of the problem, the less costly the service call.

DISINFECTION AND FILTRATION

After installation of the pump and tank, the system must be disinfected in accordance with the recommendations of the local health authority. This is necessary to kill any potentially harmful bacteria introduced during construction of the water supply system. This usually calls for swabbing or flushing the interior surface of the well casing with a chlorine solution, adding chlorine to the standing well water, and then drawing water through each fixture in turn until there is a strong odor of chlorine. The fixture is then shut off and the treated water is left to stand in the pipes for up to twenty-four hours. After that time, water is allowed to run from

each outlet until the chlorine odor disappears.

Only after the entire water supply system has been sterilized, and tests show the absence of a free-chlorine residual, are water samples taken for analysis by a licensed state chemist. State health departments analyze water either as a public service or for a nominal fee. Depending on its purity and mineral content, the addition of an automatic chlorinator, water softener, or filtering device may or may not be recommended.

Public health authorities will also require you or your contractor to file a well-construction report. The record should show the location and type of well, a geologic log of the formations penetrated, water levels, pumping test data, details of the equipment installed, and results of all water analyses.

The water that comes from a new well almost always is cleaner and purer than surface water. Deep groundwater is rarely contaminated. If there's any problem with its quality, it's more likely to be of a mineral rather than bacterial nature. Consider the fact that some of the water coming from a deep well may have been in the ground for more than ten thousand years. It's been in contact with rocks and soil much longer than suface water and has more dissolved minerals or gases in it. The amount of mineral matter and gases carried varies according to the types of rock with which the water has been in long-term contact. Limestone and gypsum, for example, are very soluble. Lava rocks, on the other hand, are relatively insoluble.

Good health requires certain of these inorganic substances and is probably not adversely affected by most of the others. But water containing more than 500 parts per million of dissolved solids may require treatment to make it wholly acceptable for domestic uses. The most frequent objections to well water are too much iron, which leaves stains on laundered clothing and on porcelain plumbing fixtures, and *hardness*, which is caused by excessive amounts of calcium and magnesium salts. Hard water makes lathering difficult, turns laundry "tattletale gray," and builds up tough scale inside water pipes, tanks, and heating equipment the way cholesterol builds up in arteries. Groundwater in arid regions is generally harder and more mineralized than water in regions with high annual rainfall.

These problems can be solved. Minerals—as well as other substances that can impart a bad taste, odor, or color—can be removed from the water supply through the use of an automatic water softener, a chlorinator, or filtration. The chemical nature of water is important. You don't want it to taste of salt, sulfur, or iron, but neither do you want it to taste flat, like dis-

tilled water. It should be soft enough to lather easily. It should have a balanced pH, which means it should be nearly neutral—neither too acid nor too alkaline.

Automatic chlorinators, using an adjustable chemical feeder to inject small amounts of chlorine solution into the water system, can kill any harmful bacteria present. The feeder can be wired to the pump to assure continuous chlorination, the most effective way of disinfecting a domestic water supply. Should the taste of the chlorinated water be objectionable, it can be removed by passing the water through a taste/odor filter after it leaves the holding tank, which should be at least 42 gallons in size. Disinfecting the water at this stage should be done only as a last resort, however. If well water becomes contaminated, make every effort to find and eliminate the cause.

Where chlorine is used to break down iron and the salts that cause hardness, an

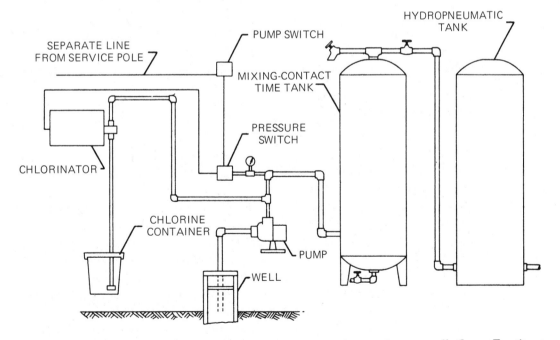

A typical chlorination-system installation for disinfecting water from a well. *Source:* Treating Farmstead and Rural Home Water Systems

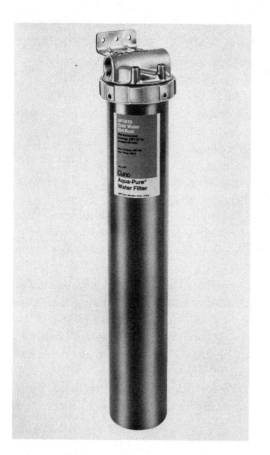

A replaceable canister-type filter can be installed in the cold-water line to remove dirt and other particulate matter or objectionable tastes and odors. Where an in-line filter can't handle the problem, a settling or other pretreatment tank may be necessary. *AMF Cuno*

additional holding tank is necessary to ensure sufficient contact time for the chlorine to work. The chlorine will precipitate dissolved iron, manganese, and hydrogen sulfide (the stuff that gives off that "rotten-egg" odor) from solution into solid particles, and these can be removed from the water with a dirt/rust filter.

The most common filtration devices are those that pass the water through a bed of chemically sticky carbon (to adsorb chlorine, sulfur, and other objectionable tastes and odors) or coarse filtering material (to

remove dirt and other particulate matter). The manufacturer's recommendations should be followed for backwashing (to clear the sludge and maintain efficiency) and cartridge replacement. Large tank-type filters (which can cost a couple of hundred dollars) are more effective and require less attention than do the smaller in-line units that are designed primarily to make municipal water look, smell, and taste as clean and fresh as that from a mountain spring.

NATURAL SPRINGS

Spring water is *not* synonymous with purity. Spring water is groundwater. It may be more refreshing and even have a bit of tang, but you face the same problems of purity and hardness with spring water that you do with well water. It all comes from the same place.

A spring is a groundwater outcropping where water flows or issues from the earth either by gravity or artesian pressure. Most springs are found on the side of a hill and should not be confused with low-lying seeps, which are nonconcentrated sources of water and are susceptible to contamination by the surface runoff that collects in valleys or depressions.

If you have a natural spring on your property, take a long look at it. If the water is not contaminated and the source doesn't have a tendency to shut down during dry spells, developing it may be a better—and less expensive—alternative than putting down a well. Have the local health officer make a sanitary survey of the area to determine the suitability of the spring before you do anything with it.

A spring has to be developed if it is to be a primary water source. This is done by

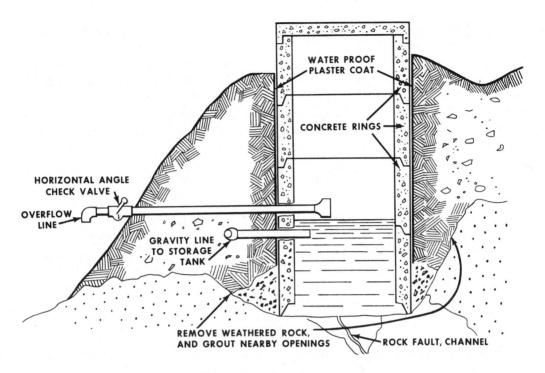

WATER PROOF PLASTER COAT

CONCRETE RINGS

HORIZONTAL ANGLE CHECK VALVE

OVERFLOW LINE

GRAVITY LINE TO STORAGE TANK

REMOVE WEATHERED ROCK, AND GROUT NEARBY OPENINGS

ROCK FAULT, CHANNEL

A spring needs to be developed if it is to be the primary source of household water. Proper protection to guard against contamination by surface sources is essential. The overflow should be above flood level. The gravity line to the storage tank should be run underground for freeze protection. *Source:* Water Supply Sources for the Farmstead and Rural Home

digging out the spring down to solid rock and building a concrete-block cistern around it, with the upper part made watertight. A filtration bed of sand and gravel is installed in the open bottom, and a lockable concrete cover is added to keep out children, animals, and debris. The cover should be removable to permit cleaning. An overflow pipe, screened to prevent the entrance of rodents and insects, will drain off any excess water that accumulates. The overflow should be channeled away from the spring via a spillway to avoid undermining the structure.

A sidehill spring that is at a higher elevation than the plumbing fixtures in your house is advantageous because it allows the water to be delivered by gravity flow. If the spring is not at sufficient elevation, however, the water can be moved with a shallow-well pump. In either case, the delivery pipe must be laid below the frost line.

SURFACE WATER

In areas where groundwater is either inaccessible or so highly mineralized that it is not satisfactory for domestic use, surface water must be considered. A surface source may also be used to supplement a well or spring that cannot fully meet your domestic water needs. Surface water should always be regarded as polluted, however, and should be used only where groundwater sources are unavailable or inadequate.

Sources of surface water for domestic water supplies include roof and surface catchments (to cisterns), farm ponds, lakes, and streams. Their susceptibility to contamination runs pretty much in that order. The old saying that "running water purifies itself to drinking-water quality" within a stated distance is about as reliable as your chances of picking the order of the first four finishers in the Kentucky Derby.

CISTERNS

In planning a cistern to store the rainfall runoff from roofs or fenced-and-paved ground catchment areas, first review local rainfall records to determine the amount and frequency of expected rainfall. One inch of rain over 1,000 square feet of surface (50 by 20 feet of roof, say) will yield 623 gallons. You're not going to be able to trap all the rain that falls on a roof, but good planning calls for a cistern capable of storing at least two-thirds of the water that is likely to fall on a catchment during the rainy season.

A cistern should be installed as close to the point of ultimate use as is practical. Monolithic concrete construction is recommended, and a round cistern is more economical than a square or rectangular one. The cistern can be installed in or above the ground, indoors or out, but should not be placed in a basement or other area that is subject to flooding.

The most common cistern is installed in the ground, with the walls extending from 4 to 8 inches aboveground. It must be made watertight to avoid leakage of

stored water and to prevent the entrance of contaminated surface water. The built-in-place cistern can be constructed of either poured, reinforced concrete, or cinder blocks, with smooth-plastered (two $\frac{1}{2}$-inch coats of 1:3 portland cement mortar) interior walls. A tight-fitting, reinforced concrete cover, with a manhole for access to the cistern interior, is required. The manhole collar should be raised above the surface to prevent contamination of the stored water through leakage.

The supply pipe to the pump and pressure tank is installed about 8 inches above the floor of the cistern and passes through a filter box containing layered sand, charcoal, and coarse gravel. To allow excess water to escape when the cistern reaches its full capacity, an overflow pipe, effectively screened to bar insects and rodents, is installed near the top of the collection box. The rainwater inlet, also screened, connects directly to the downspout.

Water stored underground will remain cool during the warmer months and will be less likely to freeze in wintertime, though you may still have to chop a bit of ice within an outdoor cistern where winters are severe. A deep cistern also needs provision for drainage, or a sump from which sludge can be siphoned, and should be cleaned out each year when the supply of water is lowest.

If you use a roof as your catchment, a diverter valve installed on the downspout will enable the roof and gutters to be thoroughly cleaned of leaves, dust, soot, and bird droppings before any water is allowed to run into the cistern. It is preferable to waste the first 15 to 20 minutes of wash rather than attempt to filter it, since heavy downpours complicate the filtering process.

A circular cistern 10 feet in diameter and 8 feet deep can hold 4,700 gallons of water—or up to about 12 inches of rainfall on that 50 by 20 feet of roof, allowing for one-third wastage. That's not an awful lot of water if you go back to the earlier allowance of 75 gallons per person per day. Unless you severely trim your water usage or get lots and lots of rain, a cistern supplied by a roof catchment, if it's your only source of supply, isn't likely to allow you to wallow in water. It can, however, supply enough for drinking and culinary requirements, and, since rainwater is virtually free of minerals that can harden water, make washday a happier occasion.

If you're handy, you could probably install a cistern for less than the cost of a water conditioner. You also can buy precast-concrete cisterns. Together with an electric pump and an automatic chlorinator, a prefab cistern installed by a contractor might come to around $1,200.

Though it's comparatively pure, rainwater off the roof or a paved catchment should be treated if it's to be drunk or used in food preparation. A rain barrel to catch water for shampooing and laundry use is one thing, but untreated water from a cistern can be as hazardous as that from a contaminated well. The cistern, too, should be disinfected before it's put into use.

Where a cistern is the only alternative, and you encounter longer than usual dry periods, you can do what many rural families do—arrange to have water delivered to the cistern by tank truck, at a cost of $10 to $15 per 1,000 gallons.

FARM PONDS, LAKES, AND RIVERS

Farm ponds are designed primarily to provide water for livestock and fire protection for farm buildings. They may also be used for swimming and ice skating. But unless you need water for a farm-type operation, installing or developing a farm pond is not the most practical alternative for providing a water supply source for mostly household purposes. For one thing, you have to have suitable acreage and a watershed that permits only water of the highest quality to enter the pond, which means water that isn't laced with fertilizers, pesticides, and other chemicals that can be highly toxic to humans and animals and are difficult even for public water suppliers to remove.

The easiest way to create a farm pond is to dam a natural catchment that drains a small watershed in which water flows only when there is a heavy rainstorm. The soil must be tight enough to hold water. Clay or a good loam is best, and sandy sites should be avoided. The pond should be capable of storing at least a year's supply of water (most are from a quarter-acre to 2 acres in size) and should be 8 to 15 feet at its deepest part. It must be fenced to keep out livestock and young children, and a spillway must be provided in the embankment to allow water to escape when the pond reaches its capacity.

Ponds have been built that filled to the brink with sediment in the first year, or during the first flood. Weeds and algae also are major problems. And in the colder areas of the country, there is always the possibility of the pond not just freezing over but freezing from top to bottom. You can't avoid the ice by dropping the screened inlet pipe, since, ideally, it should be floated within 12 to 18 inches of the surface, where the most desirable water is usually obtained.

Treating pond water for domestic use is more complicated than treating even highly mineralized well water. A typical pond-water treatment facility includes a

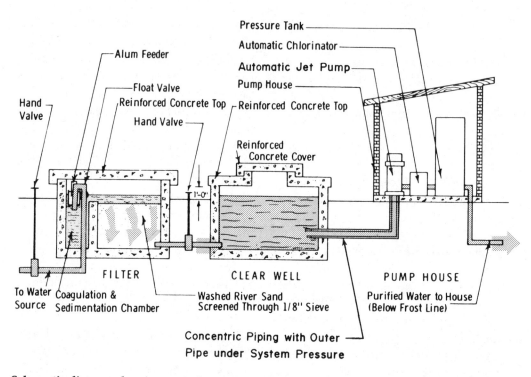

Pressure Tank

Automatic Chlorinator

Automatic Jet Pump

Pump House

Alum Feeder

Float Valve

Reinforced Concrete Top   Reinforced Concrete Top

Hand Valve

Hand Valve

Reinforced Concrete Cover

1'-0"

FILTER   CLEAR WELL   PUMP HOUSE

To Water Source   Coagulation & Sedimentation Chamber   Washed River Sand Screened Through 1/8" Sieve   Purified Water to House (Below Frost Line)

Concentric Piping with Outer Pipe under System Pressure

Schematic diagram showing a pond-water treatment system. *Source:* Manual of Individual Water Supply Systems

settling basin, with provision for coagulation if needed; a slow sand filter (up to 24 inches of fine sand on top of 6 inches of coarse gravel); clear water storage; disinfection; and further filtration before the water even reaches the pressure tank. Pumping equipment generally is of the shallow-well type. The size of the pressure tank is determined the same as for adequate well sources, though water-treatment exposure requirements may call for a larger tank or even a separate holding tank.

If you have an existing pond on your property or want to investigate the practicalities of building one, check first with local or state agricultural, geological, and soil conservation agencies and get their recommendations for the suitability of a farm pond for your particular needs. They're also the people to talk to if you're considering taking water from a lake or

stream. If you plan to divert or dam water, you must first investigate water rights and possible restrictions. You'll also need an easement if the water line has to be run through property you don't own.

Withdrawing and taking water from a lake or river calls for the same type of screened floating inlet and water treatment used with a farm pond. With a stream, you'll have the further complications of seasonal fluctuations in flow and even heavier amounts of silt to cope with during runoff periods. Pumping—which is mostly a problem of moving the water horizontally—and storage call for equipment similar to that used with a farm pond. The piping can be plastic, and unless you have gravity flow, you'll need a foot valve at the inlet to keep water from draining out of the line when the pump is not running.

Water drawn from surface sources, such

as farm ponds, lakes, or streams, is less likely to have bothersome concentrations of iron or the salts that make water hard, but don't forget that it should always be considered contaminated. Inclusion of a chlorine feeder in the water supply system is therefore a must.

DISTILLATION

If you find it too complicated or too expensive to purify your whole domestic water supply, you may want to give special attention to only the water that you require for drinking and culinary purposes, and clean up the rest as best you can. Distillation and ultrafiltration processes aren't geared to handle large amounts of water, but they are quite effective with limited quantities.

A solar still, using heat from the sun, can be used to make even water from a very brackish source fresh and pure. It's not difficult to construct—a heat trap with a shallow, black-painted basin, a pitched glass cover, and collecting troughs. A solar still for controlled evaporation should produce about one-tenth of a gallon of pure water per square foot of still area on a good day. A recommended source of plans for stills is Brace Research Institute, Publications Department, Macdonald College of McGill University, Ste. Anne de Bellevue, Quebec, Canada H9X 1CO.

For in-home distilling, portable distillers—such as the Quench Water De-Salter/Purifier, which operates with any source of concentrated heat, and the Aquaspring electric home water distiller—can deliver up to 2 quarts of bacteria- and mineral-free water every two hours. For all the energy input, the output from the stovetop and electric distillation devices is low. Some of the less expensive models can take up to four hours to dribble out a quart of distilled water. Units that deliver up to 2 quarts an hour are priced between $150 and $300.

While solar stills and portable water distillers provide yet another way to tackle a host of water problems, it is not a good idea—with young children especially—to constantly drink water from which all the good as well as all the bad has been removed. Many of the trace elements in groundwater contribute to healthy bones, teeth, and blood vessels.

Reverse-osmosis water filters are also used to make limited quantities of safe-to-drink water from virtually any source. These ultrafilters incorporate a semipermeable membrane, which under normal water pressure allows the passage of water molecules but rejects impurities, both soluble and suspended, including asbestos fibers, amoebic cysts (the cause of dysentery), and microscopic parasites. Impurities are flushed away, and the clean water passes through a carbon filter and into a pressurized holding tank that feeds a faucet. Under the right conditions, these units, which operate continuously on water pressure alone, can produce 3 to 5 gallons of drinking water a day. They do not work well with water that is overly acidic or alkaline. Culligan has both under-the-sink and freestanding models, with prices starting at about $375, plus installation.

There's even a completely portable desalinization system, dubbed the Sweet-Water System, now on the market. It's manufactured by Allied Water Corporation, and it cost about $5,000 the last time we were quoted a price. Roughly the size of a portable TV, the seawater purification device weighs in the neighborhood of 90 pounds and draws about 5 kwh of electricity per 100 gallons.

CONSERVING WATER

If you have only a limited supply of fresh water and have run out of alternatives, you'll need to adjust demand to the supply rate. This doesn't mean giving up bathing or installing a pit privy—although flush toilets and showers alone account for 70 percent of the average family's water consumption. For starters, there are waterless indoor toilets as well as water recycling. Both subjects will be examined in the next section. Water-conserving faucets and showerheads that can cut water flow in half without interfering with washing up or showering are also useful. Simply by installing a low-flush toilet and flow-control faucets and showerheads, you should be able to cut household water usage by one-third. Under the new energy-saving building codes, the use of such water-conserving devices is mandatory for new construction in many areas of the country. Finally, *be quick to stop a leak.* One drop a second from a leaking faucet adds up to 7 gallons a day. A leaky toilet tank can waste *200* gallons a day in a house's water consumption!

TWO

 BEYOND THE
SEWER LINES

THE 5-GALLON FLUSH

Thomas Crapper's flush toilet was award-
ed a gold medal at the 1884 Health Exhi-
bition in London. This official recognition
of the device that the English plumber
had patented a few years before brought
the backyard privy indoors. That the
Thunderer, as that noisy, early version of
the pull-chain convenience was aptly
nicknamed, was quite possibly the most
wasteful device ever introduced into the
home has only recently been recognized.

The typical flush toilet uses 5 gallons or
more of clean, potable water to transport
about one one-hundredth as much waste
from here to there—whether that's 20 feet
to a septic tank installed in the yard, or
half as many miles to a costly, community
sewage-treatment plant. In America alone,
we flush away more than 5 *billion* gallons
of water a day, befouling it in the process.
All of that once-pure water needs to be
reprocessed and made clean again, to prevent it from contaminating aquifers and
surface water.

With chronic water shortages in many
parts of the country, overloaded septic
systems throughout America, and the in-
tolerably high cost of fully treating wastewater in municipal plants to meet stringent Environmental Protection Agency
clean-water standards, the 5-gallon flush
has become an extravagance we no longer
can afford. Spurred by grants from the
federal government, the waste-manage-
ment industry is developing new systems
to handle the sewage-disposal problem
with efficiencies never dreamed of by "Sir
Thomas." Toilets that flush with no more
than 3½ gallons of water, as already required in new construction under some
state and local building codes, are only
the first step.

Among the alternatives to the 5-gallon
flush that already have emerged are several environmentally compatible systems
that should be of particular interest to
those building for self-sufficiency. The
usual alternative when building beyond
the sewer lines, though, is a septic tank
and subsurface absorption field. Almost
one-third of all American families use
septic tanks, and we'll look at that system
before turning to such newer alternatives
as waterless composting toilets and on-
site wastewater recycling systems.

SOIL PERCOLATION TEST

It's a mistake to buy rural property beyond the sewer lines without first having a civil engineer or a qualified representative of the local health department run a percolation test on the property. There are millions of acres of otherwise choice land on which, under existing sanitary codes, you can't get a permit to build because the soil will not support a septic system. Hardpan and plasticlike clay generally will not absorb, filter, and purify the effluent from a septic tank. Land that is poorly drained, remaining saturated during wet weather, or that has a high water table, is also unsuitable for the conventional septic system. Vermont's Environmental Conservation Agency, to take just one example, holds that no more than 20 percent of all the land in the Green Mountain State is suitable for septic tank installations. To insure your investment, have the suitability of the soil confirmed beforehand.

A percolation test begins with soil-depth measurements to establish that the high groundwater level (permanent, fluctuating, or seasonal) and any bedrock or other impermeable deposits are at least 6 feet below grade in the unobstructed area where the septic tank and absorption field are to be located. Low areas that are subject to flooding, or ground that slopes more than 15 degrees, should be avoided. One or more (if site conditions so indicate) test holes are then dug with an earth auger or posthole digger. The holes must be 4 to 12 inches in diameter, spaced uniformly over the proposed site, and about as deep as the planned absorption field—between 18 and 36 inches. Once the holes are dug, the sides are roughened to provide a natural surface, any loose earth is removed, and about 2 inches of fine gravel

TABLE TWO

MINIMUM REQUIRED SUBSURFACE ABSORPTION FIELD TRENCH-BOTTOM AREA PER BEDROOM

(Based on soil percolation rate)

Time in minutes for water to fall 1 inch during final percolation test period	Minimum required area in square feet
2 or less	85
3	100
4	115
5	125
10	165
15	190
30	250
45	300
60	330

Over 60 minutes unsuitable for absorption field.

Source: FHA-HUD Minimum Property Standards

is placed in the bottom to prevent sealing.

Clear water is then poured into each hole to bring the level up to 12 inches or more above the gravel. Water is added, as needed, to keep it at that level for at least four hours, and preferably overnight, especially during dry periods. The testing is resumed by adjusting the water level to 6 inches above the gravel and measuring the drop every thirty minutes for four hours, adding enough water when the percolation rate indicates the hole will run dry before the next reading is made to bring the water up to the 6-inch level. The drop that occurs during the final thirty minutes is used to calculate the percolation rate. In sandy soils, or other soils where the water is absorbed rapidly, the time intervals are reduced to ten minutes, and the test is run for one hour, using the drop during the final ten minutes to calculate the percolation rate. Soils with a percolation rate of less than 1 inch per hour are unsatisfactory for septic tank installations. The percolation rate also determines the size of the absorption field. The slower the percolation rate, the larger the absorption field required. Ideally, the percolation test should be made during the wet season.

SEPTIC TANKS

Don't confuse a septic tank with a cesspool. A cesspool is a covered hole in the ground, loosely lined with rocks or concrete building blocks. Sewage and other wastes (bathroom, kitchen, and laundry) flow into the cesspool, and the liquids seep into the surrounding soil. If the cesspool is not designed to be cleaned out periodically, another one must be constructed as a replacement when the first one clogs or fills with solids. It's a primitive system that can pollute a wide area and is no longer allowed under most sanitary codes.

A septic tank, on the other hand, is a large, watertight box or tank—usually either precast concrete, steel, or fiberglass, with access for cleaning—that is sunk into the ground and attached to the house wastepipe. A second pipe leads from the opposite end of the tank to the absorption field for dispersal of the effluent. In the conventional or anaerobic septic tank, sewage-digesting microorganisms that thrive in the absence of air or free oxygen slowly reduce the solids to gases, liquids, scum, and sludge. The gases are vented harmlessly into the atmosphere via the house soilstack and vent pipes to the roof. The sludge, a fraction of the original volume of the solids, settles to the bottom of the tank as an inert residue. The scum, mostly grease and light waxes, floats on the surface of the sewage. Liquefied sewage and other wastewater make up the effluent, which flows from the tank by displacement through a T-pipe outlet, as new waste (influent) enters the baffled, opposite end and raises the level of the tank content.

Septic tanks are sized according to the number of bedrooms proposed: a 750-gallon tank for two bedrooms or less, a 900-gallon tank for three bedrooms, and a 1,000-gallon tank for four bedrooms. Another 250 gallons of capacity must be added for each additional bedroom. These capacities provide for the plumbing fixtures and appliances commonly used in a single-family residence (automatic clothes

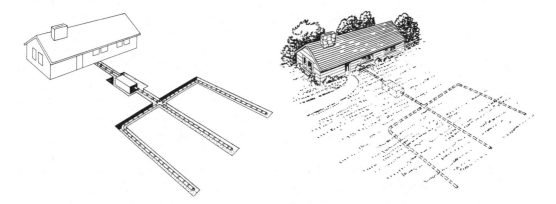

A typical layout for an absorption field: The tank and drain lines are covered with soil and planted to grass so that no part of the system is visible. *Source:* Soils and Septic Tanks

washer, mechanical garbage grinder, and dishwasher included). Exterior drainage should not enter any part of the system.

The size of the absorption field needed is determined by multiplying the minimum required trench-bottom area per bedroom, based on the percolation rate (see Table 2), by the number of bedrooms. With a ten-minute percolation rate (165 square feet of trench bottom required per bedroom) and a two-bedroom house, the minimum required trench-bottom area would be 330 square feet. Trenches should not be longer than 100 feet, and the minimum number of trenches is two. So in this example, if the trenches are 24 inches wide, 165 feet of trench would be required and this could be laid out as two trenches, each 82½ feet long. But three trenches, each 55 feet long, would be better. With 24-inch-wide disposal trenches, the minimum spacing between trench center lines is 7 feet.

A lot of juggling may be required before the designer of the absorption field comes up with a layout that can be accommodated on the property in question. In locations where the absorption field area slopes, a system of serial-distribution trenches following the contours of the land could be used. The trenches, in this case, are installed at different downhill elevations, but the bottom of each individual trench should be level throughout its length.

The problem gets more complicated with larger subsurface absorption fields. With a marginal absorption rate of sixty minutes and a four-bedroom house, the minimum required trench-bottom area is 1,320 square feet. At the very minimum, 440 feet of large-diameter clay draintile or perforated plastic pipe would be called for here. You might not have the room for an absorption field of that size. Allowances must also be made for the required separation between any part of an absorption field and the well, if there is to be one. This is a minimum of 100 feet. The well should be upgrade from the absorption field.

Generally, if you expect to include both a well and a septic tank, you should have at least 20,000 square feet of property, or about half an acre. The location and construction of the sewage-disposal installation must be such that it avoids contaminating any existing or future water source or water supply. Where the water is piped in from a public waterworks, codes *may* permit a reduction in minimum building-plot area to a quarter of an acre. However, many codes also require that the property include sufficient unobstructed area to accommodate a *second* absorption field should the first one fail.

The absorption field is formed by trenching parallel drainage beds, from 12 to 36 inches wide, and from 6 to 8 feet apart (on center), with the earth between trenches undisturbed. The drainage beds are filled with a minimum of 6 inches of pea gravel before the drain lines are laid. If draintile is used, the joints are left open about one-quarter of an inch. The trench is then filled with gravel to a minimum depth of 2 inches above the pipe. A layer of straw or building paper is placed over the filter material to prevent dirt from infiltrating the drain beds when the trenches are backfilled. With the soil planted to grass, no part of the system is visible. You therefore should make a map showing the location of the septic tank and the drain lines, including the depth to all parts of the system. Keep it handy for reference at times of inspection or repair. It could save having to tear up a lot of lawn.

Treated with respect, a septic tank shouldn't have to be pumped out more

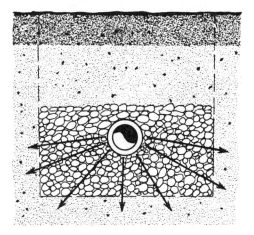

The effluent from the septic tank is carried through large-diameter clay draintile or perforated plastic pipe to all points of the absorption field. Bacteria in the soil, the living filter surrounding the drain lines, complete the reduction of the sewage to a harmless liquid. *Source:* Soils and Septic Tanks

through the filtration beds is not nearly so pure as you may have been led to believe, and particulate matter eventually fills and blocks the pores in the soil, the "living filter" surrounding the drain lines. Overloading the system hastens its demise. The usual indication of trouble is a spongy or wet surface under otherwise dry conditions or, as Erma Bombeck noted, grass that is greener than elsewhere. You'll smell it, too, since the effluent, with nowhere else to go, rises to the surface. There are chemicals, such as a hydrogen-peroxide solution, that supposedly can "unclog" an absorption field, but it usually comes down to pick-and-shovel work on your part—or an extended period of rest for the system.

often than once every two to five years. Just keep in mind that the system can handle biodegradable substances only. This means that disposable diapers, tampons, cat litter, cigarette butts, and coffee grinds should be disposed of elsewhere. Whenever possible, grease also should be kept out of the influent. Contrary to what you may have heard, normal use of detergents, bleaches, disinfectants, and drain cleaners has little or no adverse effect on the system. One thing to guard against are tree roots that might reach into the absorption field and dislodge or block drain lines. No shrubbery or vegetation with long roots should be planted above the absorption field.

Septic tanks can go wrong. In some areas of the country, especially where the depth or permeability of the soil is marginal, it is estimated that fully half of the septic tank systems installed fail within two years, usually due to clogging of the soil. The effluent that is dispersed

AEROBIC SEWAGE TREATMENT SYSTEMS

If the depth or permeability of the soil is marginal, you might save yourself some headaches by installing an aerobic, rather than an *anaerobic*, sewage treatment system. The effluent from an aerobic tank is much less likely to clog the absorption field. With an aerobic system, the sewage is agitated, with fresh air bubbled through the waste for extended aeration. This is pretty much the way it's done in central sewage treatment plants. A different, and far more efficient, strain of bacteria takes over here—one that lives and works in the presence of oxygen. In an aerobic tank, the waste reduction that is accomplished in four hours can't be matched in as many weeks in an anaerobic tank. Generally, aerobic tanks are 85 to 95 percent effective in breaking down organic waste, while septic tanks are no more than about 25 percent effective. As a result, the effluent from an aerobic tank is primarily clear, odorless water.

A dozen manufacturers have had individual on-site aerobic wastewater treatment plants approved by the National Sanitation Foundation after stringent performance testing. (The term *wastewater*, as used by NSF, encompasses all normal household plumbing wastes, whether from the bathroom, kitchen, or laundry.) All of these treatment plants differ from each other in one or more basic design characteristics, beginning with the composition of the tanks themselves. Some are reinforced precast concrete, others are made of fiberglass-reinforced plastic. Further differences include the method of aeration, which may be accomplished by mechanical stirring, or by diffusion, which requires a compressor. The effluent may or may not be filtered. If filtered, the filtration may be physical or biological. Systems may be fill-and-draw batch or "continuous" flow. With batch systems, there's usually an early morning period of enforced tank quiescence before the effluent is drawn off. The systems may also include primary sedimentation or other pretreatment units.

The most widely used aerobic system is manufactured by Jet Aeration Company, which has been in business since 1955 and pioneered in the development of both commercial and individual home sewage treatment systems. The Jet Home Plant is a central treatment plant in miniature. Constructed from reinforced precast concrete, its design incorporates three separate compartments, each performing a specific function. The primary compartment receives the household sewage and holds it long enough to allow solid matter to settle to the sludge layer at the tank's bottom, where organic solids are broken

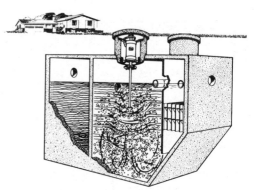

The Jet Home Plant, incorporating three compartments, each of which performs a separate function, is a central sewage treatment plant in miniature. With fresh air bubbled through the waste to speed the aerobic process, the effluent is primarily clear, odorless water. *Jet Aeration Company*

down physically and biochemically by anaerobic bacteria. The partially broken-down slurry that passes on to the aeration compartment is much easier to treat than raw sewage. The patented Jet aerator, cycled to run only part of each day, injects large quantities of fresh air into this compartment to provide oxygen for the aerobic digestion process and mixes the compartment's entire contents.

The final phase of the operation takes place in the settling/clarifying compartment, the design of which encourages the settling of any remaining settlable material. This is returned, via the tank's sloping end wall, to the aeration compartment for further treatment until the necessary oxidation takes place. A surface skimmer returns any floating material to the aeration compartment. The remaining odorless, clarified liquid flows into the final discharge line through a baffled outlet. An optional upflow filter and/or a nonmechanical tablet chlorinator can be added to the plant if local health authorities require this extra treatment.

If you think an aerobic wastewater

treatment plant could do the job where a septic tank can't, other units to look into might include those manufactured by Eastern Environmental Controls, Cromaglass Corporation, and Nayadic Sciences. All offer models with rated capacities of 400 gallons per day (gpd). Prices for aerobic systems run a bit higher than for anaerobic septic tanks of the same materials. The standard Jet Home Plant, for example, which has a 500-gpd rated capacity, would cost around $900 installed (not including the absorption field). You would also have to allow for the electrical demands of the system (most operate with a $\frac{1}{4}$-hp motor or compressor) if you're producing your own power.

Aerobic wastewater treatment plants not only are easier on the absorption field but should permit a reduction in its size, which could be an important consideration. In several localities, codes permit a one-third reduction in the size of the absorption field. Some experts hold that a two-thirds reduction should be possible. With the purity of the effluent from aerobic treatment systems, other options for effluent disposal are being investigated.

As part of a recent test—the Appalachian Regional Commission's Home Wastewater Demonstration Program, in Boyd County, Kentucky—effluent from some of the thirty-six single-family aerobic systems used in the one-year demonstration was found to be pure enough, following nonmechanical chlorination in the discharge line, to release directly into surface waters with no environmental risk, thus avoiding the need for any absorption field. (While the effluent from aerobic systems can be made acceptable for release into natural waterways, few sanitary codes will permit the practice because of the system's dependence on a power source for extended aeration of the sewage. In the event of a power failure, the system would become essentially anaerobic.) In another case, where the problem was a high water table, the effluent went into an evapo-transpiration mound—gravel and sand on an impermeable polyethylene sheet, covered with 2 inches of topsoil and planted with waterhungry juniper and other vegetation for transpiration.

Sludge accumulations in the NSF-approved aerobic tanks of the six manufacturers who participated in the Appalachian program was quite low, with pumping-out estimated to be required on a five-year cycle.

In some areas, where the water table is high or the soil has poor percolation, local health authorities, following the guidelines of the Clean Water Act of 1977, have outlawed septic tanks, while permitting installation of home aeration plants. Acceptance of aerobic treatment systems has been slow in many other areas, though, due mostly to early mechanical problems and a lack of timely repair service. They do require maintenance on a regular basis. NSF's endorsement, even where the unit would be otherwise acceptable, is granted only to those manufacturers who include a two-year initial service policy (with a minimum of two service calls annually and emergency service when required) in the original purchase price.

WASTEWATER RECYCLING SYSTEMS

Another way to surmount local restrictions is wastewater recycling. A fascinating range of systems has been developed to overcome all sorts of problems—from limited water supply to sewage disposal with soils that won't perc at all. Some systems are geared to handle "graywater" only, recycling mostly bath and laundry water for reuse in toilets or for irrigation. Other systems take on "blackwater" from the toilet, cleaning it up for reuse over and over again in the toilet system—which accounts for roughly 40 percent of the water used in most homes. There are even more sophisticated systems, spun off from the space program, that can take *all* the household wastewater and recycle it to drinking-water quality. Water conservation here approaches 100 percent, since the water is suitable for all domestic uses.

One of the least complicated solutions to home water supply and septic tank problems is the Aquasaver system. Certified by NSF and marketed nationally, the Aquasaver can reduce residential water consumption by up to 45 percent, with a corresponding reduction in wastewater disposal volume. The system captures lightly polluted wastewater from tubs, showers, bathroom sinks, and washing machines. (Kitchen wastes are specifically excluded.) The wastewater is treated and purified (by chlorination) to safe environmental standards and stored for toilet flushing and, if permitted by local regulation, lawn sprinkling. Provision is made in the system for automatic input of fresh

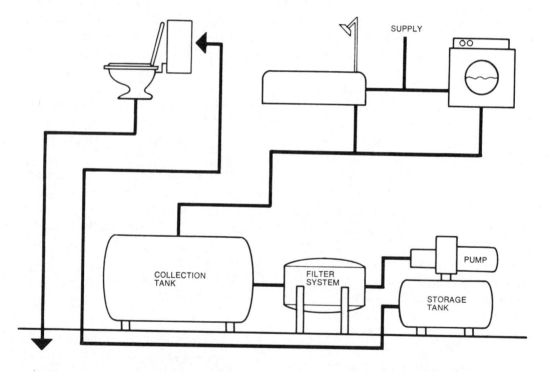

SUPPLY

COLLECTION TANK

FILTER SYSTEM

PUMP

STORAGE TANK

Water conservation as practiced in the NASA Tech House reduces the freshwater needs of a family of four by some 40,000 gallons per year. Wastewater from the bathtub, shower, and washing machine is collected, chlorinated, and filtered, then used to supply flushing water for the two toilets. The water recycling, together with the use of low-flush toilets and flow-limiting showerheads, reduces water consumption to half of what it would normally be and at the same time trims the sewage load. *NASA Tech House*

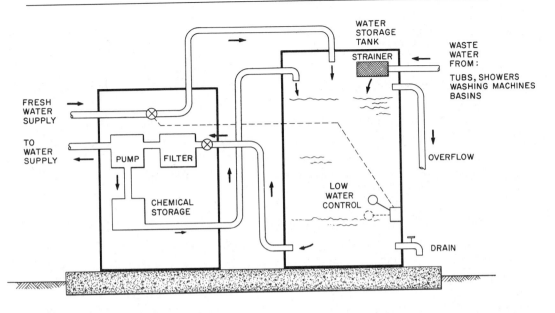

The Aquasaver residential wastewater recycling system reduces residential water consumption by up to 45 percent, with a corresponding reduction in wastewater disposal volume. *Aquasaver, Inc.*

water to the storage tank should the recycled water supply fall below a predetermined level, and for discharge of any tank overflow into a drain system. The Aquasaver costs about $2,500.

Designed to handle both graywater and blackwater, the Cromaglass Wastewater Treatment System essentially filters and disinfects aerobic effluent. The domestic wastewater treatment and recycling system is composed of an aerobic batch-treatment tank, a large prefabricated sand filter, a holding tank for disinfection by solid-state chlorination or iodination, a pressure tank, and a carbon filter. Installed cost for a complete Cromaglass recycling system, including filtration and disinfection, would be in the $6,000 range. This would provide recycled water for flush toilets, irrigation, and other nonpotable uses.

The Cycle-Let waste treatment system, manufactured by the Thetford Corporation, is designed primarily for the contin-

uous recycling of wastewater for reuse in the flushing of air-assisted, low-flush toilets and urinals in public and other large-traffic restrooms. Cycle-Let, through the innovative combination of basic biological water purification principles and electromechanical devices, converts blackwater into clear, odorless, colorless water, free of harmful bacteria. While not potable, it is quite suitable for carrying wastes. The smallest Cycle-Let, the totally self-contained Model SU-45, allows forty-five flushes per day on a regular basis and peak loadings of up to ninety flushes per day. Other Cycle-Let systems treat up to 250 flushes per day. While the off-the-shelf systems are remarkably effective, they represent a lot more engineering than is needed to serve most homes, and are priced accordingly. You're looking at a bottom price of at least $17,000, F.O.B. Ann Arbor, Michigan.

The most sophisticated household water recycling system introduced to date comes from the PureCycle Corporation. PureCycle has applied microprocessor controls and advanced water purification methods in the development of the Pure-Cycle System, which produces water of high quality and at the same time eliminates sewer requirements for wastewater disposal. The PureCycle System consists of three basic components: a 1,500-gallon tank to contain incoming wastewater; the purification system, operated and monitored by the microprocessor; and a 1,500-gallon cistern to store the purified water.

The PureCycle System is initially charged with 1,500 gallons of fresh water to be used for all household purposes. Through various domestic water uses, this becomes wastewater, to be recycled again and again through the system's five purification and treatment processes: organic reduction, ultrafiltration, adsorption, demineralization, and sterilization. Throughout the purification process, sensors send data to the microprocessor, which constantly measures the quality of the water and activates corrective maintenance programs as required. The system is sized to provide 400 gallons of potable water per day, with 7 gallons per minute at 30 to 50 pounds per square inch (psi).

Sales of the system are presently limited to 50-mile-radius areas in which at least 150 units are installed. A service center is set up along with a computer to monitor all units; the microprocessor in each Pure-Cycle System regularly transmits data to the service center through the homeowner's telephone line, if he so elects. The system is sold on a contractual basis: $5,000 (proposed price), plus a $240 annual service charge. The wastewater tank and the cistern are not included in this price.

On-site water recycling for individual homes is a brand-new industry, and with

the Clean Water Act of 1977 vigorously encouraging the development of cost-effective, alternative, nonpolluting sanitation systems, particularly for use in rural areas, many innovations can be expected here during the 1980s. In certain low-population areas, EPA grants are available for projects using "innovative and alternative" wastewater treatment processes that eliminate the discharge of pollutants and utilize recycling techniques.

We should get used to the fact that water in many places is in short supply and must be used more than once. You might not like to think you are drinking recycled wastewater, but a great many people are doing so—and with no risk to their health. Modern treatment plants are quite capable of cleaning sewage wastes from water and making it perfectly safe to drink. Many communities are already using treated water that has been discharged through the sewers of cities and towns upstream. The farther downstream you live, the more often that water will have been reused.

Some of these recycling systems, while making a notable contribution to self-sufficiency and removing the availability of sewers or good perc soil as the first priority in site selection, represent a larger investment than many of us might care to make—or can afford. But consider the PureCycle System, or one like it, since there undoubtedly will be others designed to do much the same thing. With it, you eliminate the need not only for an extensive sewage disposal system but for a well, too, which easily could represent an additional several thousand dollars. You'd also pay a lot more for a sewered site, or land with good percolation.

There are still other alternatives to be presented here, and the pluses and minuses of each system should be weighed.

There's undoubtedly one that suits your needs and/or budget, if not lifestyle, better than any other.

COMPOSTING TOILETS

For many dedicated environmentalists, the *only* answer to the sewage disposal problem is a toilet that uses natural processes to convert human wastes into a useful product. Composting toilets do exactly that. These organic waste treatment systems are exemplified by the Clivus Multrum, first imported from Sweden in 1974.

Composting toilets do not use water. Install one, instead of a conventional flush toilet, and you immediately reduce your household water needs by as much as 40 percent—the water that would normally be used in flushing. Basically, the Clivus Multrum, which translates to "inclining compost room" and handles both human wastes and organic wastes from the kitchen, is an irregularly shaped fiberglass box, approximately 4 by 5 by 9 feet, with a slanted bottom. It is usually installed in the basement, and vertical chutes connect the compost reactor to the toilet and a kitchen refuse opening. There's also a vent stack to the roof, topped by a rotary exhaust turbine.

The Clivus Multrum is "seeded" with a deep bed of peat moss, garden soil, and grass clippings when it's first installed. Human wastes enter the high end of the compost box and kitchen wastes are introduced toward the center. With the heat of the compost reaction, up to 95 percent of the waste goes up the vent pipe and into the atmosphere as carbon dioxide and

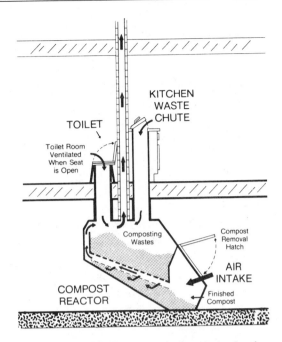

The Clivus Multrum organic waste treatment system—or composting toilet—uses no water. Install one, and you immediately reduce your water needs by as much as 40 percent and the waste disposal problem to graywater only. *Clivus Multrum U.S.A., Inc.*

water vapor, the main products of bacterial decomposition. Screened air ducts and baffles speed the essentially aerobic decomposition. With the exhaust stack, natural air convection creates a downdraft when the lid of the toilet or kitchen waste chute is raised, and keeps any odors from escaping into the house.

There is no effluent. The peat moss absorbs urine until it can be evaporated, and keeps the system from becoming waterlogged and anaerobic. The residue slips down the precisely calculated slope at glacial speed and eventually reaches the storage compartment at the lower, front end. It takes from two to four years for waste to make its way to the storage bin. By this time, the residue is a dry, potash-rich humus, which is safe for use as plant fertilizer and soil conditioner. The waterless toilet generates from 3 to 10 gallons of compost per family member per year.

The basic Clivus Multrum can serve three adults year-round, with allowance for visitors. Optional midsections can boost this capacity. The price of the basic Clivus Multrum package is $1,685, and includes all the components necessary to install the unit, except a cradle for the tank.

Most sanitary codes were written in the Dark Ages and give blanket approval only to hookups to central sewer systems; the installation, by professional crews, of septic tanks and absorption fields; and, in some areas, pit privies. Installation of a Clivus Multrum in most states requires special permission from local public health officials. However, three states— Maine, New Hampshire, and Kentucky— have formally approved the system. Massachusetts and Pennsylvania have okayed it in principle. Iowa has given de facto approval of the system, and so has Vermont. Oregon has granted tentative approval. Units have been installed in most states under permissive state laws that allow the local health officials to approve or reject applications for so-called alternative systems. The U.S. licensee for the Clivus Multrum system has prepared a packet of information, which could be useful if you find that the local agencies are unfamiliar with this answer to the extravagantly wasteful flush toilet. It has been fully approved by Swedish and Norwegian national health authorities.

There are a number of smaller composting toilets scaled for vacation-home use— or year-round use by one or two people. The advantage with most of the smaller units is that, unlike the Clivus Multrum, which has to be accommodated into the design of the house, the unit sits entirely within the bathroom and requires no additional installation except the vent pipe.

The disadvantage may be that almost all of them require electrical assistance—to power a built-in fan to circulate air for oxygen supply and odor removal, and a backup heating coil, usually thermostatically controlled, to maintain composting temperatures at an efficient level.

The Clivus Multrum, which is preinsulated with a half-inch of foam, generates nearly ideal temperatures for composting and doesn't require supplementary heat so long as the area in which it is installed is heated during the winter months. The smaller units don't generate as much heat in the composting process; and since waste-digesting bacteria become dormant at temperatures much below 68° F., interior backup heat is needed. Various temperatures suit the different types of microorganisms, but the most effective range for aerobic reaction is 85° to 95° F. Like the Clivus Multrum, the smaller composters are seeded with peat moss for better moisture control. They, too, appreciate kitchen scraps, though in limited quantity. Odors, carbon dioxide, and water vapor are drawn off through the ventilation pipe.

The Bio-Loo, another Swedish import that is marketed here by Clivus Multrum U.S.A., isn't much larger than a chemical toilet with a holding tank. Even when serving only two people, the Bio-Loo needs to be "cleaned out" every ninety days or so. The compact Bio-Loo includes a mixing lever, which is pushed back and forth five or six times to turn a steel rotor and mix the wastes after each use. This is to prevent solidification—a problem with some small systems. Wastes are periodically moved from the storage chamber to a pasteurization chamber located in the "footstool"; this is done simply by opening a door in the Bio-Loo base and turning the mixer rotor a few times. The door is then closed and a pasteurizer is switched on. It will shut off automatically in about six hours. When the storage chamber next needs emptying, some months later, the pasteurizing chamber is opened and the "biologically safe" compost is added to the garden soil. With the Bio-Loo, a 25-watt fan maintains a constant draft within the unit, assuring that no odors enter the bathroom. The 100-watt heater coil and the 160-watt pasteurizer run intermittently. The Bio-Loo costs $795, delivery included, in the forty-eight contiguous states and Canada.

The Mullbänk composting toilet is still another import from Sweden. Formerly known here as the Ecolet, this self-contained system is the most widely used of the composting toilets, with nearly four thousand owners in the United States and forty thousand throughout the world. Somewhat larger than the Bio-Loo, the Mullbänk will serve two to four people year-round, or four to six for a summer season. The waste material rests on a grate, which is also the heating coil. To speed the natural biological decomposition process, the air intake is located below the waste pile; a silent fan, which runs continuously, sucks air through the waste. The 140-watt heating coil, which is thermostatically controlled, yields a high temperature of about 120° F. The residue—a powder-dry humus—is removed from the collecting tray at the bottom of the unit once or twice a year. Because it operates at slightly higher temperatures than other composting toilets, the Mullbänk requires the addition of water from time to time to keep the waste pile moist if the toilet is used by only one or two people. The fan and heating coil consume no more energy per month than a pair of 60-watt bulbs. List price of the Mullbänk is around $800.

Self-contained Mullbänk composting toilet is nonpolluting and odor-free. A thermostatically controlled heating element hastens the natural biological decomposition process, vaporizing liquids and leaving only a powder-dry humus that is removed from the collecting tray once or twice a year *R.E.C. of U.S., Inc.*

The newest composting toilet is the Carousel. For a switch, this one is manufactured in California. There are two sizes: the smaller Carousel will serve two persons; the larger model, four persons. For continuous year-round use, the larger model requires an accessory heating coil and a blower to accelerate the composting process. Aptly named, the Carousel is cylindrical, with four chambers. When one chamber is filled, the inner container is rotated a quarter-turn to place another chamber in position below the commode. This is done every six months. At the end of two years, when all the chambers are full, the odor-free compost is removed from the first chamber. Each chamber is

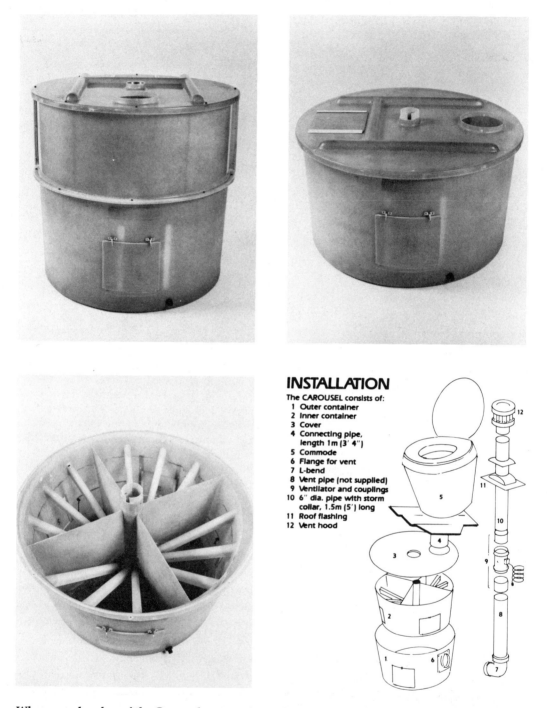

INSTALLATION

The CAROUSEL consists of:
 1 Outer container
 2 Inner container
 3 Cover
 4 Connecting pipe,
    length 1m (3' 4")
 5 Commode
 6 Flange for vent
 7 L-bend
 8 Vent pipe (not supplied)
 9 Ventilator and couplings
10 6" dia. pipe with storm
    collar, 1.5m (5') long
11 Roof flashing
12 Vent hood

When one chamber of the Carousel composting toilet (top left to right, complete unit, small container assembled; bottom left, view into small container) is filled, the inner container is rotated a quarter-turn to place another chamber in position below the commode. The first chamber normally is not emptied until two years after the toilet has been placed in service. *Enviroscope, Inc.*

emptied in turn, at six-month intervals. The larger Carousel is approximately 50 inches high. The composting container can be placed under the bathroom floor or steps can be built up to the commode. The space provided for the container, or the container itself, would have to be insulated for winter use. With the blower and heating coil, the larger Carousel costs $1,370; the smaller model is about $985.

OXIDIZING TOILETS

There are those who hold that any toilet employing a heating element to aid decomposition is a dehydrating or oxidizing toilet and not a true composting toilet. It's a matter of degree, with some composting toilets relying on supplementary heat more than others. For a true oxidizing toilet, the Destroilet deserves attention. Introduced more than fifteen years ago, the Destroilet uses heat provided by a gas burner, safely concealed in an insulated cabinet, to convert waste into nonpolluting vapor, carbon dioxide, and residual traces of sterile ash. Proven in tens of thousands of installations around the world, the combined toilet and incinerator is considered to be the granddaddy of indoor waterless toilets in this country.

Destroilets operate on either natural or liquefied petroleum (LP) gas. Installation amounts to connecting the gas supply, attaching a vertical flue having a good natural draft to the outside, and connecting a source of electricity. The oxidation cycle—12-to-16-minute oxidation period followed by a 6-minute cooling cycle—is started simply by closing the lid after use.

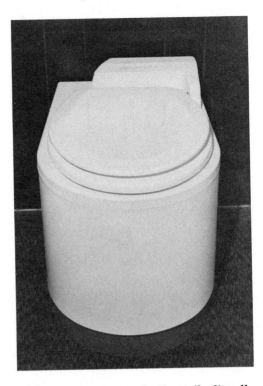

A true oxidizing toilet, the Destroilet literally incinerates waste, reducing it to dry sterile ash. *Marland Environmental Systems, Inc.*

Lowering the lid moves a heat shield into place and triggers the burner. The cycle can be interrupted for use of the toilet at any time. When the lid is raised, the burner shuts off and a blower exhausts all heat, steam, and odors to the outside via the flue.

A Destroilet can accommodate the full needs of twelve people, with up to sixty individual uses a day. The blower keeps the double-walled cabinet cool at all times. The seat is never too hot for comfort. Periodic removal of the sterile ash is the only maintenance required. Destroilet models are designed to operate specifically with natural or LP gas, and 115V AC, 220 to 240V AC, or 12V DC. Prices start at $699, not including flue materials.

GRAYWATER DISPOSAL

Any of these waterless toilets reduces household water needs significantly and eliminates the blackwater disposal problem. But for the average family there's still the matter of dealing with up to 200 gallons of graywater a day—the water from showering, bathing, dishwashing, and laundering, all of which is comparatively uncontaminated. Septic tanks are overdesigned for graywater treatment and, with toilet wastes excluded from the water to be dispersed, there should be no need for one. Filtration of the graywater is recommended, though, with a washwater roughing filter, or trickle filter, installed in the waste line to serve as a partial grease trap and to strain out lint, hair, food particles, and other solids that could clog an absorption field.

Unless you encounter a health officer who's adamantly upholding an antiquated code, you should be able to reduce the size of the absorption field by 40 to 50 percent over what would be required for a total wastewater disposal system. Approval for graywater disposal into tight soil conditions may be obtained where total wastewater would not be allowed. Variances that would permit the discharge of graywater into a drywell—a deep cylindrical pit, lined with cinder blocks and surrounded by 6 inches of gravel—or an evapo-transpiration mound may also be possible. After passing through a containerized washwater roughing filter, graywater might be found acceptable for shallow subsurface lawn or garden irrigation, or for irrigation in greenhouses and other indoor soil ditches where there is plant life.

The higher the quality of the graywater, the greater the number of alternatives for accommodating it. Passed through a sim-

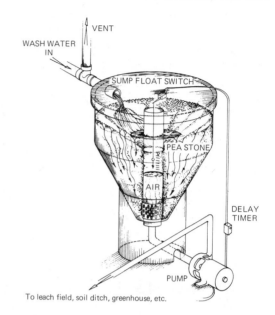

The Clivus Multrum washwater roughing filter for use with graywater disposal systems. *Clivus Multrum U.S.A., Inc.*

ple cone-shaped gravel filter where aerobic conditions prevail, the effluent will take up oxygen and be virtually odorless. Generally, however, you are not permitted to discharge graywater into surface water because of the potentially high concentrations of nitrogen and phosphorus in the wastewater.

LOW-FLUSH TOILETS

All sorts of water-saving gimmicks have been tried with standard flush toilets. There's the brick-in-the-tank trick, for one. The city fathers of Cherry Hill, New Jersey, purchased 34,000 bricks a few years ago and distributed them to the town's homeowners, telling them that if each of them placed a brick in his toilet tank, the town would be able to save 34 million gallons of water a year. The city fathers didn't know a whole lot about plumbing, however. They failed to tell the cooperating citizens that a brick laid horizontally in a toilet tank won't save any more water than it initially displaces. When a toilet is flushed, the tank doesn't completely empty. The level holds at between 2 and 3 inches from the bottom of the tank. This is just enough to keep the U.S. standard brick submerged, so it doesn't save another drop. To save water, any object placed in the tank must extend above the maximum drainage level.

Most of those water dams that are sold for installation in a toilet tank aren't much good either. Toilets designed for a 5-gallon (or better) flush get nearly as much water from the inflow during the flushing action as drains from the tank. Furthermore, if you shortchange the flushing shock, you all too frequently have to reflush to clear the bowl.

Low-flush toilets must have the saving designed into them. This means not simply reducing the size of the reservoir tank but engineering the bowl with a smaller-diameter trapway for positive, thorough flushing action with less water. All the major manufacturers of toilets have introduced low-flush models with shallow-trap bowls that use approximately 3½ gallons of water per flush. This can represent a significant saving when you figure that the typical family of four, with a 5-gallon-flush toilet, flushes away some 40,000 gallons a year. With 3½ gallons per flush, there's a saving of 12,000 gallons a year. And 12,000 fewer gallons a year to be disposed of down the line. Reducing the production of wastewater helps prevent septic tank overloads. It also cuts down on the energy needed to pump the water, and you could settle for a smaller-capacity well system.

But why stop at 3½ gallons? Microphor Low Flush toilets do it with 2 *quarts* of water, for a 90 percent saving in water when compared to the standard 5-gallon-flush toilet. The Microphor toilets get an assist from compressed air, supplied by a ½-hp compressor or, in nonelectric households, pressurized bottled air. When the flush lever is depressed, water and wastes are immediately deposited into a lower evacuation hopper built into the structure of the toilet. There is a complete water wash of the bowl before it refills with water to form a seal. At this point, the secondary chamber is pressurized with compressed air and the waste is discharged into the household waste line.

These toilets are in wide use in boats, trains, air terminals, and park restrooms, being particularly suited to areas where water conservation and/or reduced sewage volume has to be achieved. Price of the toilet is about $450, with another $200 or so for a ½-hp compressor with a 12-gallon air tank.

With a low-flush toilet, septic tank influent is more concentrated. But that shouldn't cause any problems, since it adds to the retention time in the tank. The effluent is clearer and there is less to dispose of.

Oil-flush toilets, which are closed-loop, recirculating toilets, and vacuum-flush toilets, which use a minimum of water, were designed originally for use aboard ships and in industrial complexes and commercial applications where no public sewers exist. Oil and water don't mix, so with oil-flush toilets it's easy for the system to separate the sewage, by gravity and sanitizing means, from the transport medium and recycle the clear, odorless, low-viscosity mineral oil. But the system requires a sewage settling/holding tank, which has to be pumped out by a servic-

TABLE THREE

A COMPARATIVE LOOK AT THE PERFORMANCE OF THE MICROPHOR LOW-FLUSH TOILET VS. ALTERNATE TOILET SYSTEMS IN A VARIETY OF KEY OPERATING AREAS

	Microphor	Oil Flush	Vacuum System	Chemical System
Low initial installation cost	Yes	No	No	Yes
Lowest maintenance cost	Yes	No	No	No
Easiest retrofit	Yes	No	No	No
High volume usage capability	Yes	No	Yes	No
Can be used with existing treatment system	Yes	No	Yes	No
Noise level compared to standard toilet	Lower	Lower	Higher	Lower
Can be used with existing plumbing	Yes	No	No	No
Low power requirement	Yes	No	No	Yes

Source: Microphor, Inc.

ing company when the sewage reaches a certain level. And if millions turned to recirculating toilets, there'd be a huge problem of solid-waste collection. They do not solve the problem of human waste disposal. Vacuum-flush toilets share the same disadvantages. The waste and about 3 pints of water are moved by air with each flush and collected in a tank, which holds the sewage for removal by truck.

One of the advantages of a vacuum system, such as Envirovac, is that the waste pipe, which is rigid 2-inch PVC, can be routed uphill and around obstacles if the terrain makes that necessary. Constant pressure of 7.5 psi is produced by a vacuum pump driven by a $1/2$-hp electric motor. Cost for an Envirovac toilet system with an 80-gallon holding tank would be $2,500 or more, while a central collection system for an entire subdivision might range from $1,200 to $2,000 per house. A

visual and audible alarm is activated when the sewage in the tank reaches 90 percent of the tank's capacity.

PORTABLE TOILETS

You probably wouldn't want to have to depend on one for full-time, year-round use, but there are some very well-engineered portable flush-type toilets that might meet your needs in a hideaway with no running water or a vacation home that doesn't get a lot of visitors. These toilets come with detachable holding tanks (the top section includes the cover, seat, bowl, and water supply) and typically can accommodate up to eighty flushes—with a small charge of water from a 4- or 5-gallon supply—before the holding tank has to be taken to a permanent sewage facility for dumping. (Teach the family to urinate

Portable flushing toilets might serve your needs in a vacation home or hideaway that doesn't get a lot of visitors. They have a detachable waste-holding tank that separates from the seat and water supply section for transportation to a permanent sewage facility for dumping. *Mansfield Sanitary, Inc.*

elsewhere, wherever possible, and you can stretch out the time between trips to the dump.) These are the toilets that helped make self-contained recreational-vehicle (RV) travel/camping so popular. A bacteriostat keeps the contents of the holding tank odorless and reasonably sterile. Floor hold-down brackets are usually available. The waste could even be piped to a larger holding tank to be pumped out by a servicing company. Cost of these toilets, which are mostly hassock-style, ranges from less than $100 to around $285. They're sold by Sears and the other mass merchandisers and RV suppliers.

URINALS

With more conventional plumbing and a predominantly male household, you might also consider installing a urinal. The vitreous china restroom-type urinal costs around $100 and uses only about a pint of water per flush.

THREE

HEATING AND COOLING

It would be foolish today not to integrate energy efficiencies into your building plans—doubly so, when you're seeking self-sufficiency. This means not only observing the new energy codes that require higher R-values of insulation, control the percentage of glass in new construction, and require "Energy-Guide" labeling (giving annual operating cost estimates) for most major home appliances, but also designing a house that *relates to its environment.* Do not waste this opportunity by designing the house before finding a site for it!

To reduce its heating and cooling energy requirements, a house should not only be positioned for access to the sun but should be located to take full advantage of the geography of the area surrounding the site, including seasonal windflow patterns. Socrates was on the right track circa 430 B.C., when he wrote: "We should build the south side loftier to get the winter sun and the north side lower to keep out the cold winds."

Early-nineteenth-century New Englanders were even more energy-wise. They built their houses with thick walls and small windows, and located fireplaces and chimneys centrally for more efficient heating. Screening the house from the cold north wind and shading it from the summer sun were common Yankee practices. And what better application of Socrates' teaching than the traditional New England saltbox design, which slopes from two-story front to one-story rear?

As you plan your house and its placement on the site, here are some points to consider:

- The seasonal path of the sun across the site.
- Orientation of the house (its physical placement in relation to the sun's path) to benefit from natural solar gain.
- The prevailing windflow patterns around and through the site.
- The presence of trees and earth formations that may usefully block the sun or wind.

In cold climates, the major axis of the house ideally should run north-south, with major glass areas facing south, to

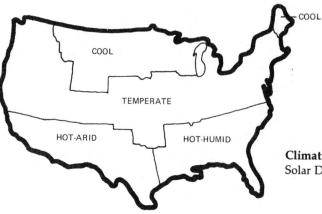

Climatic regions of the United States *Source:* *Solar Dwelling Design Concepts*

TABLE FOUR

SITE ORIENTATION CHART

OBJECTIVES	Cool	Temperate	Hot Humid	Hot Arid
	Maximize warming effects of solar radiation. Reduce impact of winter wind. Avoid local climatic cold pockets.	Maximize warming effects of sun in winter. Maximize shade in summer. Reduce impact of winter wind but allow air circulation in summer.	Maximize shade. Maximize wind.	Maximize shade late morning and all afternoon. Maximize humidity. Maximize air movement in summer.
ADAPTATIONS				
Position on slope	Low for wind shelter	Middle-upper for solar radiation exposure	High for wind	Low for cool air flow
Orientation on slope	South to southeast	South to southeast	South	East-southeast for P.M. shade
Relation to water	Near large body of water	Close to water, but avoid coastal fog	Near any water	On lee side of water
Preferred winds	Sheltered from north and west	Avoid continental cold winds	Sheltered from north	Exposed to prevailing winds
Clustering	Around sun pockets	Around a common, sunny terrace	Open to wind	Along east-west axis, for shade and wind
Building orientation*	Southeast	South to southeast	South, toward prevailing wind	South
Tree forms	Deciduous trees near building. Evergreens for windbreaks	Deciduous trees nearby on west. No evergreens nearby on south	High canopy trees. Use deciduous trees near building	Trees overhanging roof if possible
Road orientation	Crosswise to winter wind	Crosswise to winter wind	Broad channel, east-west axis	Narrow, east-west axis
Materials coloration	Medium to dark	Medium	Light, especially for roof	Light on exposed surfaces, dark to avoid reflection

* Must be evaluated in terms of impact on solar collector, size, efficiency, and tilt.

Source: Solar Dwelling Design Concepts

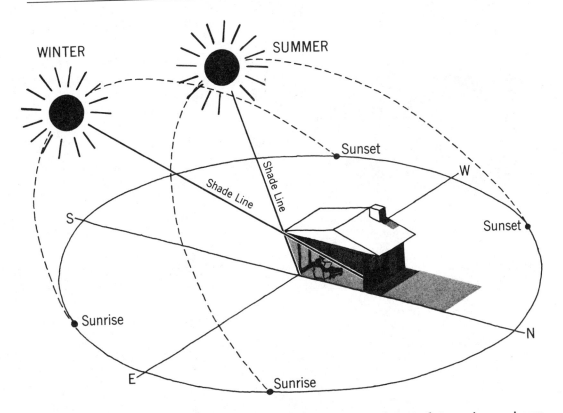

WINTER

SUMMER

Sunset

W

Shade Line

Shade Line

S

Sunset

Sunrise

N

E

Sunrise

Orienting the house so that the main rooms and large glass areas face south to receive maximum sunlight in the winter reduces the house's requirements for heating energy. Roof overhangs can shield the south-facing windows from direct sun during the summer months. (Illustration shows position of sun at noon for latitude 40° north.) *Source:* Home Heating—Systems . . . Fuels . . . Controls

take advantage of natural solar gain during the months when the sun rises and sets well to the south of the east-west line. These south-facing windows should be shielded from the high-arcing summer sun by overhangs or projecting eaves calculated to shade them in summer and allow maximum heat gain through the windows in winter. Windows to the north and northwest should be minimized where winters are severe.

In warm climates, an east-west major axis is best, with the short sides placed toward east and west to limit the wall and window areas exposed to low-angle sun. When the sun is high during the day, wall and window exposure is minimal, with

most radiation falling on roof surfaces. In hot climates, prevailing winds should also be considered to allow maximum ventilation for natural cooling.

Temper your desire for a great view with the knowledge that the best views, particularly with respect to mountain properties, often are from the worst possible locations for a house. If the view you want is from a hilltop looking north or northwest, you'll likely need a lot more energy for winter heating than self-sufficiency can comfortably provide. In cooler regions, however, south-facing slopes can provide maximum exposure for passive or active solar heating. The thing to remember here is that it's generally more com-

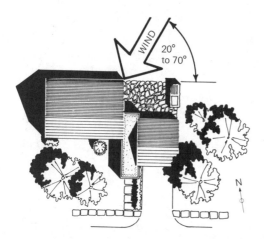

Orientation for natural ventilation begins by locating the facade through which breezes will enter at an angle of 20 to 70 degrees between the wall and the wind direction. This increases turbulence and provides better ventilation. *Source:* Passive Design Ideas for the Energy Conscious Architect

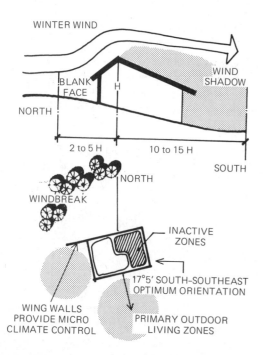

Site orientation in cool regions should have as its objective the maximizing of the warming effects of solar radiation and the minimizing of the impacting winter wind. *Source:* Solar Dwelling Design Concepts

fortable halfway up a slope than it is at the top or in a valley.

If your design for a northern home has long east and west sides, consider extending the north face 3 or 4 feet at each corner to serve as a windbreak. Or plan to add equivalent stockade fencing or dense shrubbery at the northeast and northwest corners. These barriers can alter wind-pressure patterns and reduce heat loss through east and west walls and windows.

Even in built-up areas, orientation should be to the sun or prevailing wind, rather than to the street. If this means aiming the rear of the house toward the street, so be it. In colder climates, putting the garage or carport between the house and the prevailing winter wind will provide additional protection. You might also consider adding a vestibule at one or more entrances, especially if your family includes youngsters or pets who are in and out of the house several times a day. Entryways isolated from living areas can cut your heating needs significantly.

Trees, too, can be used to good advantage in an energy-saving plan. On the east, south, and west, such deciduous trees as oaks, elms, and maples, placed to shade the house from the summer sun, will lose their leaves in the fall and allow the low-lying winter sun to stream into south-facing windows and solar heat collectors. To the north and northwest, a shelter belt of evergreens can lend variety and help baffle winter winds.

INSULATION

Neither orientation of the house for direct solar gain nor strategic landscaping is as effective as insulation when it comes to saving energy. Insulation is where energy saving *really* begins. The payback period (return on the investment in money saved through reduced energy needs) is shorter for a superior job of insulation (including reducing window area and using double- and triple-glazed windows where heat loss in winter is the primary concern) than it is for any other energy-saving device or strategy that directly relates to heating and cooling the house. It is money well spent. Pay heed to heating and cooling authority Seichi Konzo, who recommends that "everyone should prepare his structure as if it were heated by the most expensive fuel of the future."

By now, your state undoubtedly has written and adopted an energy code covering new construction, based more or less on a model code produced by the American Society of Heating, Refrigerating, and Air-Conditioning Engineers (ASHRAE). This model code, called ASHRAE Standard 90-75, Energy Conservation in New Building Design, became the accepted guide in 1977 when adopted by the National Conference of States on Building Codes and Standards. In most areas, homes built under the new codes are expected to cut energy needs an average of 20 percent over comparable noncode construction.

Key provisions of a typical state code are likely to include:

- Limiting the percentage of glass in a home to no more than 13 to 17 percent of the total wall area.
- A *minimum* R-19 insulation requirement, equivalent to 6 inches of fiberglass batt insulation, for attics.
- No sliding glass doors or picture windows without extra insulation, protective overhangs, or permanent-type shutters that can shield the glass from the direct summer sun.

Insulation needs don't vary all that much from the northern-tier states to the sunbelt. You need nearly as much insulation to keep cool efficiently when the temperature soars as you do to keep warm when it plummets. Indeed, in south Florida, where the temperature from May 1 to November 1 seldom drops below 75°F. (and that's at night!), the new state energy code requires builders to insulate homes for the first time, with a minimum of 6 inches of fiberglass batt insulation or the equivalent placed over ceilings of typical concrete-block-and-stucco homes.

There *is* such a thing as too much insulation. A house could be blanketed to the point where, even on a frigid day, it could be kept heated to 68°F. solely by the body heat of the occupants. But they'd probably suffocate from lack of oxygen before they got comfortable. There's also the law of diminishing returns. While more may be better, each additional inch of insulation is a little less effective than the one before. You eventually reach the point where the cost of the additional insulation is not justified by the energy saved.

It is realistically possible, however, with a well-insulated house designed to capture passive solar energy through triple-glazed south-facing windows, to cut heating needs by two-thirds, with 80 percent of the savings achieved through superior insulation.

Until recently, "6 and 3" (6 inches in the ceiling, 3 inches in the walls) was considered the optimum insulation in northern states, "3 and 2" in southern states. But those formulas are no longer acceptable to those who would conserve energy. Nor, with the many different types and brands of insulation, is the thickness of the batt, fill, or slab an acceptable measure of the insulation's effectiveness. All insulating materials are *not* created equal.

You'd do well to think of insulation

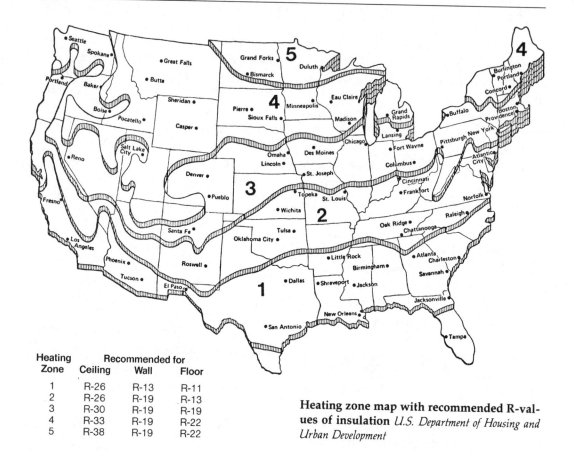

Heating	Recommended for		
Zone	Ceiling	Wall	Floor
1	R-26	R-13	R-11
2	R-26	R-19	R-13
3	R-30	R-19	R-19
4	R-33	R-19	R-22
5	R-38	R-19	R-22

Heating zone map with recommended R-values of insulation *U.S. Department of Housing and Urban Development*

only in terms of its R-value—not inches. This is a numerical measure, determined by laboratory testing, of the material's ability to resist heat flow. The greater the effectiveness of the insulation in preventing heat from leaking out of or into a house, the higher the R-value. While many in the construction industry arbitrarily assign an R-value of 1.0 to 1 inch of wood, different woods of the same thickness have different R-values, as do different kinds of factory-produced insulations. For instance, 1 inch of northern white cedar, which is widely used for modern log houses, has an R-value of 1.41. Sugar maple, on the other hand, has an R-value of 0.8. Redwood is the only wood to which the U.S. Department of Agriculture (USDA) assigns an R-value of 1.0, and it would take a redwood wall

roughly 19 inches thick to give as much protection as a 6-inch blanket of pink Fiberglas.

While wood is less efficient than most factory-produced insulations, it insulates 6 times better than brick, 15 times better than concrete, and 1,770 times better than aluminum—which should be reason enough to choose wood-framed rather than aluminum-framed windows for an energy-efficient northern home. Another recent test, conducted by researchers at the University of Illinois, that speaks well for wood construction, showed that a wood house uses 26 percent less energy in winter and 18 percent less in summer than an identical masonry house.

Our concern here, however, is not with primary construction materials, other than to point out the inherent advantages of

TABLE FIVE

R-VALUES CHART

| | BATTS OR BLANKETS | | LOOSE FILL (POURED IN) | | |
	Glass Fiber (inches)	Rock Wool (inches)	Glass Fiber (inches)	Rock Wool (inches)	Cellulosic Fiber (inches)
R-11	3½–4	3	5	4	3
R-13	4	4½	6	4½	3½
R-19	6–6½	5¼	8–9	6–7	5
R-22	6½	6	10	7–8	6
R-26	8	8½	12	9	7–7½
R-30	9½–10½	9	13–14	10–11	8
R-33	11	10	15	11–12	9
R-38	12–13	10½	17–18	13–14	10–11

Source: Department of Energy

wood when building for self-sufficiency; it's with providing an efficient thermal envelope for that structure. Insulation has become an increasingly complex subject, but basically there are only four types of insulation.

Flexible insulation is a soft and woolly mineral fiber made from glass, rock, or slag. Available in easy-to-handle rolls (sometimes called blankets) or batts (shorter lengths, either 4 or 8 feet long), it comes in 15- and 23-inch widths and in thicknesses up to 12 inches. Both rolls and batts are available faced with kraft or foil (to form a vapor barrier on the "warm" side of the insulation) or unfaced. In new construction, flexible insulation is installed between wall studs, either 16 or 24 inches (with 2 by 6 studs) on center; between attic floor joists; and over unheated areas such as crawl spaces. In crawl spaces, the insulation is installed from below, vapor barrier up, and supported by chicken wire or cross braces. Kraft- or foil-faced insulation usually includes

flanges at the edges on the vapor barrier side for easy stapling installation. Flexible mineral-fiber insulation is by far the most widely used insulation going into new homes.

Pushing 6-inch fiberglass insulation batts into place between attic floor joists. Note that batts are unfaced and are being installed atop loose-fill insulation. *CertainTeed Corp.*

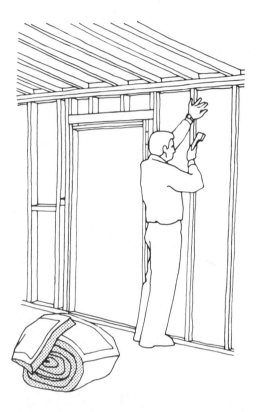

With the vapor-resistant membrane faced toward the area to be heated, flexible insulation is fitted into standard-width stud spaces and the flanges are stapled every 6 to 8 inches to the studs. Insulation should fit tightly at top and bottom plates. *Johns-Manville*

Loose-fill insulation is made from glass, rock, slag, or even macerated paper. It is poured between attic floor joists or, in mostly older construction, "blown" into wall cavities through small holes drilled in the outside walls. It is sometimes used in ceilings in combination with flexible insulation, the one on top of the other. In the late 1970s, with many fly-by-nighters selling loose fill made in backyard operations from flammable and corrosive wood-cellulose materials, loose fill, in general, gave the insulation industry a black eye. Be very careful here and deal only with reputable insulation dealers and contractors. It takes a trained professional to achieve uniform insulating efficiency with blown materials.

Rigid-foam insulation comes as boards or panels of polystyrene or polyurethane, either 2 or 4 feet wide by 8 feet long, and in thicknesses from $\frac{3}{4}$ inch to 4 inches. This type of insulation can be very useful if you're building for maximum energy efficiency. In wood-frame construction, it's beginning to replace plywood sheathing. A significant new entry here is Styrofoam TG brand insulation. It is four

The tongue-and-groove edges of Styrofoam TG brand insulation interlock to assure a tight seal. Applied roofline to frost line, the rigid-foam insulation covers and insulates both the wood frame and the masonry foundation—two critical areas of heat loss that are usually ignored. *Dow Chemical U.S.A.*

Foam insulation, which initially has the consistency of aerosol shave cream, flows easily into gaps and crevices and then hardens to form a thermal barrier.
Homefoamers

times as resistant to heat loss as ordinary sheathing and, with tongue-and-groove edges, greatly reduces the possibility of air infiltration. Rigid foam insulates the entire wall, not just the spaces between studs, and can make flexible, in-the-wall insulation more effective. It can also be used to insulate slab-on-grade floors, with perimeter insulation placed along and under the edges of the foundation before the concrete is poured, and outside foundation walls, down to or below the frost line. It's excellent for post-and-beam construction. With A-frames, chalets, and other structures featuring an open-beam ceiling, this is what you'd use between the roof decking and the roofing felt and shingles. Rigid-foam insulation can pack a lot of resistance, and some urethane brands offer R-values as high as 8.0 per inch, or twice that of extruded polystyrene. One caution: Styrene and urethane are combustible and must be covered by a minimum of a half-inch of fire-code gyp-

sum wallboard or equivalent material when used in interior construction.

Foam insulation is the term that applies to all foamed-in-place insulating materials, such as urea-formaldehyde and Tripolymer. It consists of two basic ingredients—a foaming agent and a plastic resin. These are mixed together in an application gun and pumped under pressure into wall cavities, where they harden almost instantly into millions of tiny air cells. Foam is most often used to upgrade insulation in older structures, but it has also been used effectively to insulate geodesic dome houses, applied either to exterior or interior wall surfaces. There are improved puff resins, such as Tripolymer, which NASA used to insulate its Tech House, but here again, we would urge caution. Some foams have a tendency to "shrink and stink." Others disintegrate at attic temperatures. They should be installed by professional contractors.

If you're looking for a recommendation,

we would use both flexible *and* rigid-foam insulation in any new house we were building, taking all necessary precautions with the rigid foam to guard against its potential for introducing toxic fumes in a fire. We would further recommend that you follow the map on page 62 for *minimum* recommended insulation R-values for ceilings, walls, and floors in the six heating zones spanning the United States. The R-values suggest economical amounts of insulation based on electric-resistance heating and cooling (the "most expensive fuel" of today when purchased from utilities in most areas of the country). To accommodate flexible R-19 wall insulation, studding will have to be 2 by 6 (to deepen stud cavities) rather than the usual 2 by 4. However, if you use rigid insulating sheathing in combination with flexible insulation, 2 by 4s will provide all the depth needed for R-11 or R-13 batts. One inch of rigid-foam insulation as exterior sheathing and R-13 Fiberglas batts produce a through-the-wall R-value of 20-plus.

If you have to skimp, it's better to put a *little* insulation everywhere before you put a *lot* of insulation anywhere. The important thing is to include insulation in any barrier separating conditioned (by heating or cooling) space from unconditioned space. If you do the job yourself, be sure to follow the manufacturer's directions carefully.

Here are four tips to help you get the most out of insulation:

1. Flexible insulation is made fluffy on purpose. Do not cram it into a space that is too small for it. Squeezing the material lowers its R-value.
2. Route wiring and piping through a raceway along the sole plate to avoid interfering with the correct placement of in-the-wall insulation.
3. Face vapor barriers toward the warmer-in-winter side of the structure. In the attic floor, the vapor barrier should be down; in walls, the vapor barrier should face the interior of the house. If you use two layers of faced insulation, in the attic, for example, the vapor barrier must be stripped from the upper layer.
4. Most important of all, *do not buy any insulation that does not have the R-value plainly marked on the package.*

Insulation does not stop with the roof, walls, and floor of the house. A thermal jacket for an underinsulated water heater, wrap for exposed air-handling ducts, and insulation sleeves for long hot-water pipe runs all can more than pay their way in energy savings. Pay particular attention to the water heater. In most households, it's the second biggest user of energy. While water heaters are constructed with a layer of insulation between the glass-lined tank and the steel outer jacket, the insulation is sometimes pretty skimpy. If the jacket of the functioning water heater is warm to the touch, invest in a Johns-Manville Water Heater Insulation Kit (cost: about $25). The J-M kits are designed for easy, do-it-yourself insulation.

A word of caution: Underwriters Laboratories, the national electrical products testing organization, advises that insulation should not be placed over the access doors to the water-heater controls or over the house-wiring connection box. Underwriters Laboratories makes a good point. Insulation should not be packed around electrical connections, or fixtures containing lights, fans, or other heat-generating electrical devices. The danger of overheating, leading to shorts or fire, becomes too great.

While it is generally accepted that, square foot for square foot, insulation does the most good in the attic, air infiltration is the primary cause of heat loss in most homes. Warm air rises and will escape through even a well-insulated ceiling. This heated air is replaced by cold air drawn into the house mostly through cracks and gaps around windows and exterior doors. In a loosely constructed house, you have a chimney effect that can destroy a heating budget, with huge volumes of cold air sucked into the house by temperature and pressure differentials. No house should be made completely airtight, but cracks and gaps around windows and exterior doors *must* be closed up to make the house energy efficient.

Don't count on in-the-wall insulation doing the job for you. Batts and blankets, even when carefully installed, lose much of their effectiveness at "loose" edges bordering door and window frames. The most effective way to reduce air infiltration is to seal wall-to-ceiling, wall-to-floor, and wall-to-wall seams during construction and to embed window and door frames in caulking as they are installed. No amount of caulking applied later will do as good a job. Quality weatherstripping also is a must, even with windows and doors that appear to be properly fitted.

WINDOWS

Window glass, in the standard window thickness, is one of the least effective of all insulating materials. Single-strength window glass has an R-value of 0.89 and is one of the great villains in heat loss—

and unwanted heat gain. Insulating glass, also known as double-glazing, or Thermopane—two panes with a trapped air space between—is only moderately effective when it comes to preventing heat loss in winter or heat gain in summer. Its R-value is a feeble 1.65. Adding a storm window, for triple-glazing, boosts the R-value of insulating glass only modestly, to 2.13. When it's 0°F. outside and 68°F. inside, the temperature of the inner face of a single-pane window will be 15°F. Double-glazing brings the inside surface temperature up to 45°F., triple-glazing, to 55°F. In an otherwise well-insulated house, most of your heat loss will be via the windows.

Most architects accept the fact that heat escapes through windows and there's not much you can do about it, other than reducing the number and size of windows, especially on those sides of the house that will be buffeted by winter winds. On a frigid day, a 3-by-5-foot north-facing, double-glazed window can lose as much as 15,000 BTUs. On the other hand, an unobstructed, south-facing, double-glazed window of the same size, on a sunny though frigid day, can contribute a gain of 9,500 BTUs. That's a difference of 24,500 BTUs—the equivalent of one quart of oil with an oil-fired furnace or 7 kwh with conventional electric resistance heating. But then, if your south-facing window is not shaded from the direct sun during the summer, you'll throw all that additional heat onto the cooling system. And what happens in the wintertime when you don't see the sun for weeks?

Reducing energy losses through windows is not easily accomplished. We would, however, recommend the use of double-glazed windows in both northern and southern climates, with triple-glazing in the northernmost states and in Canada.

They do contribute to energy efficiency. Placement of major glass areas should be carefully thought out, not only to take advantage of winter solar gain but to admit cooling summer breezes and take advantage of natural cross-ventilation. You'll also have to include overhangs in your design to block the sun from south-facing windows where the focus is more on summer cooling than on winter heating.

Beyond that, there are several window-management strategies that may or may not work for you. In sunbelt states, the use of Scotchtint, Nunsun, Reflecto-Shield, and other sun-control films applied directly to window and sliding-door glass has become fairly common. In general, the thin plastic films reject up to 80 percent of solar heat and reduce winter heat loss through the glass by from 7 to 22 percent. It's difficult to strip some of the sunscreening materials from glass, however, and homeowners tend to leave it on year-round, which means that what they gain in summer they may lose in winter. The reflective film also severely restricts the amount of sunlight entering the house. You may have to make this up with additional incandescent or fluorescent lighting during the day.

Ford Sunglas and PPG Solarcool are tinted reflective glasses that stop as much as 24 percent of the sun's heat by absorbing and reflecting the sun's rays. They allow much more daylight to enter the house than do the sun-control films.

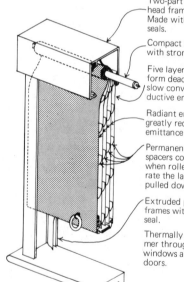

Two-part extruded plastic head frame for easy access. Made with integral head seals.

Compact single roll design with strong spring return.

Five layers expand to form dead air spaces that slow convective and conductive energy transfer.

Radiant energy flow greatly reduced with low emittance materials.

Permanently shaped spacers conform tightly when rolled up yet separate the layers when pulled down.

Extruded plastic jamb frames with integral jamb seal.

Thermally effective summer through winter at windows and sliding glass doors.

The IS High "R" Shade develops a resistance of about R-15 with a double-glazed window. When the shade is drawn, spacers separate the five layers of the shade to form dead air spaces for a high resistance to heat flow through the shade. *Insulating Shade Co., Inc.*

Where the climate can be blistering, you might consider one of these energy-saving environmental glasses for your windows and sliding doors.

Window shades and drapes can make an energy-saving contribution, but unless you move up to *insulating* shades and *thermal* drapes, it's likely to be a small one. With a house designed for passive solar heating, insulating shades and thermal drapes can help retain much of the heat gained during the day. Shutters are another window-management alternative that can be used effectively to block the heat of the sun or to limit heat losses. We're not talking about the decorative aluminum shutters now in vogue, but European-type roll shutters, with slats of extruded PVC material and interlocking design. Made by Pease (Ever-Strait), Rolladen, and others, the shutters mount on the outside and are operated from the inside for almost complete light control, from near total darkness to total use of the window or glass-door area. Stopping the sun by shutters or shading *before* it hits the glass is many times more effective in heat reduction than using inside shades and drapes.

DOORS

A thick, well-fitting, prehung entry door does not transmit much heat or cold—unless it has glass panels. In most cases, adding a storm door makes only a minimal contribution to energy saving. For efficiency, your best investment would be a single urethane-core door with magnetic weatherstripping. A number of manufacturers, including Lake Shore Industries, Steelcraft, Nord, and Simpson, offer ther-

mal doors. Lake Shore and Steelcraft feature insulated steel doors that duplicate the look of wood-paneled doors.

VENTILATION

A snug house is not without its problems. Two of them are summer heat build-up in the attic and winter moisture condensation, also in the attic. The problems, compounded by the use of higher R-values of insulation in the ceiling, make good attic ventilation an important part of any well-insulated house.

In a poorly ventilated attic, under typical summer sunbelt conditions, the under-the-ridge temperature can reach 160°F. and stay up there for weeks. Even with the new recommended R-values for ceiling insulation, enough heat will work its way down to maintain the ceiling temperature at 85°F. This heat, absorbed and held by the heavier insulation, will then be radiated to the living areas below. In the evening, when the house ought to be cooling off, there you sit, inside an oven.

During the winter months, in colder climates, with the house windows closed tight, moisture-laden air from the living areas makes its way up to the attic. Breathing, cooking, bathing, washing clothes and dishes—all add water vapor to the air. With a family of four, the amount of vapor added to the inside air in just one week can exceed *18 gallons*! Elimination of high humidity at the source, by kitchen and bath exhaust fans, helps; but, because of a phenomenon called vapor pressure, enough of this moisture can force its way through plaster, wood, and other building materials to create serious condensation

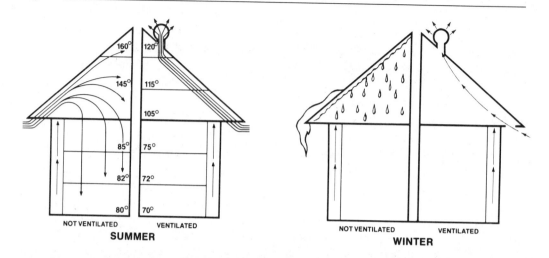

The cure for high attic temperatures in the summer months and moisture condensation problems in the winter months is moving air, using either natural ventilation or an inexpensive powered exhaust system. The solution here combines soffit venting with wind-rotated turbine ventilators. *Triangle Engineering Co.*

problems in the attic. Vapor barriers can only reduce, not halt, the flow.

Warm air can hold more water vapor than cold air. When the moisture-laden air from the living areas reaches the colder attic, it condenses, sometimes as visible droplets, on rafters, trusses, and the cold underside of the roof sheathing. This water can soak insulation, compressing its volume and reducing its effectiveness. It can also work its way into cracks and joints in the roof structure. When the attic temperature dips below freezing (with today's heavier ceiling insulation, attic air and outside winter air are nearly the same temperature), the trapped water expands as it turns to ice, enlarging the crevices. Each freeze-thaw cycle refills the now enlarged spaces with more water, and the destructive process continues.

Short of air conditioning the attic for summer relief and installing a large-capacity dehumidifier for winter, the cure for both of these problems is *moving air*, which is another term for ventilation. If you move a sufficient volume of air through the attic space, the attic tempera-

ture will remain within 10° of the outside air temperature in summer, substantially reducing heat transfer to the living areas below the attic. You can also carry off moisture before it condenses in winter, or evaporate any slight condensation on structural members or insulation, using either natural ventilation or an inexpensive, powered exhaust system. Since we're concerned here with self-sufficiency, we'll look first at those systems that do not require a power source.

The same principle that enables an airplane to fly makes natural ventilation systems work. When wind hits a building, it slows down and builds up pressure. When it flares out, to go over or around the structure, it speeds up, thereby creating an area of low pressure. To take advantage of prevailing breezes and these pressure differences, the ventilating air ideally should enter through under-eave soffits, or louvers *low* on the windward side of the attic, and exit through outlets at the peak of the roof, or *high* on the leeward side. The higher vent is always the exhaust vent.

In the past, natural ventilation systems

almost always relied on louvers in the gables or end walls of the attic, with or without soffit intake venting. Today, ventilation experts generally agree that the most effective and efficient natural attic ventilation system is provided by intake venting at the soffits balanced with a continuous ridge vent for outward air flow. Turbine ventilators, however, are not without their advocates, especially in latitudes where attic heat build-up is the primary concern.

Ridge venting is designed with louvers inverted to block rain and snow infiltration, a not uncommon problem with end-wall louvers. When installed correctly, with equal net free area of ventilated soffit, a ridge-vent system creates a natural air flow within the attic space that sweeps across the underside of the roof sheathing, where ventilation is needed most—for maximum effect in reducing radiation of heat to the attic floor in summer and preventing condensation in winter. Even when there is no wind, warm air rises to exhaust at the ridge. When even the slightest wind is blowing, it creates a venturi effect as it passes over the ridge-vent baffle, reducing the pressure. This negative pressure draws air from the attic

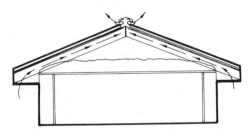

The most effective and efficient attic ventilation system is provided by intake venting at the soffits balanced with a continuous ridge vent for outward air flow. Providing continuous and uniform air flow across the underside of the roof sheathing combats heat radiation in summer and moisture condensation in winter. *Air Vent, Inc.*

through the vent, with cooler, drier replacement air entering the attic space through the soffit venting. A change of wind direction does not change the effectiveness of the system.

Aluminum ridge-vent systems by Air Vent, Inc., and H.C. Products Company (Alcoa) are being used today on hundreds of thousands of homes from Florida to Alaska. These continuous ridge-vent systems can be installed on virtually every type of roof and adapted to every type of roofing material. Most manufacturers of ridge vent also offer prefabricated intake strips, or ventilated soffit, that can provide a continuous vent opening for uniform distribution of intake air across the underside of the roof sheathing. Vent-strip openings are sized to bar bees, wasps, flies, and other insects. For best results, approximately 50 percent of the required venting area should be placed at the ridge and 25 percent in each opposing soffit. Hip-type roofs should have all four soffits vented.

Vent sizing gets complicated. It's based on net free area, which excludes framing and interstices. FHA Minimum Property Standards call for 1 square foot of vent area for each 300 square feet of ceiling for attics with a vapor barrier, 1 square foot of vent area for each 150 square feet of ceiling for attics without a vapor barrier. But that's for unobstructed vents, or at most, those with $\frac{1}{4}$-inch hardware cloth. Adjustments have to be made for finer screening, and for rain and snow shields. Where $\frac{1}{4}$-inch hardware cloth with rain louvers is used, the adjustment factor is 2, or two times the vent area specified in the MPS. With $\frac{1}{16}$-inch mesh screen and rain louvers, the adjustment factor is 3.

The summer requirement for air flow sufficient to prevent heat build-up is greater than the winter requirement to re-

PINK FLASH
INSULATION
BAFFLE

Insulation baffles are used to prevent today's thicker ceiling insulation from spilling over into the soffit or choking off the critical air ventilation passage where plate and rafter meet. Polystyrene Pink Flash baffle, with self-positioning, preformed troughs that fit over the rafters, is being installed here before roof sheathing is applied. *Air Vent, Inc.*

move moisture. If good summer heat removal as well as good winter moisture removal is desired, a ridge-vent system providing $1\frac{1}{2}$ square inches net free area per square foot of attic floor area is recommended. This is designed to furnish $1\frac{1}{2}$ cubic feet per minute (cfm) of air flow per square foot—ample for both summer and winter conditions with an effectively buttoned-up home. Keep in mind that the ridge-vent system is the most efficient of the natural ventilation systems. Other natural ventilation systems may need higher percentages of vent area.

Soffit venting can be combined with all types of high ventilation for a balanced system. Among the alternatives to ridge vent: gable (triangular) and end-wall (rectangular) louvers; stationary roof ventilators; wind-rotated turbine ventilators; and powered ventilators. As with the ridge-vent system, the most effective systems are those that combine two types of venting. Soffit-to-soffit venting merely moves air across the attic floor; it does little to change the air temperature and even less for the condensation problem. Gable-to-gable venting zips a stream of air through the attic when the wind is right, but it doesn't really come to grips with

heat or moisture. To do the job, the airstream should contact all surfaces where moisture tends to collect in winter and all surfaces that get hot in summer.

An acceptable though less effective alternative to a ridge-vent system might combine gable louvers with soffit vents, or turbine ventilators with soffit vents. Turbine ventilators use centrifugal action and are superior to fixed louvers. The spinning blades of the turbine produce a nimbus of low pressure and draw air from the attic when actuated by the slightest breeze. One 12-inch turbine, located near the peak of the roof to receive wind from all directions without interference, should ventilate 600 square feet of floor area, provided the system includes at least 2 square feet of net free inlet, and the vertical distance between the inlet and the turbine is at least 3 feet.

A turbine system for a house with 1,500 square feet of attic floor area (see Table Six) would call for two 14-inch turbines and a minimum of 5 square feet of net free inlet area, which could be provided by gable vents at each end of the attic, or preferably, by opposing soffit vents. Turbine ventilators, which are available with automatic and chain-operated dampers,

TABLE SIX

SIZING TURBINE VENTILATOR SYSTEMS

Square Feet Attic Floor Area	Number Turbine Ventilators Required	Size Turbine (inches)	Minimum Square Feet Inlet Louver Area Required	Minimum Number * and Size (inches) Eave Vents	OR	Minimum Number and Size Gable Vents	
						14 × 24 inches	12 × 18 inches
1,200	2 each	12	4.0	9 ea. 8 × 16		3	5
1,500	2 each	14	5.0	12 ea. 8 × 16		4	7
1,800	3 each	12	6.0	14 ea. 8 × 16		5	8
2,100	3 each	14	7.0	16 ea. 8 × 16		6	9
2,400	4 each	12	8.0	18 ea. 8 × 16		7	10

* Use twice the number of 4-by-16-inch eave vents.
Source: Triangle Engineering Co.

are not effective unless an adequate supply of outside air is allowed to flow through the attic.

The most effective ventilation system is the one that moves the greatest volume of air. For summer comfort under sweltering conditions, the ideal would be to approach the "Tahiti method"—with the entire roof raised at least 10 inches above the ceiling and left open all around. (Don't be overly concerned about winter heat loss with a well-ventilated attic. If you have sufficient ceiling insulation, the energy efficiency of the house is not perceptibly changed.)

Powered roof ventilators are designed to do the same job that natural ventilation systems do, only more effectively—moving more air with better control. Powered roof ventilators are not to be confused with attic fans. Attic fans, which are misnamed, are meant to move air throughout the house for personal comfort and can be an energy-saving substitute for air conditioning.

A typical line of powered roof ventilators, such as that offered by Leslie-Locke, includes $\frac{1}{10}$- and $\frac{1}{5}$-hp models that can be installed on the roof or a gable wall. Mushroom or similarly shaped covers protect roof-mounted ventilators from the elements. Louvers that close by gravity and are blown open by exhaust action generally protect wall-mounted units. An adjustable thermostat enables the fan to operate automatically only when necessary. A humidistat control that will actuate the fan on cold days when the moisture inside the attic reaches a certain level is usually offered as an option. With capacities to match a range of attic sizes, prices go from about $50 to $150.

There are two ways of determining the proper capacity for powered roof ventilators. One is based on the volume or air-change method, which requires knowledge of the roof pitch and special tables to calculate the attic volume. The other involves taking the attic area to be vented and multiplying by 1 cfm per square foot. This gives the total cfm required. Add 15 percent for dark roofs for summer heat removal. If the system is to be used primarily for winter moisture removal, about one-third less fan capacity can be used. To size the intake vents, allow 1 square foot of net free opening per 300 cfm of fan capacity, or a minimum of one-half square inch of net free inlet area per square foot of attic floor area, whichever is greater. Since the powered ventilator puts the exhaust at a single point in the attic, it is important to space the inlet vents (preferably soffit vents) around the perimeter of the attic to ensure good air flow under the roof.

Attic fans, more properly called whole-house fans since they cool the whole house and not just the attic, draw air into the living areas through windows open about 6 inches from the bottom and discharge it through the attic. They are larger and move much more air than do normal window fans. Run mostly at night, when outside air is often appreciably cooler than trapped air, they are sometimes referred to as the poor man's air conditioner.

A whole-house fan not only lowers the temperature inside the house by replacing heated air with cooler air but makes us feel more comfortable even at high temperatures because moving air cools the skin by speeding the evaporation of body moisture. With the air around us moving at between 100 and 300 feet per minute—or between 1 and 3 mph—we feel as comfortable at 85°F. as we do in still air at 78°F.

Whole-house fans generally are installed horizontally in the attic floor. Over

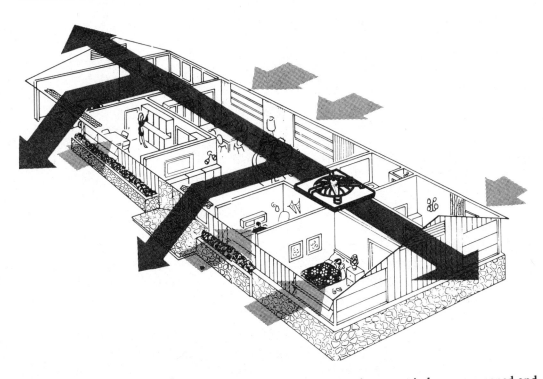

Whole-house fan pulls cooler night air into house through whatever windows are opened and discharges heated air through soffits and gable louvers via the attic. *Triangle Engineering Co.*

a central hallway is the ideal location. But perpendicular end-wall installations also are common, especially if that places the fan away from bedrooms, where the running noise and vibration, if not sufficiently dampened with antishock mountings, can disturb light sleepers. Units designed for installation in the attic floor include a ceiling shutter, with louvers that open automatically when the fan is running and close when it's not. Insulated seals that fit over fan shutters to save heat in winter are available.

The size of the fan required is determined by calculating the volume of the total living space to be vented. Excluding garage, closets, and the attic itself, multiply length times width times height of each room in feet, then total. This will give you a cfm figure for southern states and other areas where summers can be de-

scribed as stifling. For northern states and areas where summers might be uncomfortable but not murderously so, divide this figure by 2.

A 30-by-40-foot total floor area and an 8-foot ceiling works out to 9,600 cubic feet. You won't always find a fan with a cfm rating that exactly matches the cubic footage figure, so choose the fan with the next highest rating. In this case, it might be a 36-inch (blade diameter), 10,500-cfm fan. With a $1/3$-hp motor, a fan of this capacity typically sells for about $175. For cooler areas, the choice might be a 24-inch fan rated at 5,200 cfm.

A whole-house fan requires a minimum exhaust opening of 1 square foot per 750 cfm. For the 10,500-cfm fan, this would mean 14 square feet of opening; for the smaller fan, 7 square feet. The vent area can combine ventilated soffits and gable louvers or ventilated soffits and roof ventilators. It is advisable to supplement a whole-house fan with natural attic ventilation at or near the peak of the roof. Turbine ventilators are the usual recommendation.

With a whole-house fan, you can pull air through every room or just one or two, merely by closing a few doors and windows. Most of the time you won't need the full capacity of the fan; two speeds or an optional variable-speed control can be useful. A timer is also a good idea, to shut the fan off early in the day, before the outside temperature starts to climb. Close the windows about the same time the fan shuts off, draw the shades and drapes, and you can retain much of the cool air through the day.

The average whole-house fan operates on less than half the wattage of a typical room air conditioner and approximately one-tenth the energy required by a central air conditioner. While it doesn't filter, dehumidify, or actually cool the air, a whole-house fan does help keep you comfortable, and it is *much* more economical to operate than an air conditioner, one of the biggest consumers of energy in homes today.

If you're producing your own energy for self-sufficiency, you're not likely to include the luxury of air conditioning, unless it's in the form of an energy-efficient solar- or groundwater-assisted heat pump (which both heats and cools). But if you also have air conditioning, be careful how you use it with a whole-house fan or powered roof ventilator.

A whole-house fan must not be operated unless at least a few windows are open, which lets in both heat and humidity and greatly reduces the effectiveness of air conditioning. Turn on a whole-house fan with the house shut up tight for the sake of the air conditioner, and you'll not only quickly exhaust any conditioned air but fill the house with soot sucked from the chimney or, if you don't have a chimney, burn out the fan.

The only advantage here is when the whole-house fan is used *instead* of the air conditioner. Using the air conditioner when daytime temperatures are relatively high, and the whole-house fan at night or when the outside temperature drops below 82°F., can bring significant energy savings.

Many families have also tried using their powered roof ventilators to reduce air conditioner usage. But an efficient attic fan operating at the same time as the air conditioner sucks cool downstairs air through ceiling leaks into the attic and increases the load on the air conditioner. Research by the National Bureau of Standards and the Department of Energy shows an increase in energy consumption without any significant cooling gain when both units are cycling. In homes with air conditioning, powered ventilating fans should be shut off promptly when their job is done.

Again, with a well-insulated, well-ventilated house that relates to its environment, you aren't likely to have a real need for air conditioning. Chances are you won't even need a whole-house fan. For those occasional breezeless days and nights, an old-time paddle-bladed fan, or Casablanca cooler, will stir the air sufficiently to keep you comfortable. Back in style because of the high costs of energy, Original Olde Tyme Ceiling Fans by Hunter, The Parlour Fan by Fasco, and Casablanca Ceiling Fans by Emerson Electric add a unique addition to the decor of any room. They come in a number of blade diameters, the most common being 36 and 52 inches. Priced at about $100 and up, most units consume less energy than a 100-watt light bulb.

PASSIVE SOLAR HEATING

It's much easier to promote a product than a concept—which is why the federal effort to boot this country into the solar age has centered on active solar heating systems requiring highly visible rooftop collectors rather than on passive solar residential designs that use elements of the structure itself to collect, store, and circulate the sun's heat. With the Solar Heating and Cooling Demonstration Act of 1974 as its mandate, the Department of Energy has handed out hundreds of millions of dollars to pump up the solar industry. But it wasn't until 1979, with the granting by the Department of Housing and Urban Development (HUD) of 242 awards for passive solar residential designs, that the government took its first firm step toward accelerating the commercialization of passive solar designs. It was a step long overdue. For there is a growing awareness that the energy-saving potential of passive solar residential heating far exceeds that of rooftop collector systems, which for the most part are overpriced, inefficient, and probably not worth considering—except for domestic water heating.

In the late 1940s, architect George Keck and a few other visionaries designed and built a number of "solar houses" to use the free and abundant heat of the sun. The solar-oriented design of this Keck house, located in a Chicago suburb, continues to work to the advantage of the homeowners. Entry of solar heat through the south-facing, double-glazed (Thermopane) window wall in winter reduces natural-gas bills, while a protective overhang shields the window area in summer when the sun travels in a higher arc through the sky. *Libbey-Owens-Ford Co.*

Passive solar design goes several steps beyond relating the house to its environment. As important as the savings to be achieved through superior insulation and windows oriented to capture free heat from the sun may be, those savings can be significantly extended by an architect who fully understands natural energies and the thermal characteristics of buildings and building materials. An effective passive design maximizes the use of natural radiation, conduction, and convection processes.

Many different designs for passive systems are possible, but the most widely accepted definition of a passive solar heating (and cooling) system is one in which thermal energy flows through a building—from collection to storage mass to distribution—by natural means, enabling the system to function without external power. (When a mechanical device, such as a small fan, is used to assist the natural energy flow, the system is classed as a hybrid.) Three basic passive solar concepts have been defined: direct gain—sun to living space to storage mass; indirect gain—sun to storage mass to living space; and isolated gain—sun to collector space to storage mass to living space. Recognizing that these definitions may be confusing to solar neophytes, we'll try to be as helpful as we can here, especially in view of the contribution passive solar heating can make toward low-impact self-sufficiency.

DIRECT-GAIN SYSTEMS

Direct-gain systems represent the most common passive solar solutions and are related to the old sun porch or sun parlor. They depend, as do rooftop collectors, on the "greenhouse effect." When sunlight passes through glass, it is transformed from short-wave solar radiation to long-wave infrared radiation—or heat. Since glass is nearly "opaque" to reflected-heat wavelengths, most of this heat can't be radiated back through the glass. This "natural solar gain" is greatest when glass with a low iron content is used. With a south-facing wall of glass, substantially more heat can be trapped in the living space behind the glass than is needed for immediate comfort. With a direct-gain system, floors and/or interior walls are actually "solar slabs," which are designed to soak up much of that excess heat and release it slowly after the sun goes down and on sunless days. Walls in direct-gain

South-Facing Window as a Solar Collector   Heat Storage in Massive Floor

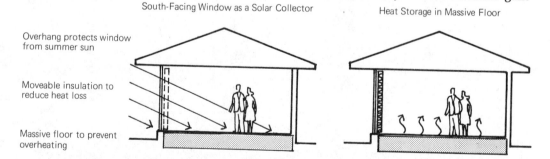

Overhang protects window from summer sun

Moveable insulation to reduce heat loss

Massive floor to prevent overheating

Direct-gain systems represent the most common passive solar solutions. Floors and/or interior walls are "solar slabs" designed to soak up heat from the sun during the day and release it slowly after the sun goes down. *Source:* Solar Dwelling Design Concepts

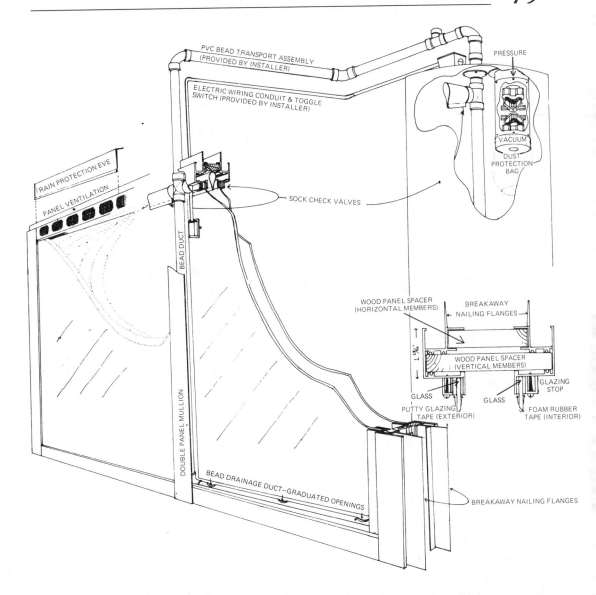

There are two main parts to the Beadwall system: the panels and the motor-storage unit, which can be placed in any sheltered location up to 40 feet from the panels. Zomeworks provides all the essential components except the glazing, which the installer can buy better locally, and the electrical and bead-transport connections between panels and motor-storage unit, whose length will depend on the tank's placement. Components provided are as follows:

• Panel frame members and glazing stops of .062 inch 6063-T5 aluminum extrusion, screen-vented against air pressure; 3/4-inch plywood panel spacer members to provide thermal break and standard 2 1/2-inch distance between glazing surfaces; putty glazing tape for exterior glazing and foam rubber tape for interior to allow removal for cleaning.

• Storage and panel bead-duct assemblies of 1 1/2-inch schedule 40 PVC pipe and standard wide sweep fittings; sock check valves of silicone-impregnated, aluminized fiberglass fabric.

• Construction grade expanded polystyrene insulating beads, flame-retardant treated; anti-static agent to keep beads from clinging. *Zomeworks Corp.*

systems are solid masonry, and floors are either thick concrete slab-on-grade, brick, slate, adobe, adobe beneath brick, or tile on concrete, with rigid-foam insulation around the perimeter to reduce heat loss to the outside. A scatter rug or two is acceptable, but the floor should not be carpeted. And while a heat sink works best when the surface exposed to the sun is dark-colored, the floor itself should be light enough to avoid uncomfortable temperatures underfoot.

In direct-gain systems in temperate climates, the total amount of south-facing glass should equal between 20 and 25 percent of the floor area to be heated; in colder climates, it should equal between 25 and 35 percent of the floor area. With all that glass, which may present a building-code conflict requiring a variance, an insulated, operable blind is essential to modulate the input of solar energy and to minimize heat loss at night and on days when the sun doesn't shine. While thermal drapes and tight-fitting, insulated shutters (either internal or external) can do the job, you might also consider a Beadwall insulating system, one of several solar-related innovations developed and patented by Zomeworks Corporation.

The Beadwall system combines the functions of wall, window, insulation, and sunscreen. When heat loss is to be minimized or summer heat excluded, the Beadwall panel—two sheets of tempered glass separated by a 2½-inch air space—turns into an insulated wall as white polystyrene beads are blown into the inner space. When heat or light gain is to be maximized, the panel becomes a window again as the beads are sucked back into the concealed storage/motor unit, which can be placed in any sheltered location up to 40 feet from the panel. The beads, round and randomly sized, provide a fas-

cinating visual texture when the panel is filled. The filling-draining process can be stopped at any point to leave the panel partially filled. While operating most efficiently in the vertical position, Beadwalls have been used successfully at angles of up to 45 degrees. Angling the Beadwall— and any other large expanse of glass— helps prevent glare, one of the common problems with direct-gain glazing.

Zomeworks also developed the sophisticated Skylid insulating system, with plump louvers that open and close automatically in response to the presence or absence of sunlight. They operate most efficiently at 15 to 75 degrees from horizontal and are designed to be used beneath skylights, greenhouse roofs, and sloping clerestory windows. A Skylid unit consists of either two or three aluminum-faced, fiberglass-filled louvers that pivot silently in a wood frame and require no external power source. One louver is the "driver" for the set and has refrigerant-charged canisters mounted on opposite faces. When the sun shines on the black canister on the sky side, liquid flows through a copper tube to the silver-painted canister on the room side, shifting the drive louver's balance and causing all the louvers in the set to open. After the sun disappears, the silver canister becomes the warmer of the two, liquid flows back, and the louvers close. The louvers can be locked in any position with simple override cords.

Solar-heating ceiling tiles (Sol-Ar-Tiles) are another recent development in passive systems. Consisting of a polymer-concrete envelope surrounding a chemical core of eutectic salt, the core melts at daytime room temperatures, absorbing heat. At night, as the room temperature drops, the core slowly returns to its solid state, releasing the heat stored during the day.

Developed by Zomeworks, Inc., the Skylid insulating system opens and closes automatically in response to the presence or absence of sunlight *Source:* Passive Design Ideas for the Energy Conscious Architect

Mirrored window louvers are used to reflect solar heat to the ceiling tiles. This reduces the amount of heat transmitted to the floor and walls, however. You can't have both, but the ceiling tiles might be useful upstairs and in other living areas where a solar slab would be impractical. The inch-thick Sol-Ar-Tiles were first used in 1978 in an experimental building at the Massachusetts Institute of Technol-

ogy. The building was designed and constructed to supply more than 85 percent of of its own heat through passive solar heating.

INDIRECT-GAIN SYSTEMS

In the second passive concept, indirect gain, the storage mass is placed *between* the

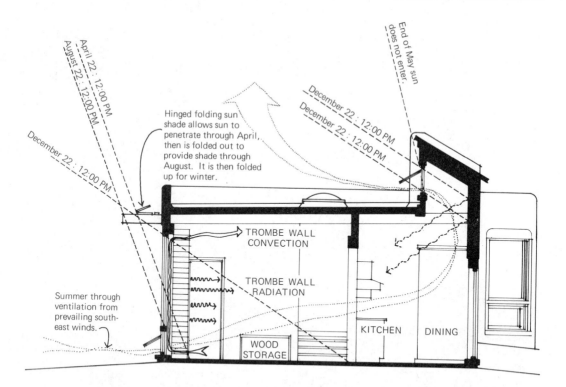

April 22 : 12:00 PM
August 22 : 12:00 PM

December 22 : 12:00 PM

End of May sun does not enter.

December 22 : 12:00 PM
December 22 : 12:00 PM
December 22 : 12:00 PM

Hinged folding sun shade allows sun to penetrate through April, then is folded out to provide shade through August. It is then folded up for winter.

TROMBE WALL CONVECTION

TROMBE WALL RADIATION

Summer through ventilation from prevailing south-east winds.

KITCHEN   DINING

WOOD STORAGE

One-bedroom residence designed by architect Ken Brooks for a high-elevation site in northern New Mexico incorporates a 14-inch-thick adobe mass (Trombe) wall and a concrete-slab floor that provide natural solar heating in winter and cooling in summer. Thermal losses are controlled with urethane night insulation panels that adhere by magnetic clips to double-glazed windows. Two wood stoves, a large one in the living area and a smaller one in the bedroom, provide backup heating as needed. *Source:* The First Passive Solar Home Awards

sun and the living space. The best example of this is the Trombe wall, originated in 1956 by Professor Felix Trombe and architect Jacques Michel of France. A massive masonry wall is installed about 6 inches from a south-facing glass wall. Darkened on the sun side, it absorbs solar heat and reradiates it at a comfortable rate into the living space. The speed with which it does this and the amount of heat released are calculable and depend on the thickness of the wall and the thermal properties of the material used. Concrete is the most effective mass-wall material. To operate at maximum efficiency, the wall should be about 10 to 12 inches thick. Where the surface will have direct exposure to the sun, figure at least 150 pounds of masonry for each square foot of south-facing glass.

The space between the glazing and the Trombe wall is a plenum in which air can be heated to high temperatures and then tapped for distribution by natural convection. Ducts at the top of the storage mass direct heated air into the living space. The convective loop is completed as cooler room air is drawn through lower vents back into the plenum. With the openings controlled by dampers, the convected heat can be turned on and off to suit the comfort of the house's occupants. To control the release and retention of heat within the wall, movable insulation can be used on either or both sides of the wall. Adding two or even three sheets of glass outside a Trombe wall can also be very advantageous, especially in colder climates.

In one modification of the Trombe wall, additional thermal storage in the form of a rock bed is located beneath the floor. Using blowers, heat from the wall or plenum can be diverted and stored in the rock bed, to be drawn upon via ducting, just as with conventional forced-warm-air heating, to heat any area of the house. The rock bed increases the storage capacity of the system considerably to provide heat for extended sunless periods.

Trombe walls can be built with windows to admit light. Another variation is to install a grid of PVC piping within the wall to preheat water for the hot-water

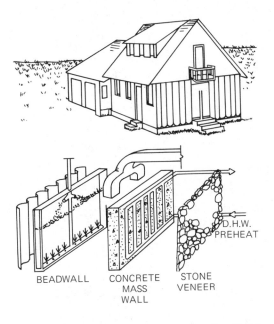

BEADWALL   CONCRETE   STONE
         MASS   VENEER
         WALL

D.H.W. PREHEAT

Designed by Larry Honeywell, the Kuhl House in Croghan, New York, uses two 9-by-9-foot Beadwalls to control heat storage in two 12-inch-thick Trombe wall segments in the south wall. Additional mass is provided by a 6-inch veneer of stone on the inside face of the poured-concrete wall. *Source:* A Survey of Passive Solar Buildings

supply, as was done in the Kuhl House (Croghan, New York), designed by Larry Honeywell. In summer, inside louvers are entirely closed, thereby maximizing the water-heating potential. The installation contributes 50 percent of the energy required to heat domestic water in winter, 100 percent in summer.

Water Trombe walls operate on the same principle as mass Trombe walls to provide both radiant and convected heat. Many container variations have been employed, but 55-gallon steel drums (oil drums, appropriately enough!) appear to be the most popular storage units in water Trombe systems. The water-filled drums are placed on their sides in racks, about 6 inches from a floor-to-ceiling glass wall, with the drum ends that face the sun painted black to absorb heat. While water has the highest heat capacity per pound of any common material, making it an attractive storage and heat-transfer medium, a 55-gallon water-filled drum weighs in the neighborhood of 500 pounds. Be sure your floor and foundation can support the load. The rule of thumb is 30 pounds of water for each square foot of south-facing glass. A corrosion inhibitor in the water might delay the unhappy day when one or more of the drums rusts through.

The use of a drum wall for passive solar heating was pioneered by Steve Baer of Zomeworks Corporation. To retain heat after the sun goes down, his design includes a huge, insulated shutter operated from inside the house. Lowered like a drawbridge during the day, it is winched up to cover the glass at night. The inside face of the shutter is surfaced with aluminum to reflect additional solar radiation on the glazing and the drum ends. Inside, heavy curtains control the flow of warm air from the drums to the living space.

Drum wall developed by Steve Baer is similar to the mass Trombe wall. Oil drums filled with water are placed on racks just inside the glass wall. The drum ends facing the sun are painted black to absorb heat, and an insulated shutter operated from inside the house is pulled up at night to retain it. *Source:* Passive Design Ideas for the Energy Conscious Architect

A water Trombe wall has an added advantage in that it can be "reversed" for summer cooling. Shutters and windows are opened at night to cool the containers by radiation to the cool night air. With the windows and shutters closed during the day, the cooled water will absorb indoor heat to provide more comfortable summer temperatures. The water-wall concept has been commercialized, and several manufacturers are producing reinforced plastic cylinders or stackable tubes designed for water-wall applications. Kalwall, for example, offers fiberglass-reinforced Sun-Lite cylinders up to 10 feet tall and 12 to 18 inches in diameter. Filled with water and placed in a row behind an expanse of south-facing glass, they become solar collector, storage medium, and heat distribution system—without any need for pumps or plumbing.

Rooftop thermal "ponds," with the water held in large plastic bags, are another variation on the water Trombe wall. In a solar concept designed and developed by Harold Hay, the water-filled collectors, located within the flat roof structure above the living space, are exposed directly to the sun's rays. Solar radiation warms the mass of noncirculating water, which in turns warms the supporting metal deck.

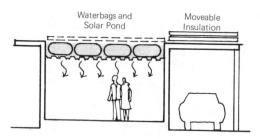

Waterbags and Solar Pond

Moveable Insulation

In a patented solar concept by Harold Hay, water-filled collectors located within the flat-roof structure above the living area absorb heat from the sun and radiate it through the supporting metal deck to the interior of the dwelling. The system can be reversed for cooling. *Source:* Solar Dwelling Design Concepts

The deck/ceiling radiates the collected solar heat to the interior of the dwelling. At night, insulating panels, mounted in aluminum tracks and controlled by a $\frac{1}{2}$-hp motor, cover the ponds to keep heat from escaping to the night air.

Cooling is provided in summer by reversing the procedure and sliding back the panels at night so that the heat which the ponds have absorbed from the house during the day can be dissipated by nocturnal cooling. Radiation to the sky, evaporation, and at certain times, convection all play a part in the nocturnal cooling process. This system works best in climates with low humidity and cool nights, as in the Southwest. The house, of course, would have to be engineered to support the extra weight of the water.

ISOLATED-GAIN SYSTEMS

Isolated-gain systems, the third passive concept, depend on a collector-storage component separate from the primary living space. A greenhouse attached to the south wall of the house as an incidental heat trap is an excellent example of what we're talking about here. Because it can provide ventilation and natural illumination, as well as serve as a solar collector, the greenhouse becomes a particularly valuable building component in integrated solar dwelling designs—whether used for indoor gardening or not.

The typical greenhouse exposes more glass area to solar radiation than would a direct-gain window filling the same wall area, which means it has the potential of

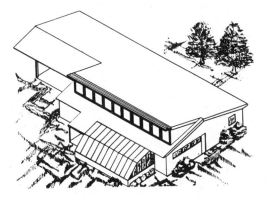

Three-bedroom house designed by Thomas Goodson uses sunspace (solarium) and roof monitors to collect solar energy. Heat is stored in solar slab (concrete floor) and water-filled steel drums. Operable insulating shades and vents control access to sun and summer ventilation. *Source:* The First Passive Solar Home Awards

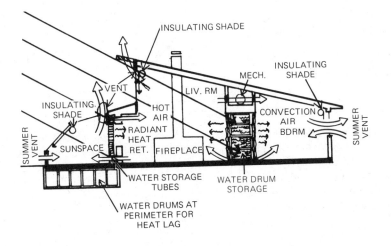

collecting substantially more BTUs than are needed to keep it heated—at least while the sun is shining. This excess heat can be transferred via wall openings and natural air flow directly to the living space, or by blower into a heat-retaining, rock-filled bin beneath the house, where it is stored for forced warm-air distribution when needed.

The major problem with a greenhouse is excessive heat loss through all that glazing at night and on sunless days. While the greenhouse can be closed off from the house to reduce the net area that needs to be heated when the temperature drops, insulated shutters or shades are required to retain the heat after the sun goes down. Soil and clay pots will retain and reradiate a certain amount of heat, but not enough to keep a green thumb from turning blue. To guard against big temperature drops within the greenhouse itself, you need additional heat-absorptive materials, such as a slate or concrete floor, a rock pile, or a

number of black-painted, water-filled drums to capture heat by day and reradiate it to the greenhouse at night. Insulated end-wall panels left in place during the coldest months also improve the solar-gain/heat-loss relationship.

Both greenhouses and atriums come under the general passive solar design heading of sunspace systems. Atriums have been around since Roman times. Traditionally, an atrium is a centrally located court within a structure, surrounded by enclosed space and open to the sky. With most glass areas facing inward to the atrium, heat loss through the exterior walls can be minimized. The atrium also makes a very useful heat trap. If the floor of the atrium is designed to be a heat sink, and the atrium is covered with a skylight (and an insulating shutter to keep the heat in when the sun goes down and to provide shading during times of unwanted solar gain), the atrium can be made to deliver heat virtually round the clock. Slid-

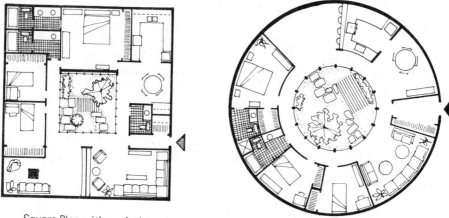

Square Plan with an Atrium   Circular Plan with an Atrium

Atriums can make a significant energy-saving contribution in passive solar design. With a major fraction of the building's exterior glass oriented inward to the atrium, heat losses through and around windows of the structure are minimized. The atrium can also be designed to act as a heat trap, with a skylight and an insulted shutter to keep heat in after the sun goes down. The shutter would also provide shading during times of unwanted solar gain. *Source:* Passive Design Ideas for the Energy Conscious Architect

ing doors to rooms opening off the atrium can be adjusted to admit sun-warmed air as needed for comfort.

There is a design problem here, however. A centrally located open court is not going to be able to capture all that much winter sun, especially in northern latitudes. You'd have to calculate your sun angles as the sun travels across the winter sky to see whether and where an atrium would work for you. A south-facing greenhouse, on the other hand, can capture sun all day long—all summer long, too, if you don't provide trees and other shading devices to screen it from the direct sun.

Thermosiphoning represents another isolated-gain heating design. In this passive collector concept, heat that is built up within a wall or roof cavity is "siphoned" out and supplied to the living space or a storage element. It's a hot-air system of limited capacity, not unlike the plenum in a mass Trombe wall system. To avoid overheating in summer, the space where the heat builds up must be insulated from the interior of the house and vented to the exterior.

Several manufacturers have introduced self-contained solar heating devices that are installed in the wall and supply heat to the interior of the house by thermosiphoning. These "thermal diodes" are close cousins to rooftop solar collectors. They are constructed with transparent covers to admit sunlight into a shallow chamber where it heats a blackened metal absorber plate or water held in fiberglass tubes. Operable vents in interior wall openings allow solar-heated air to enter the house as cooler air is drawn from the house to be heated in turn, completing the siphoning cycle. Most of these manufactured "hot boxes" are glazed with plastic, and we have yet to be convinced that plastic can stand up to collector stagnation temperatures and ultraviolet light long enough to outlast the payback period.

EARTH-SHELTERED HOUSES

One of the most effective of all tools for passive design is the very earth we build on. Burrow 10 to 15 feet into the ground and take the temperature of the earth. You'll find it's around 56°F. This may vary a few degrees with latitude, but whether there's snow on the ground or fire in the sky, earth temperatures below the frost line remain nearly stable throughout the year—and a whole new school of energy-conscious architecture is taking advantage of this fact.

Ten years ago, there weren't ten underground, or more correctly, earth-sheltered, houses in this country. Today, there are over a thousand, with as many more under construction or in the planning stages. And while a few shortsighted critics would dimiss earth-sheltered houses as being suitable only for moles and miners, there's nothing dreary or cavelike about these houses. Many are carved into hillsides, with one face of the house exposed, its wall virtually all window, to fill the house with light and provide a pleasant and often spectacular panorama to the outdoors. Others are sunk into the ground, with atriums for natural lighting and a sense of openness. Still others are more conventional structures, built on the surface and with earth bermed against one or more sides. In general, however, an

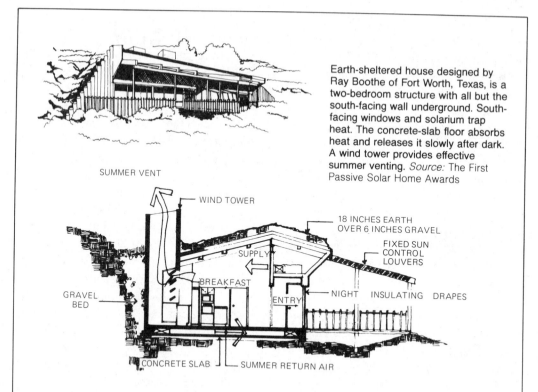

Earth-sheltered house designed by Ray Boothe of Fort Worth, Texas, is a two-bedroom structure with all but the south-facing wall underground. South-facing windows and solarium trap heat. The concrete-slab floor absorbs heat and releases it slowly after dark. A wind tower provides effective summer venting. *Source:* The First Passive Solar Home Awards

SUMMER VENT

WIND TOWER

18 INCHES EARTH OVER 6 INCHES GRAVEL

SUPPLY

FIXED SUN CONTROL LOUVERS

BREAKFAST

GRAVEL BED

ENTRY

NIGHT   INSULATING   DRAPES

CONCRETE SLAB

SUMMER RETURN AIR

earth-sheltered house is defined as one with 60 percent or more of the wall area and 80 percent of the roof covered by earth.

With the moderate, stabilized temperature provided by the depth of surrounding earth, and no air infiltration from those surfaces, the main advantage of an earth-sheltered house is its dramatically reduced energy requirement for heating and cooling. Insulated from wintry blasts and the relentless summer sun, it requires no air conditioning, and with passive solar heating, only minimal supplementary heating during the colder months. Think what this means in climates having extremes in temperature, such as in Minnesota, where aboveground temperatures typically range from $-30°$F. in winter to the 90s in summer. Not surprisingly, Minnesota is the hotbed of earth-sheltered housing.

There's no great saving in construction costs when you build below the ground. Some architects claim a 5 to 10 percent saving over aboveground construction. Others say that building underground costs 5 to 10 percent more. What you save on unneeded siding and shingles, fewer windows, and less labor is largely offset by the cost of the tons and tons of concrete and masonry that go into the walls, roof, and floor, and the steel I-beams needed for roof reinforcement. Rigid closed-cell insulation is also required, as a barrier between the building exterior and the earth—or the colder earth will draw heat away from the interior of the structure.

To keep a below-grade house from becoming a swimming pool, you must carefully waterproof the entire structure. Butyl sheeting could be used to provide both waterproofing and a vapor barrier. But waterproofed or not, a low-lying area with a high water table would be a poor location for a house sunk into the ground. The ideal location is a gentle, south-facing slope that gives sunlight for passive solar heating and positive drainage, though a gravel drainage base to prevent moisture build-up may still be needed.

Other than overcoming a possible psychological barrier to living partially underground, humidity is the most serious problem you're likely to encounter in an earth-sheltered house. It's not that you'll have to contend with groundwater seeping through the floor and walls, at least not in an adequately waterproofed house, but that the house can't breathe in the normal house-breathing manner. The humidity problem usually can be kept under control through forced-air circulation, with good ventilation to the outside. But a dehumidifier will likely be needed in naturally humid regions. Something else that may take getting used to is the intense quiet that is characteristic of living underground, with the cycling of the refrigerator (or dehumidifier) often contributing the only noise.

With earth-sheltered buildings, there's little damage to the environment. The natural contours of the landscape can be preserved. Roof soil coverings generally range from 18 to 48 inches in depth and can be seeded with grass or planted with a garden. Skylights are sometimes extended through the soil to illuminate interior rooms. Other designs might include air cowls to provide additional ventilation.

Not all earth-sheltered houses are being built in extreme northern climates. There's "underground" activity from Texas to Connecticut, and some of the most attractive earth-sheltered houses we've seen have been built into sand dunes in Florida, overlooking the Atlantic Ocean. Nestled in the earth, they're also giving comfort in regions where tornadoes are an annual threat.

A number of architects, including Malcolm Wells of Cherry Hill, New Jersey; William Morgan of Jacksonville, Florida; and John Barnard of Osterville, Massachusetts, specialize in earth-sheltered designs. But the best single source of information is the Underground Space Center, University of Minnesota, 221 Church Street S.E., Minneapolis, Minnesota 55455. *Earth Sheltered Housing Design—Guidelines, Examples and References*, a 300-page report prepared by the center, is available for $11, including postage and handling. Make checks payable to American Underground-Space Association. The center can also provide information on association membership and subscriptions to *Underground Space*, a bi-monthly journal.

ACTIVE SOLAR HEATING

Solar heating, based on rooftop collector systems, has been hyped higher than the moon, and a good understanding of its limitations is in order if it is to be included in a house designed to be largely self-sufficient. Listen to some solar proponents and you'd think all you had to do was install a bank of solar collectors and a thermal storage unit and you'd have all the "free" energy you'd ever need to provide domestic hot water, heat the house, and run an absorption chiller for air conditioning. It's not nearly that simple—at least not without unlimited funds.

In any heating system, active or passive, the basic unit of energy is the calorie, the amount of heat required to raise the temperature of 1 gram of water 1°C. For convenience, however, since not all that many of us have gone metric, we'll deal here in British thermal units. One BTU (252 calories) is the amount of heat required to raise the temperature of 1 pound of water 1° F.

Let's say your family requires 80 gallons of hot water a day, for bathing, dishwashing, and other domestic purposes. At 8.35 pounds to the gallon, that's 668 pounds of water. If you draw the water from a well at 60°F. and want to raise its temperature to 130°F., a difference of 70°, you need a heat source that can supply 46,760 BTUs (668 × 70) per day—day in and day out. Using the sun to provide the energy to heat that water, you must capture a *minimum* of 46,760 BTUs per day via solar collectors. Realistically, you'll probably need a system sized to "collect" at least twice that amount, to allow for heat losses and to see you through a sunless day or two.

We know to the decimal how much solar energy strikes the earth's outer atmosphere: 429.2 BTUs per square foot per hour. This quantity is known as the solar constant. A large amount of this energy, however, is lost by absorption in the atmosphere and by reflection from the clouds, and it cannot be regained regardless of collector design. Vapor, dust, and smoke content, as well as lower sun angles, which lengthen the path of radiation through the atmosphere, further diminish the amount of radiation striking the

Opposite: Annual mean daily insolation on a horizontal surface, in Langleys. To convert Langleys to BTUs per square foot, multiply by 3.69: i.e., 300 Langleys equals 1,107 BTU/ft², 500 Langleys equals 1,845 BTU/ft². *Source:* Climatic Atlas of the United States

The Quechee Energy House in Vermont was conceived to demonstrate that a home can be heated cost effectively with solar energy in the more extreme cold northen climates. Using 16 Sunstream Model 60 collectors in combination with a heat pump for maximum efficiency satisfies approximately 50 percent of the heating requirements for this 2,300-square-foot home. The slack is picked up by an oil-fired system. Energy-saving features include triple-glazed windows, no north-facing glass, the equivalent of 6 inches of insulation in the walls, and a solarium (with insulated shutters for night) for passive solar gain. *Grumman Energy Systems*

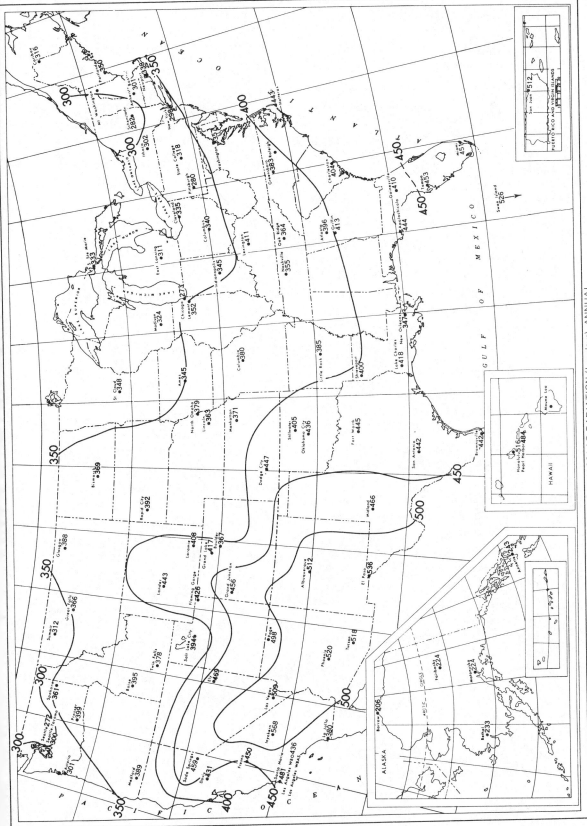

MEAN DAILY SOLAR RADIATION (Langleys), ANNUAL

earth's surface. The amount of solar energy that will fall at a particular point on the earth, therefore, depends as much on weather patterns and sun angles as on the solar constant, with the annual daily mean radiation in the forty-eight contiguous states ranging from around 1,100 BTUs per square foot in northern-tier states to around 1,850 BTUs per square foot in Arizona and south Florida. Allowing for collector inefficiencies and other heat losses, you would then need approximately 50 square feet of collector in Phoenix or Fort Lauderdale and 85 square feet of collector in Boston, Minneapolis, or Tacoma. And unless you do all your bathing and other washing during sunny periods, you'll still need a backup water heater, fired by conventional fuel, to supply from 20 to 50 percent of the energy needed annually to maintain the hot-water supply.

When we're told how well solar heating works, it's almost always in reference to domestic hot-water systems in south Florida, southern California, or Arizona, with the projected savings invariably based on the high electric rates of the Northeast (when, in fact, the majority of conventional water heaters are fired by natural gas). Indeed, solar heating *does* shine deep in the sunbelt. For one thing, the daily mean radiation in midwinter there is around 1,100 BTUs per square foot; in the northern-tier states it drops below 500. Additionally, the water to be heated comes into the house at higher temperatures in the sunbelt than it does in northern states. And, most importantly, you don't have the heat-exchange losses you have with the more complicated—and more expensive—collector systems required in the colder parts of the country to avoid disastrous freeze-ups.

We don't mean to turn you off active solar heating. But there are many misconceptions to cut through before you decide whether or not to go solar. For self-sufficiency, natural gas, an increasingly scarce commodity, not being available, we probably *would* turn to solar energy for domestic water heating. Beyond that, there are other alternatives to be considered.

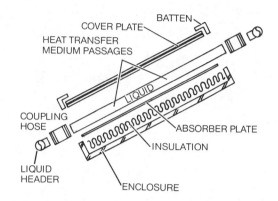

An exploded view of a flat-plate collector.
Source: Solar Hot Water and Your Home

The collector is the key component in an active solar heating system. It functions much the way a greenhouse does, admitting most of the visible energy from the sun and converting it to longer-wavelength heat energy—which is then carried off by a heat-transfer medium to storage or to the point of use, depending on energy demand. Collectors are becoming increasingly sophisticated, but the flat-plate collector remains the basic design and is by far the most common active-system solar-collection device. It is used in both domestic water-heating and space-heating systems. Although there are numerous variants, a flat-plate collector generally consists of a transparent cover; a blackened metal absorber plate, insulated on the underside; and usually, metal tubing circulating the medium to be heated—all contained within, or secured to, a shallow rectangular case.

Collector covers may be tempered glass or rigid plastic, either a single or double layer, and sometimes in combination. Their job, in addition to keeping out moisture and dust, is to trap heat within the collector and retard cooling of the absorber plate. Proponents of plastic cite its high strength, lighter weight, and resistance to hailstones and vandalism (thrown rocks). On the negative side, however, plastic is not as effective as glass in blocking reflected heat coming off the absorber plate, making for a less efficient heat trap. In long-term use, it's also subject to degradation from ultraviolet radiation, ozone, and high temperatures.

The most widely used material for absorber plates is copper, which has the best heat-transfer characteristics of any common metal—twice that of aluminum and eight times that of steel. To increase the heat-absorbing capability of the absorber plate, which may be flat, corrugated, or grooved, the surface that faces the sun is darkened with a high-absorptivity black paint or a selective chemical coating. While Dr. Erich Faber, founder of the University of Florida's Solar Energy Laboratory, one of the country's top two or three solar labs, discovered that a shade of green approximately that of an elm leaf was the most effective color for absorbing the sun's rays, he subsequently went back to flat black in all test applications to avoid having to endlessly explain to science reporters and others why *his* collectors were green instead of the usual black. (The color change didn't really make that much difference.)

To minimize heat loss through the back of the collector, the absorber plate must be backed with insulation. Insulation is also needed around the inside frame of the case. The insulation must be of a type that will remain stable under stagnation temperatures that can reach as high as 400°F. When the heat-transfer medium is not circulating, no heat is being drawn off and the temperature within the collector can soar on a sunny day. At elevated temperatures, under no-flow or dry-plate conditions, insulation containing an organic binder can "boil off" as a gas and condense on the underside of the cover, ruining the collector's efficiency. Outgassing of insulation, absorber-plate coatings, and sealants is a common problem that few manufacturers took into consideration until recently.

Where flat-plate collector designs differ most noticeably is in the configuration of tubes, ducts, fins, and other extrusions that serve to transport the heat-transfer medium over, through, or under the absorber plate and maximize the removal of heat. There are as many variations here as there are manufacturers of collectors. But essentially, there are just two classes of transfer media—liquid and gas (usually air)—and three types of flat-plate collectors.

Closed-channel liquid collectors employ potable (tap) water, silicone oil, or an antifreeze solution as the transfer medium. The fluid is pumped through a grid of headers and parallel tubes, usually corrosion-resistant copper, bonded to or integral with the absorber plate. There it is solar-heated before being delivered to the hot-water storage tank or, when oil or antifreeze is used, routed through a heat exchanger in the storage tank.

Air collectors feed air drawn from the house or the cold end of the heat reservoir (usually a rock bin) over, through, or under the absorber plate and return heated air to the storage medium or directly to the living areas. Control is by automatic dampers. Unlike liquid collectors, an air system is not subject to freezing, leakage, or corrosion problems. However, air col-

Flat-plate collectors should be mounted facing within 15 degrees of true south and tilted at an angle corresponding to the geographic latitude of the site for optimal gain of direct radiation. *Libbey-Owens-Ford Co.*

lectors do require relatively large, insulated ducts for their "transfer medium" and often require more mechanical transfer energy per unit of solar energy delivered. Solaron is rated the country's largest manufacturer and supplier of air-type collector systems.

Trickle collectors use corrugated absorber plates for an open flow of the transfer medium, in this case water, preferably free of minerals. Trickling down the sun-warmed troughs from a manifold or spray distributor at the top of the collector to an insu-

lated gutter at the bottom, the water collects heat and flows by gravity to a large, insulated storage tank. When collection is not occurring, the transfer medium drains back into storage. Sensors tell the pump when the absorber plates are warm enough to contribute useful heat, and a solenoid starts the water flowing. The principal manufacturer of trickle-type collector systems is Solaris.

For optimal gain of direct radiation, flat-plate collectors should be mounted facing true south and tilted at an angle corresponding to the geographic latitude of the site. A flat-plate collector provides good heat collection from both direct and diffuse light, however, and variations of 10 degrees on either side of the tilt optimum and 15 degrees to either side of true south are acceptable. Let local weather patterns influence pinpoint panel orientation. If you have frequent morning fog or haze with little direct sunlight before noon, face the collectors more toward the southwest. If you have frequent afternoon rain showers, deviate toward the southeast. The snowfall characteristics of the area should also be taken into consideration. An adjustment in the tilt angle toward the perpendicular may be necessary to avoid snow build-up on the collectors. On the other hand, snow on nearby surfaces can be a plus, since reflected sunlight can increase collector output by up to 30 percent.

Solar collectors do not have to be mounted on the roof of the house. They can be mounted anywhere the sun shines—on a garage or shed roof, on a separate support structure, or even on a vertical wall if the sun angles are low and the directional orientation is right. Installed on the ground, they should be set on concrete pads. But a word of caution from the insurance companies here: Solar collectors installed on or close to the ground can be an invitation to vandals.

The very thought of adding solar collectors to the roof of a well-designed house makes most architects cringe. Aesthetically, solar collectors don't do a thing for a house. But a number of manufacturers, including Grumman, have introduced low-profile, watertight panels, constructed with a flange as part of the collector chassis, for integrated, in-the-roof design.

When they are recessed in the roof so as not to disturb its clean lines, you might be persuaded that they look more like skylights than solar collectors.

Active collector systems include automatic controls, with thermostats, electronic sensors, and low-energy electric pumps, or blowers (with air systems), so that heat is collected only when the sun shines on the collector with enough intensity to warm the heat-transfer fluid above the temperature of the storage medium. The transfer fluid then circulates only as long as the system is delivering a net heat gain. When the differential thermostatic controller detects that the temperature of the transfer fluid leaving the collector has fallen to within a few degrees of the input temperature, the circulator shuts off.

SOLAR WATER-HEATING SYSTEMS

All solar water-heating systems have three basic components: the solar collectors (usually at least two), the hot-water storage tank, and the circulation system. Where solar heating is used to provide domestic hot water only, the collectors almost always are the closed-channel liquid type, although it is possible to use an air system (with an air-to-water heat exchanger). Potable water can be used as the heat-transfer fluid in domestic-water-heating systems, but only where there is no danger of its freezing. Using potable water as the transfer fluid allows an open-loop system, with the water heated by the sun returned directly to the storage tank from which it is drawn. Where the transfer fluid is an oil or antifreeze solution, or water to which an anticorrosion agent has been added, it must be confined within a

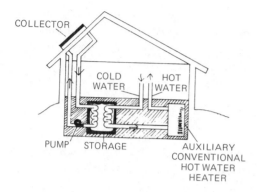

COLLECTOR

COLD WATER   ↓↑ HOT WATER

PUMP   STORAGE   AUXILIARY CONVENTIONAL HOT WATER HEATER

The active (with pump) solar hot-water system usually is designed to preheat water from the incoming water supply prior to passage through a conventional water heater. A double set of coils, as shown, or a special heat exchanger is required so that anticorrosive additives and antifreeze solution in the solar collectors cannot contaminate the potable water system. *Solar Heating and Cooling Information Center*

closed, recirculating loop, and routed through or around the storage tank via a built-in or wraparound heat exchanger. The heated fluid delivers heat energy to the water held in storage, then returns to the collector as the cycle is repeated. Generally available in 66-, 82-, and 120-gallon sizes, the storage tank/heat exchanger receives water from the cold-water supply and serves as a preheat tank, feeding hot water to a conventional water heater. When the water in the delivery tank falls below a preset temperature, the heater (electric, gas, propane, or oil) fires up automatically. Direct systems also include a backup heating element for extended periods of limited or no sun.

During the winter months, not only is the sun unreliable, at least in colder climates, but freezing becomes a major problem with solar water heaters. To avoid burst channels in the collector, protection against freezing is essential. Until recently, the most common answer to the freeze problem was to use an antifreeze solution

or silicone oil as the heat-transfer medium. But both of these fluids have their drawbacks as transfer media, and a lot of energy is lost in the heat-exchange process. There's always the danger, too, that the heat-transfer fluid will contaminate the potable water system. The state of the art has been advanced, though, and there now are domestic hot-water systems, from Rheem, Libbey-Owens-Ford, Sunworks, State Industries (Solarcraft), and other manufacturers, that automatically shut off the circulator and drain all liquid from the collectors and all exposed pipes if a freeze threatens. After the sun has returned and had a chance to heat up the absorber plates, the system automatically resumes circulating liquid through the collectors.

Other freezeproof systems are designed for temperate climates where freezing temperatures occur only rarely. These systems send warm water from the storage tank through the collector when a sensor in the collector activates the frost-cycle circulator, and continue to supply sufficient heat to maintain the collector temperature in the mid-40s.

These freezeproof systems allow the use of tap water as the heat-transfer medium in cold climates as well as in warm ones. Tap water, though, should be used only with noncorrosive copper. When the fluid-carrying system is constructed of aluminum or steel, it is necessary to use distilled water or treat the water with an inhibitor to ensure the integrity of the protective oxide films. This requires a closed-loop system. Do not, in any case, permit hard (scaling) water or salt water to flow through the solar absorber. Heat transfer could be severely reduced by the scale that can build up on the walls of the fluid passages.

Solar heating is based on a simple idea, but it involves technical difficulties. If you want to build your own domestic water-heating system, be warned that many of the do-it-yourself solar collector and systems designs that appeared in magazines and books in the 1970s just won't work—at least not efficiently, or for very long. Too few of those designs addressed the problems of overheating, freezing, and corrosion. Critical pipe diameters were often omitted from the diagrams, as well as specifics on the "solder" required to bond fluid passages to the absorber plate, or the type of "paint" to be used for coating the absorber. Most authors suggested that you could find everything you'd need in neighborhood hardware and plumbing

supply stores. But it's a rare suburban retailer who carries coatings, such as 3M's Nextel Black Velvet, formulated especially for use on collector plates; immersion thermistor sensors; $\frac{1}{20}$-hp circulator pumps, or combination pressure/temperature relief valves.

Makeshift doesn't work here. If you're investing time and money, make sure the job gets done right the first time and is designed to last. We don't recommend tackling a home-built collector system unless you have a pretty good grounding in plumbing. And that doesn't mean knowing how to fix a leaky faucet or adjust a toilet-float valve. It means knowing more

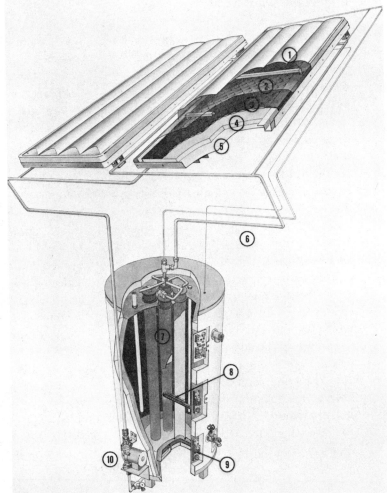

Self-contained Solarcraft automatic, all-climate, solar water-heating system includes standby heating element and 82- or 120-gallon storage capacity. Features of the system: (1) transparent cover plate, (2) Teflon glazing, (3) heat-absorbing coating fused to the collector plate, (4) insulation, (5) galvanized-steel backplate, (6) piping carrying heat-transfer fluid (distilled water) to heat-exchange chambers in the hot-water tank, (7) the heat-exchange chambers, (8) standby electric heat element, (9) thermostats and temperature sensors that automatically control circulation of solar-heated fluid, and (10) pump that recirculates distilled water into the collector panels to be reheated by the sun. The fluid is automatically stored in the heat-exchange chambers at night and on extremely overcast days to prevent the system from freezing. *State Industries, Inc.*

than a little about hydraulics and fluid-handling controls. If you want to study a set of plans to judge whether you are capable of constructing your own solar water-heating system, two reliable sources for plans are the nonprofit Environmental Information Center, 935 Orange Avenue, Winter Park, Florida 32789 (a minimum donation of $3 to the Florida Conservation Foundation, to cover printing and mailing costs, will get you a copy of *Build Your Own Solar Water Heater*), and Brace Research Institute, Macdonald College of McGill University, Ste. Anne de Bellevue, Quebec, Canada H9X 1CO (*How to Build a Solar Water Heater*; $1.50).

A number of solar manufacturers and solar component distributors cater to do-it-yourselfers. But we checked one list of such sources, and less than 20 percent of those who were in business three years later indicated that they still sought retail mail-order customers. New solar energy equipment companies look for whatever business they can get. But once they line up a few distributors or begin selling to other principals, who manufacture from their components, they often shut down the mail-order end of the business. There have also been a lot of failures in this industry.

No matter how good the plan, there's no way a do-it-yourselfer can construct an absorber that will match the efficiency of an absorber plate that's been metallurgically bonded and mechanically expanded to form integral flow passages. If you're looking to economize, your best bet would be to buy ready-made collectors and other components from a distributor (check the Yellow Pages under "Solar Energy Equipment") and handle the installation yourself. If you don't find what you're looking for through the Yellow Pages, contact the federally financed National Solar Heating and Cooling Information Center, P.O. Box 1607, Rockville, Maryland 20850. The center can provide you with lists of solar equipment manufacturers and distributors for specific product types and/or specific geographic areas. Before any construction is begun, local plumbing and building codes should be checked and the necessary permits obtained. You may find that you can't get a building permit for a solar collector unless you involve a licensed plumber, even though he may know less about the subject than you do.

SOLAR SPACE-HEATING SYSTEMS

Because of the significantly larger capacities, combined space- and water-heating systems can be a lot more complicated than domestic hot-water systems. The thermal-storage facility for space heating has to be many times larger than for solar domestic water heating. A 1,000-gallon storage tank for liquid collector systems is not unusual, nor is an insulated bin holding 15 tons of heat-storing rocks with an air collector system. There's also almost always an auxiliary heating system—forced warm air or hydronic—through which the stored heat is fed when heat is needed in the living areas. And while solar collectors for space-heating systems generally are the same types used for domestic water heating, there are many more of them. But down-sizing may become general here.

As a rule of thumb, the collector area for a space-heating system utilizing conventional flat-plate collectors should equal one-fifth to one-third the floor area of the house. Early systems required a collector area sized 50 percent or more of the

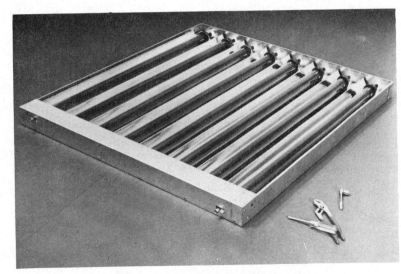

General Electric's high-performance TC-100 Vacuum-Tube Solar Collector is designed with a specially shaped cusp-type metal reflector that optimizes the concentration of sunlight onto the solar absorber vacuum tube, improving the collector's efficiency in direct and diffused sunlight. *General Electric Co.*

floor area, but solar components are being improved dramatically. A new breed of collectors makes still smaller arrays possible. If you reduce the amount of air contained in the collector, you reduce heat loss and increase the efficiency of the collector. General Electric and Owens-Illinois have done this with their evacuated-tube collectors, which are said to provide up to twice the annual energy collection capability of flat-plate collectors employing double glazing and selective absorber coatings.

Capable of supplying up to 300°F. fluid temperatures (as compared to a maximum of about 190°F. with flat-plate collectors—the average is closer to 150°F.), each collector is actually three tubes in one: a small feeder tube at the core to distribute the working fluid (air or liquid) through the system; a specially coated absorber tube, which traps the solar energy; and a clear outer tube, pumped to a high vacuum as a barrier against heat loss and to protect the highly absorbent selective coating. Both G.E. and Owens-Illinois mount eight tubes to a module, with prefabricated header assemblies for interconnecting the evacuated-tube collectors. With the G.E. system, a protective module cover of Lexan or acrylic plastic is an option. A cover is generally a good idea, though, to minimize collector maintenance.

There are patented design differences between G.E.'s Solartron and Owens-Illinois's Sunpak evacuated tubes and headers, but both systems are provided with built-in protection against freezing, or boil-out in a no-flow condition, as well as storage over-temperatures, all controlled by an energy-management module. With both systems, the tubes are mounted parallel to one another, each at the focal point of a mildly concentrating cusp-type metal reflector. What solar radiation the tubes miss, the reflectors bounce back to them. The reflectors are stationary yet "track" the sun, collecting both direct and diffuse solar radiation up to ten hours a day. With these advanced collectors, the angle of installation becomes less critical than with flat-plate collectors. The high-temperature, high-performance collectors can be used for solar cooling (with an absorption chiller) as well as heating. Given their high efficiency, installing these systems to provide hot water only is like assigning a man to do a boy's job. A mixing valve is necessary to provide water at usable temperatures.

Designing heat-storage systems for active solar space heating is a major challenge that has not been resolved with much elegance. We know of only two practical ways to store heat collected from the sun. To have heat available for use at night and during inclement periods (which, if you become solar dependent, you'll pray won't last too long), a large part of the heat collected from the sun must be stored—in water, which has the highest heat capacity per pound of any common material, or rocks, which retain heat under static conditions and have a good ability to either absorb or give off heat when exposed to moving air. The normal rule with a water-storage system is 2 gallons of water for each square foot of collector area, although the trend seems to be toward larger tanks, with a 1,000-gallon minimum. With present air systems, 1 cubic foot of small rocks per square foot of collector area is about right.

Using the same heat-transferral methods found in solar domestic-water-heating systems, solar-heated water for space heating is typically stored in a cylindrical, glass-lined steel tank or a polyethylene-lined precast concrete tank located in the basement and insulated on the outside with 2 to 3 inches of rigid foam or up to 6 inches of flexible insulation. To hold heat-storing rocks, an enclosed bin is constructed of reinforced concrete blocks and surrounded on all sides with an inch or more of rigid-foam insulation. The bin may be located in the basement, in a crawl space beneath the house, or in the ground. The rocks can range in size from crushed

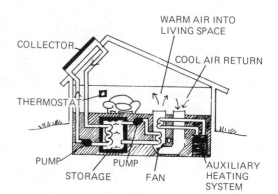

Typical air collector–rock storage system with forced warm-air heating. Depending on the amount of heat in storage, the auxiliary system is used to supply some or all of the heat needed. *Solar Heating and Cooling Information Center*

stone or large gravel to fist-size river rocks.

At the present time, it's virtually impossible to store solar heat for more than a few days. And there will be those periods, and sometimes too many of them, when you will have to fall back on a standby, or auxiliary, heating system that uses one of the conventional fuels. As a consequence, most active solar heating systems, solar water heaters included, are held to be supplementary, since they almost always are paired with a full-sized conventional heating system.

Distribution of stored solar heat is most easily and most often effected via forced warm-air systems. In an air-type solar heating system, upon demand, air is drawn through and warmed in the bin of hot rocks and then circulated through the house by a central air-handling unit. With liquid heat storage, the heated liquid is pumped through a suitably sized heat-exchange coil in the return-air duct of the warm-air distribution system. From there, fan-blown air, heated over the coil, is distributed to the living areas.

The backup system ties into the warm-air distribution system downstream from the solar system's fan or blower. In this way, a subsystem is available to provide an energy boost to the heated air coming either from storage or directly from the collector, if heat requirements are greater than can be met solely by the solar heating system, or to provide the full load of required heat until solar heat becomes available again. The backup may be a coil in the duct, circulating boiler-heated water, an electric resistance element, or a furnace supplying hot air. The auxiliary and solar system operation is maintained and monitored by an integrated control component.

A circulating hot-water heating system is also possible in a solar-heated home, with heated water from storage (a supply temperature in excess of 180°F. is needed) piped through hydronic baseboard units in the living areas. It's also possible to install a forced warm-air solar heating system without including an auxiliary heating plant. This might be the case if you're designing for self-sufficiency and prefer to rely on a high-efficiency wood stove or two in the living areas rather than a basement backup heating plant. In warmer, sunny climates, some solar homes get by nicely without backup heating systems.

With combined solar space-heating and hot-water systems, the cold-water supply line to the auxiliary water heater is routed through the heat storage, using a suitably sized coil for heat transfer, or a preheat tank submerged in the storage tank or embedded in the rock bin. Heated water could also be pumped from the liquid storage tank and sent through a heat exchanger in a domestic hot-water preheat tank outside of storage, or into the water heater itself. If the liquid from storage is toxic, a double-wall heat exchanger is required for extra protection; water is circulated through a second coil in the tank, heated, and drawn off for domestic use.

Trickle collectors aren't well suited for domestic hot-water needs, operating as they do at temperatures between 70°F. and 120°F. much of the year, but they are worth some additional comment. Developed and patented by Harry Thomason, the collector is about as simple and cheap as an active solar collector can get—costing from $5 to $8 per square foot installed.

Thomason's Solaris collector is essentially corrugated aluminum barn roofing, insulated on the underside, painted black, and covered with a single layer of glass. Factory-produced panels measure 4 by 16 feet, but collectors can be constructed on-site to almost any size, and they frequently cover the entire south-facing roof of a house expressly designed for the Solaris system by Thomason or one of his licensees. A perforated pipe runs along the top of the collector at the roof ridge line, and water pumped from storage flows in thin

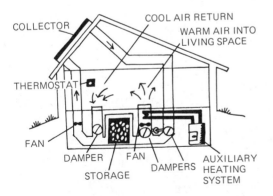

COLLECTOR
COOL AIR RETURN
WARM AIR INTO LIVING SPACE
THERMOSTAT
FAN
DAMPER   FAN
STORAGE   DAMPERS
AUXILIARY HEATING SYSTEM

Typical liquid collector-liquid storage system with forced warm-air heating. Auxiliary heat from a conventional heating system is necessary to provide a backup for the solar heater. *Solar Heating and Cooling Information Center*

streams from the holes, picking up heat as it runs down the corrugated valleys to a gutter and from there returns by gravity to a 1,600-gallon tank in the basement. The tank, a long, uninsulated steel cylinder, lies on its side in a 7-by-6-by-20-foot insulated bin that also holds 25 tons of rocks. When heat is needed, a small blower fans air through the warmed stones that surround the tank and up into an interior wall/distribution system that eliminates the need for conventional ductwork.

To minimize corrosion problems, collected rainwater is used for the open-flow system. There are no freeze-up problems. When the system shuts down, the water drains back into the storage tank. Any moisture left on the collector is evaporated by residual heat. When unfavorable weather gets the upper hand, an oil-fired domestic water heater sends hot water through finned copper pipes in the rock bin. The 40-gallon water heater functions as the sole backup heating system, supplying heat to supplement whatever stored solar heat remains.

For the domestic hot-water supply, cold water is preheated in a tank installed inside the main storage tank. Water flows from the preheat tank into the 40-gallon oil-fired water heater, allowing for a portion of the home's hot water to be produced by the sun. The contribution is much greater in the summer months than when the collector is functioning in winter temperature ranges.

GOING SOLAR WITHOUT GETTING BURNED

One of the big problems with solar heating is the seeming simplicity of it all. President Jimmy Carter and his energy advisers believed that all you had to do was get a few thousand government-subsidized solar collectors up on rooftops and the public demand for collectors would, through increased assembly-line production, quickly bring lower prices affordable by nearly all homeowners, and make an important contribution to relieving the energy crisis. But it didn't—and doesn't—work that way. For one thing, the President's advisers lost sight of the fact that it takes as much energy to manufacture a solar collector as the collector can gather in 6½ years. Furthermore, the megabucks potential of the industry, as projected by government officials, attracted hundreds of fly-by-nighters and backyard entrepreneurs, who, in the absence of federal or state regulation of the industry at least

until recently, delivered some very shoddy products, botched installations, and generally turned a great many prospective buyers away from solar. Not only that, instead of coming down in price, the installed cost of collectors has been spiraling right along with inflation.

If you're looking at solar as an optional source of energy, and not as a step toward self-sufficiency, cost effectiveness must be taken into consideration. How does the installed cost of a solar water-heating system stack up aginst the cost of fuel for a conventional oil-fired water heater, for example? Oil burned in a water heater at typical 60 percent efficiency delivers 84,000 BTUs to the gallon. To raise the temperature of that daily 80 gallons of water from 60°F. to 130°F. would require .55 gallons of heating oil—or 200 gallons per year. Since a backup water heater is almost always needed with solar water-heating systems—to handle up to 50 percent of the annual heating load in northern climates, up to 20 percent in the sunbelt —does it really pay to have a solar water heater that might cost anywhere from $1,500 to $2,500 installed? Even at $1 a gallon for heating oil (a price not reached at this writing), a solar water-heating system, in this example, isn't likely to pay back much more than $100 a year in northern states, $160 in the sunbelt. But then who's to say, outside of OPEC, that oil won't cost $2 a gallon five years from now?

Solar heating does become more competitive as the costs of other fuels rise. It's already competitive with electric water heating in some areas; heating water by electricity at 6 cents per kilowatt-hour equates to heating it by oil at $1.50 a gallon. But this could turn around in a few years, if recent breakthroughs in solar-cell development lead to affordable sun-powered electric plants for the home. At present prices, we would be very cautious in considering whole-house solar heating. There are just too many more practical alternatives. A house that relates to its environment and is well insulated will go a long way toward lightening the annual heating load. For self-sufficiency beyond hot-water requirements, passive solar design supplemented when needed with heat from a high-efficiency wood stove, or heat generated by wind power, could likely satisfy your heating needs.

Based on $20 per square foot of collector installed, plus $2,000 for all other components, solar heating can add anywhere from $7,000 to $12,000 to the cost of a typical new home. And that's for a system designed to supply no more than 50 to 75 percent of the energy required to heat the house. Climatic data in most areas does not justify the cost of the additional collectors and storage capacities needed to supply more than that. Worse, when you need heat the most is when you have the least solar radiation. Conversely, those collectors are going to get awfully hot during the summer months unless you continue to remove heat and do something more with it than maintain the hot-water supply.

Whether you go solar for hot water only or go solar all the way, do not commit yourself to a purchase of solar hardware without fully understanding what you are buying and whether the company selling and/or installing the system will back up its product with good service. Take a long look at the manufacturer behind the product. There are many small new firms without much of a track record, but there are also some of the best-known names in American industry, including General Electric, Westinghouse, Exxon (Daystar), Grumman, Libbey-Owens-Ford, Rheem, Owens-Illinois, Honeywell, Olin, Lennox, and Revere Copper and Brass.

To implement a recent grant program offering $400 rebates to ten thousand homeowners in Florida and ten northeastern states who bought solar water heaters, HUD set down some basic standards that manufacturers had to meet to qualify their systems for use under the program. The systems had to be sized to meet at least 50 percent of the daily hot-water needs of a family of two adults and two minors—or a minimum of 70 gallons of storage. The collectors had to be able to raise that 70 gallons of stored water from 70°F. to 140°F., and to be able to withstand a thirty-day no-flow test with stagnation temperatures of up to 400°F.

You might begin with those same standards when shopping for a solar hot-water system. Ask the manufacturer or dealer for proof that claims for the system's performance have been evaluated by an independent, reputable testing laboratory. Look for a five-year warranty. Ask the seller for names and addresses of previous purchasers in your area. Contact them to see if their solar units have been performing satisfactorily. A word of caution, however: Since most systems are paired with conventional gas or electric water heaters, the homeowner often has little way of knowing how much of a contribution, if any, the sun is making.

Other things to look for in solar equipment, installation, and use:

- A solar heating system cannot produce more heat than its collector panels obtain from the sun. Therefore, the efficiency of the collector is crucial to the performance and reliability of the entire system. All other things being equal, the collector that delivers more BTUs per dollar should be selected.

- The most dangerous time in the life of a solar collector is when it is being put up on a roof. Unless it is to be put into operation almost immediately, the absorber plate should be screened from the sun by taped-on white paper or other reflective material to prevent high-temperature build-up within the collector.

- The addition of a second cover plate to a solar collector creates an air space between the glazings, providing thermal insulation, which retains heat under cold-weather conditions. As a general rule, double-glazed units are recommended for cold climates, while single-glazed units are best in temperate and warmer climates.

- Raising collectors off the roof is preferable to mounting them directly on the finished roofing. When collectors must be mounted on the roof, place them on the roofing felt rather than atop shingles or other weather cover. They can then be flashed and sealed as part of the weather surface.

- The success of a solar water-heating system in energy conservation and hot-water delivery can be strongly influenced by such a mundane thing as a particular family's use pattern. This applies particularly to solar systems equipped with automatic booster elements. If laundering, dishwashing, and bathing are done mostly in the evening hours, the backup water heater will kick on and heat the next day's supply of water before the sun gets a chance to work. A booster that can be turned on manually when needed is more efficient.

ACTIVE SOLAR COOLING

The very idea would seem to be a contradiction of the laws of physics, since we know what happens to a block of ice left in the sun on a summer day, but it is possible to use water heated to high temperatures by the sun as the energizing force to cool a house. In fact, the hotter the day, the better the process usually works. Unlike the situation with solar heating, the capability is there when it's most needed: peak air-conditioning demands generally coincide with times of greater solar radiation.

There are several different types of solar cooling systems for residential use under study or development. The one that is most advanced, and available commercially, is based on technology that was first applied to gas-fired refrigerators, which work on the absorption principle and eliminate the need for a mechanical compressor (an essential element in conventional refrigerators and air conditioners) to get the refrigerant ready for the next cycle.

The first step in the air-conditioning process begins in a *generator*, where water heated to temperatures in the 170° to 220°F. range by solar collectors evaporates refrigerant from a concentrated solution and sends it as a vapor to a *condenser*. In the condenser, the gaseous refrigerant is changed back into a liquid. The heat given up in the process is drawn off by water piped to an evaporative cooling tower, and the temperature of the refrigerant drops to around 40°F. The chilled refrigerant then moves to an *evaporator*, where it draws heat from the house via fan-coil air conditioning, and changes back into a vapor. The gaseous refrigerant is then sent to an *absorber*, where it is dissolved back into solution, with the heat from the process again drawn off, before being pumped back into the generator for another cycle.

The high heat needed in the generator to change the refrigerant from a liquid to a gas cannot be developed by most flat-plate collectors. High-temperature, high-performance collectors are required here. They must be capable of delivering and maintaining stored water at a temperature in excess of 200°F. The only collectors that can do this consistently are evacuated-tube collectors and concentrating collectors mounted on motorized tracking cradles that keep the collectors faced toward the sun.

The only solar air-conditioning system that is available off the shelf at this writ-

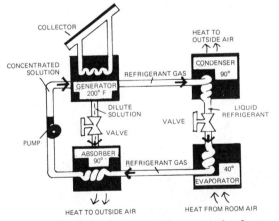

High-grade solar heat from evacuated-tube and concentrating collectors can drive an air-conditioning system using an absorption-refrigeration cycle. The method is very complicated, but the physical principle that applies is that evaporation is a cooling process, and condensation a warming process. *Solar Heating and Cooling Information Center*

ing is manufactured by Arkla Industries. Arkla's Solaire 36 sun-powered air-conditioning system is nominally rated at 3 tons (36,000 BTUs), but design flexibility allows for operation over a wide range of cooling capacities. With firing-water temperatures between 170° and 205°F., and with 85°F. entering condensing water, the lithium-bromide absorption chiller can produce from 0.5 to 3.5 tons of cooling. A ton is 12,000 BTUs per hour—or one twenty-fourth of the total energy required (2,000 by 144 BTUs) to melt a ton of ice over a twenty-four-hour period.

We're not seriously suggesting that solar air conditioning is essential for the self-sufficient home. Except where prolonged periods of high temperatures and high humidity are the norm, all the cooling you're likely to need can usually be built into the house through optimum siting, shading, insulation, and natural ventilation, with perhaps a nocturnal assist from a whole-house fan.

There's nothing cheap about solar air conditioning. Figure from $12,000 to $25,000 for a unitary system that will also provide solar heating and handle domestic hot-water needs. If you just want solar air conditioning, it would still cost about the same. Furthermore, for all the capital investment, a solar air conditioner often relies as much on an auxiliary boiler, fired by natural gas, oil, or LP gas, as it does on the sun. The boiler is needed to boost the temperature of the water supplied to the generator when insufficient heat remains in the storage tank, a not infrequent condition during periods of heavy use and short sun exposure. In Florida, for instance, where summers are hot, long, and humid, skies frequently cloud over during the afternoon, and it's possible to meet only about half of a home's summertime demand for cooling with solar energy. The inability of concentrating collectors and some evacuated-tube collectors to absorb diffuse radiation on a hazy day, the way flat-plate collectors can, places a further limitation on solar air conditioning.

Again, there are other alternatives here.

Harry Thomason, inventor of the trickle collector, offers a cooling option for use with Solaris space-heating and hot-water systems. During the warmer months, at night, when there might be more site-generated electricity available than you can store, or cheaper off-peak power from a utility, air that has been cooled and dehumidified by a 2-hp air-conditioner compressor is blown into the basement rock bin. During the day, when things begin to get uncomfortable, air from the house is cycled through the rock bin and comes out cool and dry. As an option, the compressor unit adds about $600 to the Solaris package, and typically runs from four to eight hours a night during hot humid weather.

If you have the electricity—whether generated by a wind energy conversion system or hydroelectric plant, or provided by a utility—a solar-assisted heat pump

(it also cools) or a groundwater-assisted heat pump might also be worth considering.

HEAT PUMPS

In those areas of the country where it is desirable to have both residential space heating *and* air conditioning, give some thought to a heat pump. Contrary to what their name may suggest, heat pumps can provide either warmth or cooling as needed, automatically and quite efficiently. While they do depend on electricity or mechanical energy for operation, there are solar- and groundwater-assisted heat pumps that return up to 5 BTUs of energy for every BTU of energy consumed. If we were going to have central air conditioning, our shopping list would include a heat pump rather than an active solar heating-and-cooling system that not only is a lot more expensive but relies heavily on a conventional backup heating system as well.

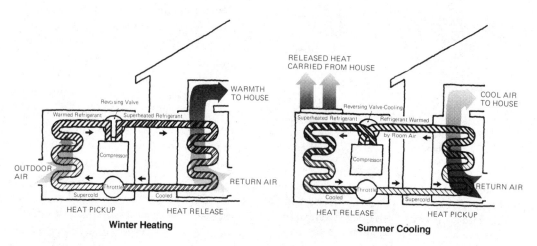

In winter the common air-to-air heat pump extracts heat from outside air, amplifies its temperature by compression, and brings that heat indoors. In summer it extracts heat from the air inside the house and expels it outdoors. *Department of Energy*

A heat pump basically is an air-conditioning unit with an indoor heat exchanger, a compressor, an outdoor heat exchanger, and an expansion device, plus a switchover valve to reverse the flow of refrigerant in the system. When the refrigerant flow is reversed, the system changes from the cooling to the heating mode. In winter the common air-to-air heat pump extracts heat from outside air (even at freezing temperatures, the air is "packed" with heat), amplifies its temperature by compression, and brings that heat indoors. In summer it extracts heat from the air inside the house and expels it outdoors.

AIR-TO-AIR HEAT PUMPS

The air-to-air heat pump has little or no advantage over a conventional air-conditioning unit of the same capacity and energy efficiency ratio. Both would deliver about the same amount of cooling power per unit of energy consumed. It's as a heating device that the heat pump excels. It delivers amazingly more energy than it consumes, whereas other kinds of central heating systems consume more energy than they deliver. Compared with ordinary electric resistance heating, which works essentially like an electric toaster, the air-to-air heat pump typically can reduce electric usage from 34 to 68 percent while delivering the same amount of heat. Give it a more stable heat source than outdoor winter air, either solar-heated air or water, or water from a well, and you can boost the heat pump's efficiency by another 50 to 100 percent or more. With cool groundwater as the heat sink, you also gain a considerable energy-saving advantage over conventional air conditioning.

Heat pumps got off to a bumpy start. In the late 1950s and early '60s, they were hailed for their efficiency, and it was predicted that few new homes would be built without one, especially with the all-electric suburban home becoming the American Dream. But early heat pumps had numerous design flaws and performed well only in the mild temperatures of the middle latitudes of the United States, such as in Tennessee. As heat pumps moved north, efficiencies plummeted and breakdowns multiplied. As one consequence, the military services barred their use in barracks and other base residences for eleven years. The major problem was with the reversing valve, which all too frequently froze up in only moderately cold weather. Though the defect was soon corrected, heat pump sales slumped nearly everywhere but in Florida. Floridian developers decided that if you're putting in a compression refrigeration system (air conditioning), you might as well give it the capacity to heat. By 1974 nearly half of all the heat pumps installed in the United States were in Florida living units.

In the late 1970s, with new gas tap-ins halted in many areas, and soaring oil prices outpacing even the rising cost of electricity, improved versions of the heat pump, with models designed for northern as well as southern climates, found increasing acceptance. By 1980 they were selling at a rate approaching 600,000 units a year. While perhaps not an ideal method of heating and cooling a house that depends on hard-to-come-by electricity, a heat pump is certainly worth considering if you have the electricity available. A tolerance for noise is also required; heat pumps tend to be noisy brutes, even with the compressor parked outside.

A heat pump works against the natural flow of heat energy, which is from a warmer place to a cooler one, by using refrigerant in a closed loop to transfer heat from a cooler place to a warmer one. Operating in the heating mode, the outdoor coil of the heat pump circulates refrigerant that is colder than the air. When the heat-exchanger fan blows air across the coil, the liquid refrigerant, which is volatile at low temperatures, absorbs a few degrees of heat from the air and gasifies. The vapor is then pumped through a compressor, where it is pressurized, becoming much hotter in the process. The heated vapor (between 100° and 150°F.) is then sent through the indoor coil and gives up its heat to air that is blown over the coil and distributed through the house via ductwork. The refrigerant cools when it releases its heat to the house and returns to a liquid state. It is then pumped back outside, passing through an expansion valve or throttle, where the sudden decompression drops the temperature of the refrigerant below 0°F. It is then ready for another run through the outdoor coil. Heat pumps cool simply by reversing the heating operation. When cooling, they absorb heat from the indoor air, pumping the heat outside, just as air conditioners do.

The measure of the heat pump's ability to produce more energy than it consumes is its coefficient of performance (COP), which is determined by dividing the heating/cooling output (in BTUs) by the energy input in watts multiplied by 3.413 (1 watt of power input is equal to 3.413 BTUs). Most heating systems have a fixed-rated COP, but with an air-to-air heat pump, the COP varies with the outside temperature. For example, a 5-ton G.E. Weathertron heat pump operated when the outside air is 47°F. delivers 62,000 BTUs of heat for every 22,900 BTUs of electricity used by the compressor (the major user of electricity in a heat

pump) and fans. As the outside temperature drops, so does the output of the heat pump. At an outside temperature of 17°F., a unit that was able to produce 62,000 BTUs at 47°F. now produces only 35,500 BTUs, but the electric input also has dropped, to 18,100 BTUs. Therefore, the COP has dropped from about 2.8 to 1.9.

The COP for a particular air-to-air heat pump may range from less than 1.0 at extremely low temperatures (there is a "balance point" at which electric resistance elements kick on to help deliver heat to the house) to more than 3.0 at much higher temperatures. It is normally about 2.0 for average winter conditions. This means that the unit produces twice as much heat output (in BTUs) as its electrical input in equivalent BTUs (watts multiplied by 3.413). Even at lower COPs, the heat pump operates at much higher efficiencies than you can expect from heating systems that burn fuel oil (COP .60) or natural gas (COP .75), or from a central electric furnace or baseboard heating system (COP .95).

GROUNDWATER-TO-AIR HEAT PUMPS

At winter temperatures below 10° or 15°F., an air-to-air heat pump generally will not offer heating efficiencies superior to conventional electric heat. However, if given an assist—a stable heat source in the 40° to 60°F. range, such as well water—it will perform at or near the top of its COP all winter long, even in sub-zero weather. Closed-loop water-to-air heat pumps, with the water maintained at temperatures in the 60° to 90°F. range by a cooling tower and a boiler, have been used in commercial and institutional applications for a number of years. But these systems incorporate the sort of energy users we're trying to avoid here and would be too expensive for residential applications. If you have a well, however, you have what you need at hand for the most efficient of all heat-pump systems. Indeed, there are those, and their number is growing, who now believe we may be looking in the wrong direction for the answer to our heating needs. Rather than overhead, the solution may not be very far beneath our feet.

Until quite recently there weren't many believers in groundwater as a viable energy source. It was thought that useful heat could not be extracted from water below 60°F. For *useful* energy, you had to drill thousands of feet—not 25 or 50 or 100—and tap geothermal sources. For a long

time heat-pump manufacturers turned a deaf ear to hydrologists and others who understood the potential of groundwater as a heat source; their advice was taken with a grain of salt, since their livelihood lay in promoting water-well development. There also were complications with well water in many geographic areas, such as scaling and corrosion, but problems of corrosion, incrustation, and iron bacteria proliferation have been largely overcome. Now heat-pump manufacturers are convinced of groundwater's potential as an energy source, and more than a score of companies, including such heating and cooling giants as Carrier, Friedrich, Westinghouse, and York, are turning out groundwater-source heat pumps. We're apparently on the brink of a boom that

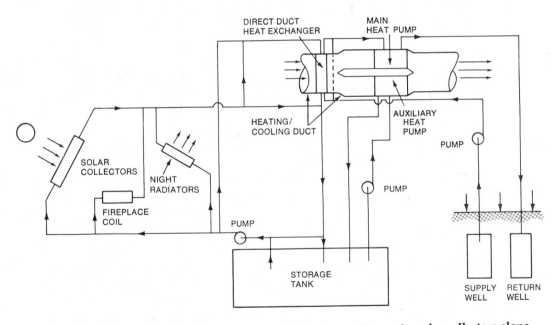

NASA Tech House heating and cooling system. Tech House relies on its solar collectors alone for much of its heating needs. But when the temperature in the solar heat storage tank drops below 90°F after a run of overcast days, the electric heat pump comes on and taps that heat to warm the house. Should the temperature of the water in the thermal storage tank drop below 55°F., well water at about 55°F. is used to supply heat to the pump. For air conditioning, the availability of cool water from the wells significantly reduces the load on the heat pump in the cooling mode. *Source:* NASA Tech House

will see groundwater-to-air heat pumps accounting for a high percentage of central-heating installations, especially in rural areas, where wells are common for domestic water supply.

The typical groundwater-to-air heat pump has a rated (average) COP of 3.2. Since its COP may climb as high as 5.0, the groundwater-source heat pump is three to five times more efficient than the *best* fossil-fuel heating system, and it will reduce energy consumption accordingly.

With a water-source heat pump, the "outside" heat exchanger merely taps a constant flow of water rather than the air for its heat source (heating mode) or heat sink (cooling mode). Invariably warmer than air in winter and cooler than air in summer, groundwater occurs at temperatures ranging from 40° to 75°F. throughout most of the United States, enabling the heat pump to operate at its peak efficiency. To save you the trouble of trying to figure out how to take the temperature of groundwater without digging a well: it's about the same as the *average* annual air temperature in the area.

The well, or other source of water, should be capable of supplying a flow of $2\frac{1}{2}$ gallons per minute per ton of heating or cooling. A typical 2,000-square-foot home in the Midwest might require about 60,000 BTUs, or 5 tons, of heating and cooling. But if that house is designed to be energy efficient, it could possibly get by with half that, or a $2\frac{1}{2}$-ton heat pump. We know of a 1,300-square-foot house in Beaumont, Texas—a size house and climate that would normally call for a $2\frac{1}{2}$-ton heat pump—that is so energy efficient that $1\frac{1}{2}$ tons is plenty.

In any case, you're going to have a lot of water that has been cooled or raised several degrees above its normal tempera-ture to dispose of after it has done its work in the heat exchanger. In scattered areas of the country, there are prohibitions against discharging fluids—even uncontaminated ones—into the ground or bodies of water. If the use of groundwater-source heat pumps soars, there's a possible risk of "thermal pollution." But at present, most of the water used with heat pumps is being safely returned to wells, ponds, or lakes, or used to meet lawn-watering, irrigation, and other outdoor requirements. The trend, however, is toward recharge/discharge well systems. Using two wells, water is drawn from one and discharged into the other. When the heat pump is reversed, the system is reversed: the well holding the warmer water is drawn from in the winter months; and the well holding the cooler water is drawn from in the summer months.

Where the well can't meet the required flow rate, a storage tank can be used. A 2,500-gallon tank, for example, is installed in the ground near the well. Water is drawn from and returned to the tank after it has passed through the heat exchanger. The temperature of the water in the tank is raised or lowered very slowly; but at a certain point, water is drawn off and additional water is automatically pumped from the well to maintain the temperature of the tank water at an optimum level. This control system reduces the amount of time that the water pump has to operate and increases the efficiency of the system.

When groundwater is used to carry heat away from the refrigerant in the heat exchanger (or the condenser, in the cooling mode), water at 50° or 60°F. can do this far more effectively than air at 80° or 90°F., reducing the input required by the heat pump—which is why the groundwater-

Friedrich hot-water
generator uses heat
normally ejected by water-
source heat pumps to
produce the household hot-
water supply. The unit,
which measures only 12 by
17 by 6 inches, can be
attached directly to the heat
pump, as shown here.
*Friedrich Air Conditioning &
Refrigeration Co.*

source heat pump gets high marks for summer cooling. Water, which has the highest specific heat of any common substance, can release (and absorb) fifty times as much energy as can the same weight of air.

The groundwater-source heat pump in the cooling mode doesn't save as much input energy as it does in the heating mode, but further efficiencies can be achieved by using ejected heat to meet domestic hot-water needs. Compact hot-water generators for use with groundwater-source heat pumps are offered by a number of manu-

facturers. Friedrich, for one, has developed an uncomplicated unit that extracts heat from the compressor's discharge and automatically maintains hot-water-tank temperatures at between 120° and 140°F. whenever the compressor is running. When the compressor is not in operation, the standard heating element in the hot-water tank kicks on (as it would to back up a solar water heater during protracted periods of no sun). Friedrich hot-water generators provide their greatest economies with electric water heaters, but they can also be used with oil or gas heaters.

Hot water is produced almost immediately when the compressor is in operation, whether heating or cooling.

The heat produced by a groundwater-source heat pump is low-grade, which means the ductwork, registers, and blower must be sized larger than would be required for conventional forced-warm-air heating. But then it's a gentle heat, coming off the heat exchanger in a steady, smooth flow. There are no blasts of hot air, and there's less drying out of the air than with conventional hot-air systems.

Groundwater-source heat-pump technology is improving rapidly, and units are being manufactured to compensate for poor water quality. One manufacturer offers a heat pump that can even operate with brackish water. It is estimated that groundwater-source heat pumps could be used for residential heating and cooling in up to 75 percent of the United States—including both suburban and rural areas—without impairing the quality or quantity of groundwater as a source for domestic water supply.

SOLAR-ASSISTED HEAT PUMPS

When we began talking with heat-pump manufacturers and other experts to bring

Modern one-story ranch house, built by students of the Moore-Norman area Vo-Tech School in Oklahoma, features a solar-augmented heat pump to provide heating and cooling. The solar system, with fourteen air collectors, 8 tons of rock for storage, and a 3-ton Westinghouse Hi/Re/Li heat pump are tied together physically by ductwork and operationally by a control unit and three-stage thermostat. When solar energy is available, it is used to satisfy the heating needs of the home. Domestic hot water is also provided. During extended cloudy weather, the heat pump operates in the normal manner to heat the house. It also serves to cool the house independently during the summer cooling season. *Westinghouse Electric Corp.*

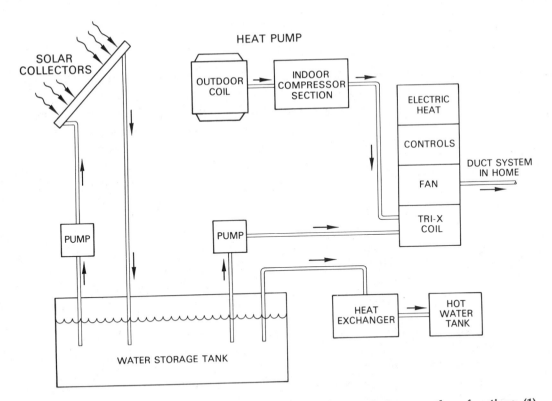

Carrier solar-assisted heat-pump system features Tri-X coil, which serves three functions: (1) transfers heat or cooling from storage water to household air, (2) transfers cooling from refrigerant to storage water during off-peak hours, and (3) transfers heat-pump heat or cooling from refrigerant to household air for normal heat or cooling when storage water is not at the appropriate temperature. *Carrier Air Conditioning*

ourselves up to date on the state of the art, we anticipated that the emphasis of our coverage would be on solar-assisted heat pumps. But then we realized that residential heat pumps, even in the heating mode, work best with a relatively low-temperature reservoir. There's no advantage with sun-warmed water at temperatures much above 60° or 70°F. With solar, it's more a matter of alternatives.

Solar-assisted heat-pump installations combine solar heating, using either air or liquid collectors, with a conventional heat pump and electric resistance heat. Tied together physically by piping or ductwork, and operationally by a control unit and a multi-stage thermostat, the systems are

designed to use whichever operating mode is functioning at its highest efficiency and can make its greatest contribution to winter comfort. Typically, when solar energy is available down to an outdoor temperature of 47°F., it is used alone to satisfy the heating demands of the house. Domestic hot water is also provided. During extended cloudy weather and between outdoor temperatures of 47° and approximately 30°F., the heat pump operates in a normal manner to heat the home. When the outside temperature falls below the heat pump's balance point, stored solar energy is used to assist the heat pump. Only when the solar storage tank or bin is depleted of heat on extremely cold days is it necessary to switch on the supplementary electric heating. With a properly designed heat-pump/solar-energy system, the collectors work at peak efficiency and the heat pump supplies only the additional heat required by the house. The heat pump also serves to cool the house independently of the solar system during the summer cooling season.

It makes for an expensive heating-and-cooling package, with the heat pump functioning as a mid-temperature-range backup to the solar-heating system. A heat pump is expensive enough, costing roughly 25 percent more than a standard furnace and air conditioner. Including ducting, a heat pump may cost between $2,000 and $3,000. We can't see investing $5,000 to $10,000 more for solar space heating (you generally can get by with a somewhat smaller system with a heat pump than would normally be required), plus the backup electric resistance heating required by most utility companies as a standby system in heat-pump installations.

If you're putting down a well anyway, for your domestic water supply, and can't live without air conditioning, a ground-water-source heat pump, plus a hot-water generator tied to the heat pump—with no active solar heating at all—would be the most practical package.

Heat pumps are just beginning to find their place in the energy-saving scheme, and further improvements can be anticipated. A few systems have been built with the compressor driven directly by a stationary engine. But until very recently, almost all heat-pump compressors were powered by electricity. In mid-1979, however, Coleman introduced a system compatible with natural gas as well as electricity. Future models from other manufacturers, still in the research and development stage, derive their compressor power from other heat sources, such as oil, synthetic fuels, and high-grade solar heat. Work is also being done on direct-wind-drive compressors. The technical barrier to commercializing these new heat pumps has been the lack of an inexpensive, efficient, and sufficiently small engine to convert heat to mechanical energy.

HIGH-EFFICIENCY FIREPLACES

You're probably not old enough to remember a time when there were no gas- or oil-fired furnaces. But it wasn't all that long ago. Even the use of coal for home heating didn't become common until the late 1800s. For almost all of man's history since his discovery of fire, wood has been the principal source of "controlled" heat energy in the home. As an infinitely renewable resource, it can be a key to self-sufficiency and a natural backup for passive solar heating. It can also relieve pressure on other energy sources.

Since the fuel-oil crisis of 1973–74, there's been a dramatic resurgence in the use of wood for home heating, the largest single user of residential energy in most climates. In the colder areas of the country, working fireplaces and wood stoves have again become as common as mufflers and comforters. In New England, much of which lies beyond the gas transmission lines, some 20 percent of all households now rely on wood-burning systems to get relief, if not independence, from the crushing costs of OPEC oil.

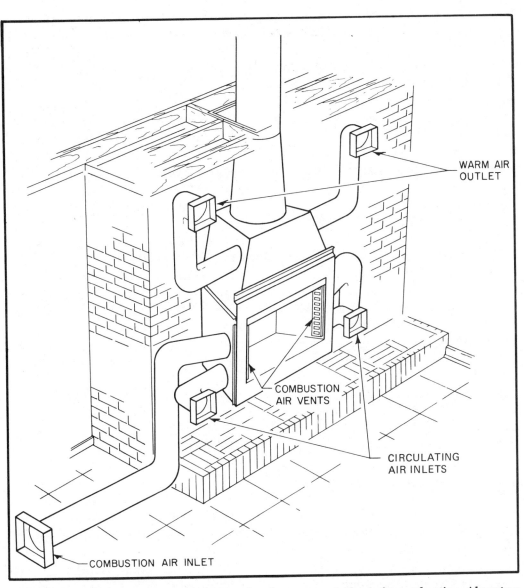

WARM AIR OUTLET

COMBUSTION AIR VENTS

CIRCULATING AIR INLETS

COMBUSTION AIR INLET

Martin Octa-Therm built-in wood-burning fireplace uses outside air for combustion. Almost no heated air is drawn from the room into the fireplace and up the chimney, and no vacuum is created within the home to draw cold outside air through cracks and crevices. Outlets are provided for ducting heated air directly into as many as three rooms, with optional blowers available for improved heat distribution. *Martin Industries*

When we think about heating with wood, most of us picture an open fireplace, with the flames dancing, the logs crackling, and the family gathered near the hearth on a winter evening. It's a warm, romantic image. But if you've sat in front of a few cheery fires, you also know that while your face and feet may get toasted, your back can feel like there's ice forming between the vertebrae. And that's always been a major deficiency with wood-burning fireplaces: radiant heat warms any solid object in its path, but has almost no effect on the room air. Even with man's long dependence on wood as fuel, improvements that would distribute the fireplace heat more effectively have been largely ignored. Most masonry fireplaces are still constructed according to design principles formulated nearly two hundred years ago in England. And we all know, at least by reputation, how poorly heated English homes are during the colder months.

The typical open-front brick or stone fireplace installed in most homes has an efficiency (the percentage of total heat from the burning logs that is converted to useful heat in the house) falling somewhere between 5 and 10 percent. It pumps far more BTUs up the chimney flue than it radiates into the room and, as the fire dies, can draw more heat from the rest of the house than the fire has contributed. But that doesn't have to be. With the reawakening of the long-dormant wood-heating industry and a raising of energy-saving consciousness, fireplaces are being intensively redesigned to serve in a utilitarian rather than a decorative capacity. That greater strides have been made here than in most other areas of energy conservation is more a tribute to Yankee ingenuity than to government funding.

Much of the discomfort associated with conventional fireplaces can be attributed to the fact that, with a good fire blazing, a typical fireplace with a 2-by-3-foot opening draws 22,000 cubic feet of heated air per hour up the chimney. That's more air than the average house contains. The fire would quickly die if it couldn't bring in outside air for combustion, which it *does*—great drafts of it, through every crack and gap around doors and windows—as the inside air pressure drops. With a well-insulated house, you soon discover that the chimney won't "draw" unless a window in the same room is opened a few inches to let in cold outside air to replace the heated air sent up the stack. There are more energy-efficient—and physically comfortable—ways to supply the fire with air for combustion, however. While the house is under construction, or even as an afterthought, ducting can be installed to bring air from outside directly to the hearth. This not only saves the supply of oxygen in the house but avoids pulling preheated room air into the fire and wasting it up the chimney. There is no drop in air pressure, so even where walls, doors, and windows are not as "tight" as they should be, cold outside air does not come whistling in through the cracks.

HEAT-CIRCULATING FIREPLACES

Heat-circulating fireplaces display an even bigger change in fireplace design. These built-ins are essentially prefabricated double-wall steel fireboxes designed to draw room air through a heating chamber sealed off from the fire, warm it, and return it to the home. The real advantage here is that a heat-circulating fireplace heats not only by radiation, which is about all that a conventional fireplace does, but also by convection, wafting heated air directly into the room and even into adjoining rooms. Take a look at a typical heat-circulating fireplace system.

The Energy Saving Fireplace by the Majestic Company, UL listed for efficiency and performance, returns 37.4 percent

The Energy Saving Fireplace by Majestic typifies change in fireplace design to prefabricated, heat-circulating systems that draw room air through a heating chamber sealed off from the fire, warm it, and return it to the living area. The addition of an Outside Air Kit on which the fireplace rests and a Glass Enclosure Kit assures greater performance and efficiency. *The Majestic Company*

Below: Majestic's Energy Saving Fireplace effectively channels 37.4 percent of the heat released by a wood fire back into the house. By adding optional duct kits and fans, heated air can easily be diverted to adjacent rooms or even upstairs, with the flick of a lever. *The Majestic Company*

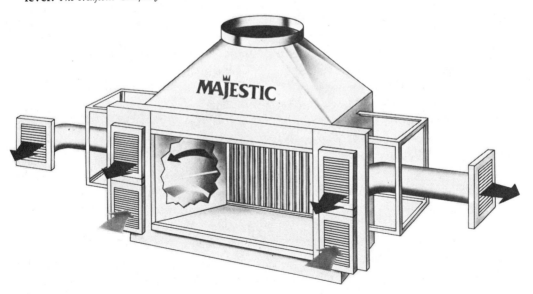

Zero-clearance, self-insulated fireplaces like the Heatilator Model 3138 can be installed against a wall, in a corner, or between rooms. Only the facing and hearth must be noncombustible materials. *Heatilator Fireplace Division of Vega Industries, Inc.*

of the total heat input to the home. Majestic's heat exchanger, with a convoluted backwall formed from 14 square feet of stainless steel, separates heat from flue gases before the heat escapes. Through a series of simple passages, cool air from the room is drawn in behind the backwall of the firebox and pushed through the heat exchanger. The hot steel heats the air and sends it back into the room at close to floor level (where it does the most good) and not up the flue. By adding optional ducts and blowers, the heated air can be diverted to adjacent rooms, or even upstairs, with the flick of a lever. The combination of convective heat in addition to radiant heat using a 14-pound fire will produce a total heat output of 46,000 BTUs per hour.

An Outside Air Kit is available for use with the Energy Saving Fireplace. Installed with flexible ducting, it brings air from outside directly to the firebox at the hearth level. A damper is provided for control of the combustion-air source. A Glass Enclosure Kit, with tempered bifold doors and louvers for limited air introduction at the hearth level, is also available. When closed, the doors permit radiant heat to enter the room while isolating the combustion chamber. The doors serve as a spark guard and limit the loss of heated air from the house via the open chimney damper as the fire burns down after you've turned in. Use of either or both of the accessories improves the existing efficiency of this fireplace.

Other preengineered fireplace units that have all the features needed for energy efficiency—convective and optional (with blowers) forced-air heating, outside air for combustion, tempered-glass doors—include Preway's Energy-Mizer Fireplace, the Heatilator EP Fireplace, Superior Fireplace Company's E-Z Heat model, and Martin Industries' Octa-Therm.

These fireplaces come from the factory with firebox, smoke dome, smoke shelf, and damper incorporated into the steel shell. There's no chance that the flue opening or the smoke shelf will be too large or too small for the fireplace, as they sometimes are with conventional masonry fireplaces built by those to whom fireplace construction is more surface art than science. Beyond their ability to deliver a much higher percentage of the heat generated by the burning logs, there are other advantages with preengineered built-ins. The units mentioned are all zero-clearance

Modern zero-clearance fireplaces enable do-it-yourselfers to install a complete fireplace system. Clockwise from lower left: Once fireplace unit is in place, chimney starter section is fastened; chimney is run through ceiling to roof, with firestop fastened to top of header at ceiling; fireplace is framed-out with studs; and exterior facings of paneling or imitation stone or brick are applied to complete the project. *Heatilator Fireplace Division of Vega Industries, Inc.*

models, which means they can be installed without expensive masonry work.

Zero-clearance fireplaces are surrounded by mineral-fiber insulation contained in an outer housing and may also include a firebrick back and refractory base. The fireplaces are sufficiently insulated and light enough in weight to sit directly on an existing wood floor. Unlike masonry fireplaces, they require no special footings. You can trim with masonry if you wish, but you can also support and surround the fireplace with standard building materials, combustible or not. Only the facing and hearth must be made of non-combustible materials.

Chimneys are usually assembled from a chimney package that includes sections of double- or triple-wall, insulated metal flue pipe. Since no major structural changes are necessary to accommodate a zero-clearance fireplace, it's always possible to add another one later, in another room on the same or a different level, if you decide it would be desirable to have more than one fireplace in the house.

Many manufacturers offer more than one size fireplace. Widths (openings) of 28, 36, and 42 inches would be typical. Some also offer open-end fireplaces in addition to open-front models. Factory-built heat-circulating fireplaces with outside air systems cost between $800 and $1,200 installed, or about one-fourth the cost of a stone fireplace built by a mason. You not only gain in heating efficiency, but you save considerable money at the outset with a heat-circulating fireplace. The savings are even greater if you handle the installation yourself—and Preway, Heatilator, Superior, and Martin promote the installation of their heat circulators as being within the capabilities of do-it-yourselfers.

CURVED-TUBE CONVECTION HEATERS

There are also ways to increase the efficiency of an ordinary masonry fireplace. This most often begins—and too often ends—with the installation of a slip-in fire grate constructed with open C-shaped steel tubes that draw cool air from the room into the bottom of the C, pass it under, behind, and over the fire, and then return heated air to the room through the top of the C by natural convection. Because of the small diameter of the heavy-gauge tubes, usually no more than 2 inches, it is questionable whether the simpler curved-tube convection heaters make a significant heating contribution, though manufacturers claim they can increase the heat output of a fireplace by 50 percent or

Easy-to-install Thermograte fireplace heater simply slides into fireplace opening, anchors in two places, and is sealed against the face of the fireplace. *Thermograte Enterprises, Inc.*

more. If the grate isn't correctly sized, or if it is improperly placed so that the heat exiting from the tubes cannot clear the fireplace opening, the flue draft may draw the heated air straight up the chimney, or the fire may draw it back for combustion. To avoid this problem, a number of manufacturers of fireplace inserts have added electric-powered blowers, usually as part of an intake manifold, to increase the speed and volume of the heated air and propel it well into the room.

The best known of the thirty or more manufacturers of fireplace systems based on the curved-tube convection heater is Thermograte Enterprises, whose president, Ted Bergstrom, invented the original tubular fireplace grate in 1970. Thermograte's tubular heat exchangers, which heat air to about 600°F., are made from stainless steel rather than the usual mild steel, to better withstand the thermal expansions and contractions that the metal undergoes, and are more expensive than most competitors' models. Thermograte's newest version of the tubular heat extractor includes a variable-speed blower unit to increase the speed and volume of hot air going through the tubes (the temperature of the air being expelled drops somewhat, but the result is an approximate 40 percent increase in heat output), and a bifold glass-door fireplace enclosure. Ducting for bringing outside air directly into the fire chamber is offered as an accessory. With this combination, Thermograte claims fireplace efficiencies of better than 40 percent. Proper fit is essential to achieve maximum efficiency and effective heat output, so Glass Door Thermograte Fireplace Heaters are offered in a full range of width, depth, and height combinations. The system can cost from $400 to $800, depending on size.

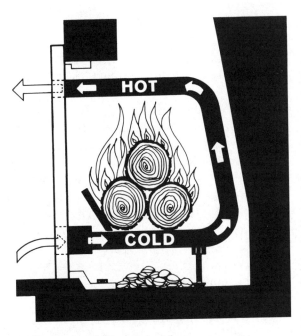

Here's how it works: Natural convection draws in cool air, heats it, and forces heated air out into the room. *Thermograte Enterprises, Inc.*

If you wish to compare claims and prices for fireplace heat exchangers, two other well-engineered systems are The Free Heat Machine, by Aquappliances, Inc., and the Hearth Heater System, by Duo-Therm. The Free Heat Machine is not unlike the glass-door Thermograte. Where Thermograte units have from six to ten tubes, the Free Heat Machine has twelve, and two low-wattage blowers, instead of the Thermograte's one, to assist cool-air intake. Duo-Therm's Hearth Heater System will fit any masonry fireplace with horizontal openings from 28 to 46 inches. Instead of the C-shaped tubular fire grate of most other fireplace inserts, the Hearth Heater System has two top-mounted plenums that extend into the fireplace opening to recover heat from flue gases. At 110°F., an automatic fan switches on to circulate heat into the room.

Still another type of fireplace insert ties into the existing central heating system and distributes heat from the fireplace throughout the house. A good example here would be the Hydrohearth, from the Hydroheat Division of Ridgway Steel Fabricators. Like the curved-tube convection heaters, the similarly shaped Hydrohearth replaces the conventional log grate. But the Hydrohearth circulates water instead of air. It is connected to the main return line of a central hydronic heating system, a liquid-to-air heat exchanger mounted in the plenum of a forced-air system, or a liquid-to-liquid heat exchanger mounted in a solar heat storage tank. The water that circulates through the Hydrohearth extracts up to 50,000 BTUs of heat per hour from a fire. This is in addition to the radiant heat energy

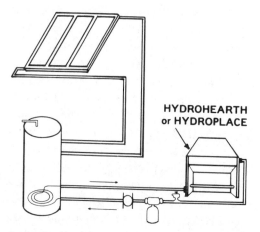

HYDROHEARTH or HYDROPLACE

Instead of handling air, the Hydrohearth and the Hydroplace circulate water and connect to a heat exchanger mounted in a solar heat storage tank, the main return line of a central hydronic heating system, or a liquid-to-air heat exchanger mounted in the plenum of a forced-air system. *Hydroheat Division–Ridgway Steel Fabricators, Inc.*

thrown off by the fire. The Hydroplace, also by Hydroheat, is similar to a conventional double-wall, steel fireplace liner, except that water circulates through its hollow walls and grate. The Hydroplace is intended as an improvement over conventional masonry fireplaces in new construction. The Hydrohearth can be installed in existing fireplaces.

FREESTANDING FIREPLACES AND FIREPLACE/STOVES

The range of styles, sizes, and prices of freestanding wood-burning fireplaces and stoves is staggering. We started compiling a list of the wood-burners advertised in just one magazine, *Country Journal*, and gave up when the count reached fifty. To help you here, we've broken the wood-burners (some also burn coal) down into two categories: (1) freestanding fireplaces, including fireplace/stoves; and (2) airtight stoves and heat circulators.

Placed away from room walls, a freestanding wood-burner radiates heat in more than one direction, which makes even the simplest units more effective, if not more efficient, than conventional masonry fireplaces. Flexibility in respect to placement and relative ease of installation (consult your local building inspection department for applicable codes if you plan to do the job yourself) are other advantages. The major disadvantage is that about 40 to 50 square feet of living area must be given up to the fireplace or stove. Hot surfaces can also present a hazard if there are young children in the home.

Conical fireplaces generally provide more ambience than BTUs. They are a favorite, however, with owners of A-frames and other contemporary vacation homes. A floor base of noncombustible material is required. *Preway, Inc.*

Freestanding fireplaces are the center of attention. They generally are placed where a comfortable furniture arrangement gives a maximum view of the fire. This is true especially with conical fireplaces, which, as the least efficient of all the freestanders, provide more ambience than BTUs. The contemporary design of the conical steel fireplace, with its integral hood, its easy-to-clean porcelainized finish, and its availability in a choice of decorator colors, has made it a favorite with owners of A-frames and other contemporary vacation homes. While they're an effective *auxiliary* heat source for taking off the chill in the spring or fall, you wouldn't want to depend on one for primary heating when the temperature drops much below 50°F.

A conical fireplace is relatively inexpensive. The price range is about $200 to $350. Majestic's Firehood, the original conical wood-burning fireplace, retails for about $275, with a 38-inch hearth opening and enough porcelain-finish flue pipe to reach an 8-foot ceiling. Allow another $50 to $100 for the chimney kit, plus about $20 for each additional color-matching 24-inch length of flue pipe needed. As with any freestanding wood-burner designed to radiate a complete circle of heat, a conical fireplace must be installed at least 36 inches away from any combustible wall (or 24 inches with a heat shield), and set on an adequately sized noncombustible base, such as a pebble bed, bricks, slate, or patio blocks.

Freestanding fireplace/stoves, which open to serve as fireplaces, have seen more improvements in the last few years than Ben Franklin devised for their original prototype, which, with its folding doors, was a remarkable improvement over the conventional masonry fireplace. Franklin stoves are available today from many manufacturers, in both traditional and modernized styling, and generally have efficiencies in the 30 percent range.

Sears's "finest Franklin Fireplace-Heater" includes a sculptured profile of Ben cast into a fascia panel as a decorative touch. But otherwise it's authentically styled and, like its antecedent, made from cast iron. With the doors closed, it's a heater; open, it's a fireplace. The stove is priced at about $250 and can accommodate a barbecue grid or a 5-quart bean pot on a swing-out hook. Other Sears Franklins start at around $125 for a 38-inch-wide model made of cast iron and steel.

The U.S. Stove Company, which has been making Franklin stoves since the 1890s, recently introduced a model with traditional styling except for the addition of space-age glass-ceramic doors. The Coronado, by Martin Industries, is an even more modernized version of the traditional Franklin, with bifold glass doors, vents on top to aid heat distribution, plus an optional blower to improve the efficiency of the stove.

One of the objections to traditional Franklin stoves is that they require a lot of attention, but most of the refined models can be dampened down to burn fuel slow-

ly. Any of these single-wall stoves, which radiate heat from five more surfaces than a built-in fireplace, is capable of maintaining comfortable temperatures in areas of up to 750 square feet.

The glass-door Franklins are part of the trend toward more efficient, freestanding fireplace/stoves that bridge the gap between built-in fireplaces and airtight stoves. Combining the function of a heating stove with the aesthetics of a fireplace, the newest designs, such as Majestic's Peabody, which includes three sides of tempered glass to allow optimum flame visibility, can be operated with doors opened or closed, and may include a heat exchanger to capture heat normally lost up the chimney, as well as a built-in fan to circulate heated air throughout the room, if not the house.

Preway's hexagonal Provider, with functional European styling, features not only a built-in high-volume heat-circulating fan, along with glass doors, but an optional Energy-Mizer air kit to bring in outside air for combustion and avoid burning substantial amounts of heated home air to support the fire. The Provider operates on manual or automatic (thermostatic) control and costs around $800. It's a far cry from the traditional Franklin stove, with an efficiency rivaling that of conventional oil- and gas-fired furnaces.

Sears's most efficient freestanding, wood-burning fireplace (which we suspect is manufactured by Preway) has a built-in fan for forced-air heating, plus a built-in heat shield that permits the rear wall of the stove to be positioned as close as 7 inches to a combustible wall, and within 20 inches at the sides. This Sears fireplace/stove features glass doors, plus a firescreen to keep ashes and sparks inside when the doors are open. It sells for about $500; an optional duct kit ($29) for bring-

Preway's freestanding fireplace, the Provider, features an air-circulating system with a built-in, high-volume fan for rapid room heating. Optional Energy Mizer air-intake kits allow the Provider to use outside air for combustion. Glass doors, standard equipment on the Provider fireplace, minimize the escape of warm air and radiate additional heat to the room. *Preway, Inc.*

ing in outside air for combustion is offered.

If you're looking for efficiency, give some consideration to Thermograte Enterprises' fireplace/stove, which has full-view bifold tempered glass doors and is the newest entry among the economical and efficient alternatives to a conventional fireplace. The Thermograte® Free-Standing Super-Heating Fireplace/Stove features a built-in stainless-steel tubular heat exchanger (six tubes), which delivers high-volume heat output by natural convection. An auxiliary blower is available to increase the output of heated air and aid in the distribution of warm air throughout the house. Thermograte claims a heat output of 55,000 BTUs per hour with a fuel load of under 12 pounds per hour, for a 63.2 percent net efficiency *without* the aid of the blower.

Fireplace and stove manufacturers are prone to exaggerated performance claims. But great strides have indeed been made in the efficiency of wood-burners. Engi-

neered to control combustion air and reduce the burning rate of fuel while increasing heat output, combustion is so complete in some freestanding fireplace/stoves that ash cleanout is necessary only after every 200 to 300 hours of burning.

AIRTIGHT STOVES AND HEAT CIRCULATORS

The airtight box stove is replacing the old-fashioned potbelly as the basic wood-burning, radiant heater. Constructed with baffles that maneuver the gases within the firebox for more complete combustion, the best sellers today burn logs from front to rear, slowly and evenly, like a good cigar, and can hold a heat-radiating fire for up to twelve hours or more on a single loading.

Modern box stoves typically have

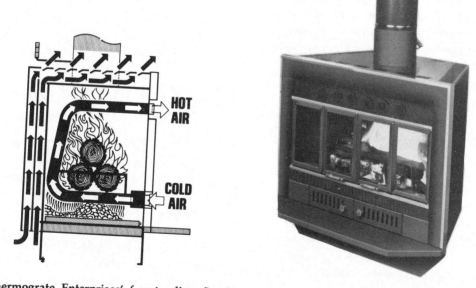

Thermograte Enterprises' freestanding fireplace/stove has full-view bi-fold tempered glass doors and features a built-in stainless-steel tubular heat exchanger, which delivers high-volume heat output by natural convection. *Thermograte Enterprises, Inc.*

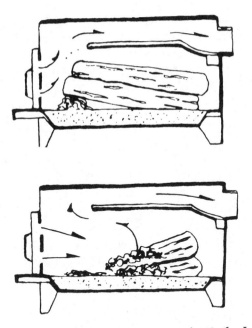

Like its bigger brother, the Jøtul 118, the Jøtul 602 burns logs from front to rear, slowly and evenly, like a good cigar. *Kristia Associates*

smooth tops to provide a cooking surface, gasket-lined loading doors to ensure that only controlled air gets into the chamber, and an upper air regulator to provide added oxygen so unburned gases and carbon particles, their escape up the flue delayed by a baffle toward the top of the firebox, may be consumed. Efficiencies of 60 percent and better—in terms of heat output—are common. These airtight stoves draw substantially less air than open fireplaces, locking out the air that contributes to uncontrollable, inefficient burns.

The most popular airtight stoves today are either step-shaped, with two unobstructed cooking surfaces, each of a different temperature, or oblong. Sears's Huntsman Wood-Burning Heater ($340), which Sears claims burns logs longer and more completely than any of their other heaters, is a step-stove, as is Fisher's popular Mama Bear, and, of course, the Canadian Step-Stove. These stoves are

fashioned from rugged steel plate, welded for an airtight body, and lined with firebrick to hold and radiate heat evenly. Most oblong box stoves, on the other hand, are made of cast iron and have no lining. We're not going to get into the cast-iron vs. welded-steel debate, but Scandinavian-type cast-iron box stoves are leading the pack and account for much of the increased volume in stove sales. Stoves like the classic Jøtul 118 and the Morsø 1B, among the imports, have done nearly as much for wood-stove sales as OPEC.

The much-publicized Jøtul 118 has been acclaimed for its ability to hold a fire. With a preheating chamber on the inside of the door, front-end combustion, and a horizontal baffle plate that extends from the back wall of the stove toward the front, the draft takes an S-shaped path through the firebox. A secondary air flow, directed at the gases given off by the burning wood, provides oxygen for double combustion. In tests performed in Norway burning seasoned wood with a 20 percent moisture content, the Jøtul 118 achieved an efficiency of 76 percent, for 22,500 BTUs, when burning 3.1 pounds of wood per hour. Burning 11 pounds of wood per hour, for 44,500 BTUs, the efficiency dropped to 54.6 percent. The Jøtul 118 can handle logs up to 24 inches long and is rated for 4,000 to 7,000 cubic feet. With an 8-foot ceiling, that works out to from 500 to 875 square feet of floor area. The dark-green-enameled 118 has a little brother, the Jøtul 602. Big enough to handle logs up to 16 inches long, it is rated for 2,500 to 5,000 cubic feet. Its top efficiency (69 percent) comes with a burn rate of 2.6 pounds of wood per hour, for 15,000 BTUs. Burning 7 pounds of wood per hour, it can deliver 27,000 BTUs.

The Morsø 1B (22-inch logs) and the

Morsø 2B (20-inch logs) have most of the same features as the Jøtuls, with a special chamber preheating and distributing intake air. The air flow is regulated by rotating a draft wheel on the door. The Morsøs' front-end combustion and an S-pattern draft flow allow hot gases to remain in the stove longer, and consequently they radiate more heat per load of wood. The heating capacity for the Morsø 1B is 6,000 cubic feet, and for the Morsø 2B it's 4,800 cubic feet. Their prices are about $600 and $425, respectively.

Among the U.S. foundries producing airtight, Scandinavian-type, front-end-combustion stoves, the Portland Stove Foundry Company and Upland Stove Company offer efficient box stoves which many authorities consider to be the equal of the imports. Depending on the health of the dollar abroad, they also tend to be somewhat less expensive than the imports.

If you're looking for a stove of this type with a greater heating capacity, the fully baffled Cawley/LeMay Model 600, which was developed by a team of industrial designers after experimenting with a wide range of wood stoves, is quite a bit larger than the Jøtul 118. It can handle logs up to 27 inches long and is rated for 5,500 to 10,000 cubic feet. This not only is a re-

Burning 7 pounds of wood per hour, the Jøtul 602 can deliver 27,000 BTUs. Its top efficiency (69 percent) comes with a burn rate of 2.6 pounds of wood per hour, for 15,000 BTUs. The decorative top is optional.
Kristia Associates

panels, the stoves are quite handsome and very European.

The heating range of any of these stoves is approximate and depends on everything from how well the house is insulated to the type and condition of the wood being burned. Since radiant heaters do not use forced convection to distribute heat evenly throughout the house, careful attention must be paid to the placement of

The American-made Cawley/LeMay Model 600 is remarkably efficient and can handle logs up to 27 inches long. It is rated for 5,500 to 10,000 cubic feet. *The Cawley Stove Company, Inc.*

markably efficient heating unit but a cook stove as well, with removable cooking lids. During months when less heat is required, the interior side baffles can be reversed to create a smaller firebox. There's an ample sweep shelf for ashes that may spill from the door, and the legs are adjustable for leveling. The stove sells for $675. A smaller version of the stove, the Model 400, handles logs up to 19 inches long, is rated for 2,500 to 6,500 cubic feet, and costs $545. With their sculptured side

Cawley/LeMay Model 400 is a smaller version of the Model 600. It can handle logs up to 19 inches long and is rated for 2,500 to 6,500 cubic feet. Legs are adjustable for leveling. Interior side baffles may be reversed to create a smaller firebox. *The Cawley Stove Company, Inc.*

the stove in relation to the space to be heated. Operable vents in floors and walls can help distribute the heat if more than one room is to be warmed.

While the great advantage with these stoves is that they will burn unattended through the night, maintaining the stove in the lower draft ranges contributes to creosote build-up in the stack. A natural byproduct of the incomplete combustion of wood, creosote is driven off as a vapor and will condense on the colder interior surfaces of stovepipes and chimneys when the stack temperature drops below 250°F. As creosote accumulates, it poses a fire hazard and is the cause of most chimney fires. With a stove set to hold a fire at lower settings, the stack cools and flammable creosote build-up increases. The problem can be avoided to some extent by burning only seasoned hardwoods in the lower fire ranges, and by briefly firing the stove in the high range each morning to dry out and flake off any creosote that has accumulated overnight. Nevertheless, with an airtight stove designed to be used in low fire ranges, it's impossible to avoid some creosote build-up. It begins as a thin, varnishlike film and builds up into a tarry substance that can seep through pipe seams. A well-insulated stack, such as Metalbestos, that runs up to the roof through the interior of the house will help reduce the creosote problem. The worst thing you could do here would be to run uninsulated stovepipe up an outside wall, exposing it to frigid air.

There are dozens of stove styles and literally hundreds of wood-burning models. The Jøtul line alone includes ten distinctly different stoves, and the Portland Stove Foundry Company offers not only airtight box stoves but Franklins and cook stoves plus *two* lines of Norwegian stoves—Trolla and Ulefos. It is not our intention, however, to inventory every manufacturer and stove model, nor are simple coal stoves or cook stoves and ranges that operate with wood or coal covered in this volume. Our aim is to fill you in on the state of the art and bring to your attention those stoves and heating systems that can save significantly more energy than most, back up solar heating (active or passive), or serve as *practical* alternatives to conventional fossil-fuel heating systems.

If you're looking for a stove that can heat more than a room or two, a circulator heater is more suitable than a radiant heater. A circulator heater is constructed with a metal jacket surrounding the firebox, and heats mainly by convection. Natural air currents (or a blower, for forced-air circulation) distribute the air heated between the jacket and the firebox. U.S. Stove Company's Wonderwood, promoted as "America's favorite wood-burning circulator heater," heats ten hours or more on one load of wood and includes a nonelectric thermostat that automatically opens and closes the damper to control the fire. A two-speed blower is offered as an option to send the heat into other rooms. The Wonderwood lists for about $230, plus $60 for the blower.

Sears's "best" circulator heater includes a cast-iron firebox liner, automatic draft/damper controls, a cover that can be removed to permit cooking atop the firebox, and an optional temperature-activated, two-speed counterflow blower that releases warm air at floor level. The stove, which handles logs up to 24 inches long and is advertised to hold a fire up to twelve hours, sells for $270. Add another $60 for the blower.

For the maximum possible transfer of heat into the house, stove designers are turning away from updraft systems that allow more than 50 percent of the heat value of wood to escape up the chimney in the form of combustible gases. As noted, the trend in radiant heaters is toward baffle reburn systems that force the draft to follow an S-shaped, horizontal path for more complete combustion; in heat circulators, it's toward thermostatically controlled *downdraft* systems. The Vermont DownDrafter exemplifies this type of combustion. The primary air source is placed above the fire but below the main load of logs, so the air pulls the gases down through the embers, where secondary air is introduced to oxidize these super-heated volatiles. A thermostatic controller senses stack temperatures and regulates inlet air supplies for extended burning. A "slo-feed" system within the stove, with the top-loaded logs isolated from the flames until they drop into po-

sition in a V-shaped grate, limits the wood consumption rate.

The Vermont DownDrafter includes an inner chamber through which room air is drawn for heating and circulation by blower. There are two models of the DownDrafter. The DD I can handle logs up to 24 inches long and can be connected directly to ducting to heat five or six rooms; it costs about $600. The DD II sells for about $400 and can handle logs up to 18 inches long to heat two or three rooms.

Other downdrafters are offered under the Ashley, Tempwood, and Nashua labels. The Deluxe Ashley Imperial Model C-60 (about $450) burns logs up to 24 inches long and can hold 100 pounds of wood for a long, slow burn that is ther-

Reflecting the understated elegance of traditional New England design, the Defiant Parlor Stove scores high for both looks and performance. With doors opened or removed, the stove offers the warmth and appeal of an open hearth. Doors closed, it's an airtight heat circulator, with thermostatic controls to set the level of heat. *Vermont Castings, Inc.*

mostatically controlled. With an optional automatic blower, the Ashley downdrafter is said to be capable of heating four to five rooms. The Tempwood, by Mohawk Industries, is made of rugged steel plate with a refractory firebox and gives immediate heat, once lit. The Nashua Doubleheat Woodstove includes 600 pounds of $\frac{1}{2}$-inch boilerplate steel and could be the most substantial stove made. It features a baffled downdraft system that recycles wood gases back into the stove to burn them almost completely, with minimal creosote build-up. It is both a radiant heater *and* a circulator heater, with a powerful blower that forces room air through superheated manifolds.

A stove that sits in the middle of a living area should be as attractive as it is functional. On both counts it would be hard to fault Vermont Castings' Defiant Woodburning Parlor Stove. In outward appearances, it's not unlike a Franklin stove, with doors that open so you can enjoy the friendly warmth of an open fire. But with the doors closed, it's an airtight heat circulator with thermostatic controls to set the level of heat. Logs fall into the flame area as the wood below is consumed. Made of cast iron, with both front and side loading, it includes a complex baffling system to provide a 60-inch horizontal draft path for effective heat transfer. The stove handles logs up to 24 inches long and can hold a fire for twelve to fourteen hours. Rated for 8,000 to 10,000 cubic feet, it has a maximum output of 55,000 BTUs and sells for $575. The Vigilant, a slightly smaller version of the Defiant, handles logs up to 18 inches long and is rated for 6,500 to 8,500 cubic feet. It sells for $470.

The Earth Stove also gets high marks for good looks and the comfort it can provide. It has a certified combustion effi-

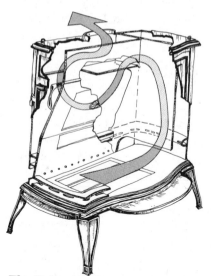

The Defiant Parlor Stove's complex baffling system provides a 60-inch horizontal draft path, which helps keep the heat inside the house instead of wasting it up the chimney. *Vermont Castings, Inc.*

ciency rating of 67 percent. A preheating draft promotes efficient and complete combustion, while a thermostatic draft automatically maintains the temperature you select. The Earth Stove can handle large "chunks" better than most stoves. Three 10-inch-diameter logs will last up to 18 hours. It, too, converts to an open fireplace. It is priced at approximately $450.

Another parlor favorite is the Belgian Efel. An attractive stove with a Pyrex door for loading and fire viewing, the clean-lined Efel is 28 inches wide, 32 inches high, and 15 inches deep. The stove comes in a choice of eight colors. The design includes a large hood, which when raised exposes the cast-iron firebox hood and reflects radiant heat into the room. When the hood is in place, the stove heats by convection. At an average burn rate, one load of hardwood lasts eight to twelve hours. Combustion is so complete in this airtight, controlled-draft stove that there is no need to empty the ash pan more than once every two weeks or more. The stove's only weakness would seem to be in the glass door, which clouds up from smoke and creosote when the stove is fired at the lower burn rates. This, however, can be cleared up with a spritz of oven cleaner, wiped off a few minutes later. The stove costs about $550.

If you haven't had any experience with new stoves, be warned that they should be broken in slowly. Like a good iron frying pan, they need to be "seasoned." Single-wall box stoves should not be fired up the first time without several inches of ashes or sand laid in the bottom of the stove to protect the bottom plate and prevent heat loss.

Follow state and local building codes when installing any wood-burning system. Whether you do the job yourself or have someone else do it, the installation, including chimney, should be checked by a building inspector before you fire up. Your insurance company should also be notified, for the addition of a wood-burner could affect your homeowner's policy.

WOOD TO BURN

Unlike the fossil fuels, wood is a renewable resource. Today, even with all our cities and highways and farmland, we have nearly 75 percent as much forest acreage as we had when the first colonists arrived. We may be running low on oil, but the sheer abundance of wood, which is environmentally compatible as a fuel, should give more than a little comfort. From new growth alone, it is estimated that—apart from meeting all other requirements—enough firewood is available to provide all the heat needed for 50 million homes.

Even if you don't own your own woodlot, wood for fuel is often free for the axing. Forests, as well as woodlots, need to be "managed"—with the removal of deadwood and selective cutting to make way for new growth. At most of the 154 national forests (not to be confused with national *parks*), as well as state forests, homeowners are encouraged to cut up and haul away deadwood and culls from specified areas. A permit, which may be free or cost a nominal amount, is required, and the wood can be taken for personal use only. Many private forest owners encourage the same practice.

Check with the nearest office of the U.S. Forest Service (listed in the telephone directory under "U.S. Government, Department of Agriculture, Forest Service") or the county extension agent.

State and local highway departments are another source of wood to burn, especially after a tree-toppling storm, or when the way is being cleared for a new road. Where open burning is not permitted, dumps and landfills can be good scavenging grounds for dead, discarded trees and all sorts of scrap lumber. Do not, however, cut up discarded railroad ties or utility poles for firewood. They are saturated with chemical substances that could prove hazardous to your health when burned.

If you have to buy your wood from a dealer, there are several things you should know. Firewood is sometimes sold by weight, but most often by the cord. A true cord is a well-stacked pile of logs measuring 4 feet deep, 4 feet high, and 8 feet long. That's 128 cubic feet, more wood than you can fit into the cargo bed of a pickup. For the convenience of the consumer, however, much of the commerce in firewood is done

TABLE SEVEN

RATINGS FOR FIREWOODS

Wood Type	Heating Values	Ease of Starting	Coaling Qualities	Sparks	Ease of Splitting
Hickory	High	Fair	Excellent	Moderate	Fair
Locust (black)	High	Poor	Excellent	Very few	Fair
Apple	High	Poor	Excellent	Few	Tough
Oak, white	High	Poor	Excellent	Few	Fair
Beech	High	Poor	Excellent	Few	Tough
Oak, red	High	Poor	Excellent	Few	Fair
Maple, sugar	High	Poor	Excellent	Few	Fair
Birch (white)	Medium	Fair	Good	Moderate	Fair
Ash	Medium	Fair	Good	Few	Fair
Cherry	Medium	Poor	Excellent	Few	Fair
Tamarack	Medium	Fair	Good	Few	Fair
Maple, red	Medium	Fair	Good	Few	Fair
Elm	Medium	Fair	Good	Very few	Impossible
Aspen	Low	Fair	Poor	Moderate	Easy
Cedar	Low	Excellent	Poor	Many	Easy
Spruce	Low	Excellent	Poor	Many	Easy
Pine, white	Low	Excellent	Poor	Many	Easy

in *face* cords, which, instead of being 4 feet deep, are only as deep as the log length required to fit the typical fireplace or stove. A face cord, which is not a legal measure, can be anywhere from 1 to 2 feet deep—one-quarter to one-half of a true cord. A *run*, which *is* a legal measure, is 16 inches deep, 4 feet high, and 8 feet long—one-third of a true cord. Know what you are buying when you see "cords" of wood advertised at what you think are bargain rates. The dealer is also likely to have three prices: undelivered, delivered, and delivered and stacked.

Commercial firewood is cheaper off-season—in the late spring or early summer. You'll pay a stiff premium if you have to replenish a woodpile in the dead of winter, even if you make the pickup yourself. Firewood is also cheaper if you buy by the true cord (4-foot logs) and make the additional cuts and split the logs yourself. Logs over 4 to 6 inches in diameter should be split before the wood is stacked, to promote faster drying. Stack the splits bark-side up and the bark will serve as a waterproof shield.

Only about 80 cubic feet of a true cord is solid wood. The rest of the stack is air. The wood can also include up to 40 percent water, if you buy *green* wood, which is one reason not to buy wood by weight. Wood should be allowed to air-dry, under cover (if you don't have a woodshed, a loose plastic or canvas tarp will do), for at least eight months after it has been cut, and preferably longer—two summers if you can manage it. Try to avoid burning any but well-seasoned wood, with a moisture content of 20 percent or less. If you throw green wood on a fire, a lot of heat energy must be expended merely to drive out the moisture as steam. Burning wood with a high moisture content also contributes to creosote build-up.

Pound for pound, all species of seasoned wood give off approximately the same amount of heat when burned—roughly 5,800 BTUs per air-dried pound. But that doesn't mean that a fire fed with white pine logs, for example, will burn as efficiently as one fueled with hickory. Hickory is a much denser wood than pine and outweighs it by

Chain saws have been a big factor in the dramatic resurgence in the use of wood for home heating. *John Deere*

A gasoline-powered log splitter can make quick work of reducing a pile of logs to a cord of firewood. *John Deere*

nearly 2 to 1. Like most of the softwoods, pine is not a good choice for a primary fuel. It burns too quickly, requiring frequent replenishment. Nor does it "coal" well, which is the ability to create long-lasting coals, the most valuable heat source. It also gums up the chimney more than most woods. This does not mean that pine has no place in the woodbin. When split to form kindling, pine and certain other softwoods ignite easily and can get a fire off to a fast start.

For efficiency and economy, fires should be maintained with the hardwoods, which, with few exceptions, have higher heating values than the softwoods. The hardwoods are mostly the broad-leaved, or deciduous, trees. Softwoods are the conifers—cone-bearing evergreens with needlelike leaves. A cord of dry hickory weighs about 2 tons and, burned in a stove or furnace with 50 to 60 percent efficiency, yields as much heat as 1 ton of hard coal or 240 gallons of fuel oil. A cord of white pine is equivalent in heating value to about half a ton of anthracite, or 120 gallons of No. 2 fuel oil.

Old-timers and fuelwood connoisseurs will tell you that the best fires are built with a log or two of resinous softwood, such as pine, fir, or spruce, for easy ignition; a larger log of hardwood, such as oak, maple, or beech, for steady, glowing coals; and, after the fire is burning well, a log of apple, cherry, or pecan for a pleasing aroma. That may be fine for an open fireplace and romantic notions—but if you're burning wood primarily for comfort, you'll likely start up your airtight stove or furnace in the fall and keep the fire glowing all winter. You will have little need for the softwoods and, unless you have a convertible fireplace/stove, will rarely get a whiff of the aromatic woods. Nor will green woods be necessary to "cool down" the fire and hold it longer (a technique that may also be recommended to you), since this can be done with thermostatic controls or a simple adjustment of the draft wheel.

When dry wood is burned efficiently, the products of combustion, other than heat energy, are carbon dioxide, water, and a small amount of residual ash—all of which, as with the natural process of decay in the forest, are easily recycled by green plants. Applied to the soil, the ash that remains from burning wood is a valuable fertilizer.

MULTI-FUEL FURNACES

With a house that's well insulated and oriented for passive solar heat gain in the winter, a conventional central heating system may not be necessary. An efficient wood-burning stove or heat circulator possibly could provide all the supplementary or backup heat you're likely to require. But this will depend on (1) the climate, and (2) the layout of the house. Whether heated by the sun or a wood stove, warm air circulates rather freely in a two-story house of "open" design—with cathedral ceilings, floor and wall louvers, wide doorways, and an airy stairwell. At the other extreme, there's little free movement of air in the typical tract ranch—with its small rooms, narrow doorways, and twisting hallways. You might meet your heating needs here with two or three strategically placed wood-burners, each of which would require its own chimney, but a central forced-air or hydronic heating system would almost certainly be more practical.

For those who require a central heating system, there are a number of interesting alternatives to the gas, oil, and electric furnaces that warm most homes today.

For starters, there are wood-burning furnaces that consume unsplit logs—green or seasoned wood—and kick out enough BTUs to warm a hangar for a 747. There also are less voracious models, in the 50,000 to 100,000 BTU range, for houses that are designed to be energy efficient. Most wood-burners intended for use in central heating systems can also be fitted with shaker grates to burn coal. With today's imperfect energy supplies, the new trend, however, is toward systems that let you burn wood or oil, wood or gas, or wood, coal, oil, or gas, converting easily from one to another. Typically, you burn wood, or whatever fuel provides maximum economy, most of the time.

The advantage of a multi-fuel system such as wood/oil (assuming that natural gas, which heats more than half the nation's homes, is not available to you) is that you're not tied to the house through the winter because of the attention a wood fire requires, and the concomitant threat of plumbing freeze-ups should you go away for more than a day. If the fire dies, you have a backup heating element that kicks on automatically when the firebox temperature drops below a preset level. Or, if you prefer not to haul wood and tend the furnace, you can heat with oil primarily and fall back on wood in the event of interruptions in your oil supply.

Wood heating, as noted, has attracted a horde of new manufacturers, and no *Consumer Reports* type of evaluations have yet been made to help steer you to the heating plant that matches your needs and at the same time represents a "best buy." For the most part, unless you can get some sound advice from a heating engineer, a reputable heating-equipment contractor, or friends or neighbors who have had experience with wood-burning systems, you'll have to go by the manufacturer's

The Riteway Model 37, with "complete combustion" design, is considered to be one of the most efficient wood (and coal) heaters around. *Riteway Manufacturing Co.*

reputation and his claims for a particular furnace.

Riteway, in business for more than forty years, is a respected manufacturer that pioneered the multi-fuel concept more than fifteen years ago—long before other manufacturers even envisioned a need for this innovative design. The Riteway Model 37, with "complete combustion" design, is considered one of the most efficient wood (and coal) heaters around. Rated at 73,000 BTUs, it will comfortably heat four to eight rooms. (Even with outside temperatures down to 0°F., a typical new,

Oil burners, natural-gas burners, and bottled-gas burners are available with Riteway wood-burning hot-air furnaces. Riteway's Model LF-20 furnace, shown here, has a fuel capacity of 13.5 cubic feet and is rated for up to 125,000 BTUs. It is equipped with a direct-drive blower. *Riteway Manufacturing Co.*

well-insulated six-room house shouldn't lose more than about 40,000 BTUs per hour.) The Model 37 is actually a radiant heater, but an accessory jacket made of galvanized steel allows it to be used as a primary heat source for a forced warm-air system, with the heated air that is gathered from above the heater blown through the house via ductwork. The unit, which holds more than 7.5 cubic feet of wood, includes a bimetal thermostat that can be set for the temperature you want. Model 37 lists for $480. The jacket costs another $92. An accessory domestic water heater is available for $95.

Riteway also manufactures thermostatically controlled wood-burning hot-air and hot-water furnaces, with four models in each series; maximum outputs range from 125,000 to 350,000 BTUs. Prices for

the hot-air furnaces start at about $1,500; for the hot-water furnaces (boilers), at $2,500. An optional oil, natural-gas, or bottled-gas burner may be purchased and mounted on any model. Riteway's furnaces change from one fuel to another automatically, with no manual assistance required. Solid fuel is burned efficiently in the same combustion chamber as oil or gas.

Another respected name in multi-fuel

A new multi-purpose boiler for hot-water heating systems, the HS-Tarm Type MB-Solo is available equipped to burn wood or coal, or it can be supplied as an oil- or gas-fired boiler. *Tekton Corp.*

Manufactured in Denmark, the HS-Tarm OT Multi-Fuel Boiler provides heat and hot water year-round from a variety of fuels. Wood can be used in combination with oil, gas, or electricity. The combustion chamber for oil or gas is on the left side; on the right is a large firebox for wood. The three center tappings are for optional installation of electrical heating elements.
Tekton Corp.

heating systems is the Danish firm HS-Tarm. The HS-Tarm Wood/Coal Boiler is a solid-fuel furnace controlled by a non-electric automatic draft regulator. It can also be installed as an oil- or gas-fired furnace that can easily be converted to solid-fuel operation should your oil or gas supply be interrupted. With four models, maximum outputs range from 72,000 to 180,000 BTUs when burning wood, and from 120,000 to 300,000 BTUs when burning oil. Prices start at $1,373, or $1,531 with a coil-type domestic water heater.

The HS-Tarm OT Multi-Fuel Boiler is designed for even greater flexibility. Wood can be used in combination with oil, gas, or electricity to provide heat and year-round domestic hot water. The OT furnace has a separate firebox for wood and another for oil and gas. If the wood fire dies down or is allowed to go out, the control system automatically switches on the backup unit—oil, gas, or electric—to maintain boiler temperature. In addition, the furnace can be fitted with shaker grates for burning coal or coke. Most OT owners report that they use firewood for 90 percent or more of their heat. Well-seasoned wood is required; the design of these units precludes the use of wood with more than 20 percent moisture content. There are four models in the OT series, with maximum BTU outputs ranging from 72,000 to 196,000 (wood), and 112,000 to 280,000 (oil). Price range: $2,000 to $3,000, including a domestic hot-water system.

Other multi-fuel furnaces are offered by S/A Energy, Duo-Matic, Oneida Heater Company, and Yukon Industries. Systems that burn wood and/or oil are offered by Charmaster Products, Marathon Heater Company, Franco-Belge, and Longwood.

Hot-air and hot-water furnaces fired with solid fuels have their own merits and drawbacks. Heating with hot water is clean and convenient, but hot-water furnaces are more expensive than hot-air furnaces, and the heat-distribution system—with piping and baseboard radiators or convectors—while taking up less space, can be more complicated than the ducting and floor or wall registers required with hot-air systems. Forced warm-air heating ductwork could also serve a central air-conditioning system and adapts more easily for solar space heating. However, hot-water heating can more easily meet domestic hot-water needs. On the other hand, wood-burning boilers run cooler than comparable hot-air furnaces and tend to produce more creosote.

If we *needed* a central heating system (which we wouldn't, if we were building for self-sufficiency), and natural gas was not available, we would favor a wood/oil system, with combustion air ducted in from outside the house for additional fuel savings. With solar water heating, we would prefer the convenience of an automatic oil-fired water heater for a backup rather than a wood burner that would have to be fired up every time the sun failed during the warmer months. If we needed oil for one system, we would extend its use, as a backup fuel, to the other system as well. With oil, even at today's prices, it would then probably make sense to install a sizable underground tank and have oil readily available as an alternate fuel.

Freestanding heat-circulating fireplaces and stoves have been improved to the point where they can heat a house nearly as well as a furnace installed in the basement. A basement installation, however, doesn't take up space in the living area, as does a fireplace or stove. It also cuts down on the upstairs housekeeping, confining the usual litter of wood-burning systems to the basement. Most wood furnaces can handle large, unsplit logs, which could save you some labor, and burn green wood, which, if you have to buy your firewood, is the most economical kind.

For a central heating system based on a furnace designed to burn wood only, or possibly wood or coal, we like the Shenandoah Model F-77 wood-burning forced warm-air furnace. It's capable of producing up to 75,000 BTUs per hour and can heat a house with between 1,600 and 2,500 square feet of living area. The furnace includes a 900-cfm blower and an automatic bimetal thermostat that controls the rate of burning and heat output.

If the Shenandoah can't meet your needs, Hydraform Products' Larger Eagle is held to be capable of heating 26,000 cubic feet from a basement location. This furnace burns unsplit chunks of green or seasoned wood up to 13 inches in diameter and 32 inches long. A full refractory firebox literally cooks the logs. It functions with the Roman Hypocaust System of central heating. Hot air from the furnace is piped to a space below the floor, without ductwork, blower, or returns.

Other manufacturers of large-capacity wood furnaces include Bellway Manufacturing Company, whose Hi-Temp furnace is equipped to burn green wood, and Sam Daniels Company. But the most interesting furnace we've come across is in a test house at the University of Maine. Called the Ultimate Wood Furnace, it was designed and built by Professor (of Alternate Energy) Richard Hill, and Otey Reynolds, a student. A grant from the Department of Energy financed construction of the furnace, and there are no patents or copyrights on it. Compatible with either a forced-air or hot-water heating system, it boasts nearly 100 percent combustion efficiency. After burning 1,000 pounds of wood, only a cupful of ashes remains—and there is no creosote build-up at all in the chimney. The furnace consists basically of seven components and could be built from readily available materials for approximately $1,800. Details of the furnace appeared in the February 1979 issue of *Mechanix Illustrated*. If you're a do-it-yourselfer, you might check this one out at the library, or write to *Mechanix Illustrated*, 1515 Broadway, New York, New York 10036, and order repros of the article, "Better Than the Potbelly."

BOTTLED GAS

Liquefied petroleum (LP) gas, or propane, as it's commonly called, is a popular alternative fuel where piped-in natural gas is not available. Easily transported and stored, it has become a traditional part of "cabin" living. Its versatility as a source of energy helped fuel the recreational vehicle travel/camping boom during the 1970s.

LP gas is extracted from natural gas, or produced as a byproduct during the refining of crude oil. Liquefied by compression and cooling, it occupies 1/270th the space of gas and returns to the gaseous state when released to the atmosphere under normal pressure. To burn, LP gas must be vaporized and mixed with large quantities of air. A gallon of highly concentrated propane (4.24 pounds), when allowed to mix with air in combustible proportions, will yield as much as 1,560 cubic feet of fuel. It burns hotter than natural gas.

The cost of LP gas has been climbing right along with OPEC crude, and we wouldn't recommend that you heat the house by propane, but it has its usefulness as an auxiliary fuel. The backup for a solar water heater could be a water heater that burns LP gas. If your home is equipped with an electric generating plant that can't always handle the load imposed by a refrigerator, there are three-way refrigerators that can run off 12V batteries, 115V AC house current, *or* LP gas. When the wood stove is not fired up, you might fall back on an LP-gas range or cooktop. There's also LP-gas lighting, but here we have a personal preference for noiseless Aladdin Kerosene Lamps.

We once heard LP gas described as being "clean, dependable, and as convenient as toothpaste." It's all of that. Packaged under pressure in 6½-ounce disposable cartridges, it's a handy fuel for backpackers' mini stoves and low-candlepower lanterns. Popular sizes for RV use are 20- and 30-pound capacity "bottles" (refillable at over 28,000 propane refueling stations located throughout the United States). For the rural home, you might buy or lease a bulk storage tank, or arrange for exchange cylinders. Bulk LP gas usually can be purchased either on a gallonage basis, as delivered, or on a metered basis, as consumed.

If you don't know where to look for appliances that run on LP gas, try any RV supplier. They carry everything from LP-gas stoves and catalytic (flameless) heaters to refrigerators and generators. Sears and other mass-merchandisers also carry a variety of LP-gas appliances. The current Sears catalog features 30- and 40-gallon water heaters that burn LP gas, a three-burner LP-gas range, a two-burner LP-gas cooktop, and a three-way Norcold refrigerator. Most refrigerators that run off LP gas are on the small side, with capacities of from 4 to 7 cubic feet, but Dometic has a 10-footer that sells for around $800. Coldstar is another refrigerator manufacturer with a good range of three-ways.

The LP-gas supply tank should not be located inside the house. All LP-gas tanks have a relief valve, and a freshly filled tank may vent on a warm day. The gas is heavier than air and will "puddle" unless the storage area is well ventilated. In the tank, itself, the gas is not explosive, but a puddle of gas in an enclosed area could be ignited by a spark. An odorizing agent is added to LP gas at the refinery, and your nose will usually tell you in time if you have a flameout or a leak in the system. There also are LP-gas alarms that will sound off before the problem gets out of hand.

FOUR

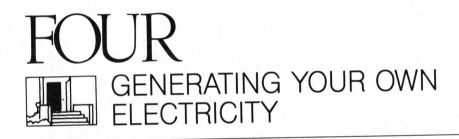

GENERATING YOUR OWN ELECTRICITY

If you are planning to construct a home on a building site that is some distance from a high line, you may already know that it can cost several dollars a foot to bring in electricity. The power company may provide the first 100 feet; but from there on, you'll pay for every pole and section of line. You'll also have to arrange to have a 20-foot-wide path, free of tree limbs, cleared to your site. All this can cost a considerable amount of money. Even where power lines are convenient, you may prefer not to become dependent on the local utility and rising electric rates. With the dramatic increases in the cost of subscribed electricity and in the cost of bringing commercial power to remote sites, there has been a surge of interest in alternate-energy systems. For many, power *independence* is shaping up as the new American Dream.

Generating your own electricity, whether by harnessing the wind or burning one of the fossil fuels to drive an engine, takes capital investment. Even where you are blessed with the essential site conditions for developing useful wind or water power, hardware prices are high, and the cost escalates with the rated ca-

pacity of the system. If you expect to use electricity as freely as you would when purchasing it "painlessly" from a utility—to run everything from an automatic toothbrush to central air conditioning—you may find that you can't afford to live beyond the power lines.

The first thing to do here is to make a careful assessment of your power needs. Depending on how much you're willing to pay for electrical self-sufficiency, you'll most likely rule out the use of electricity for space and water heating, for starters. With a well-insulated house, sited and oriented to make the most of natural solar heating and cooling, an efficient wood stove might give you all the additional heat you'll need and provide a facility for stovetop cooking as well. To meet hot-water needs, we recommend a solar water heater. So right there, you've removed two, if not three, of the biggest uses of electrical energy in many homes—with no great sacrifice in comfort.

We don't expect you to do without conveniences. Generally, electricity will be needed for refrigeration, lighting, television, stereo, a water pump, a pump for the solar water heater, maybe a fan or

TABLE EIGHT

APPROXIMATE MONTHLY KWH CONSUMPTION OF ELECTRIC HOUSEHOLD APPLIANCES

Food Preparation	Average Wattage	Monthly kwh
Blender	386	1.0
Broiler/rotisserie	1436	8.5
Coffee maker	894	9.0
Deep-fat fryer	1448	7.0
Dishwasher	1200	30.0
Egg cooker	516	1.0
Frying pan	1196	15.0
Hotplate	1257	7.5
Oven (microwave)	1450	16.0
Range (with oven)	12200	98.0
Roaster	1333	17.0
Sandwich grill	1161	3.0
Toaster	1146	3.0
Waffle iron	1116	2.0
Waste disposer	445	2.5

Food Preservation (cubic feet)	Average Wattage	Monthly kwh
Freezer (16)	341	99.0
Freezer—frostless (16.5)	440	151.0
Refrigerator (12)	241	61.0
Refrigerator—frostless (12)	321	101.0
Refrigerator/freezer (12)	326	125.0
Refrigerator/freezer—frostless (17.5)	615	188.0

Laundry	Average Wattage	Monthly kwh
Clothes dryer	4856	83.0
Iron (hand)	1088	12.0
Washing machine (automatic)	512	9.0
Washing machine (nonautomatic)	286	6.5

Comfort Conditioning	Average Wattage	Monthly kwh
Air cleaner	50	18.0
Air conditioner (room)	860	*
Dehumidifier	257	32.0
Electric blanket	177	12.0
Fan (attic)	370	24.0
Fan (circulating)	88	4.0

Comfort Conditioning	Average Wattage	Monthly kwh
Fan (rollaway)	171	11.5
Fan (window)	200	14.0
Heater (portable)	1322	15.0
Heating pad	65	1.0
Humidifier	177	13.5

Health and Beauty	Average Wattage	Monthly kwh
Germicidal lamp	20	12.0
Hair dryer (hand-held)	381	1.0
Heat lamp (infrared)	250	1.0

Home Entertainment	Average Wattage	Monthly kwh
Radio	71	7.0
Radio/phonograph	109	9.0
TV (black and white, solid state)	55	10.0
TV (black and white, tube type)	160	30.0
TV (color, solid state)	200	37.0
TV (color, tube type)	300	55.0

Housewares	Average Wattage	Monthly kwh
Floor polisher	305	1.0
Sewing machine	75	1.0
Vacuum cleaner	630	4.0

Water Heating and Supply	Average Wattage	Monthly kwh
Domestic supply pump (½hp)	460	20.0
Water heater	2475	350.0
Water heater (quick recovery)	4474	400.0
Well pump (deep well)	⅓–1hp	10–60
Well pump (shallow well)	½hp	5–20

Lighting	Average Wattage	Monthly kwh
4–5 rooms	—	50.0
6–8 rooms	—	60.0
Outdoors, 1 spotlight, all night	—	45.0

* This figure will vary widely depending on climate and size of unit.
Note: Each dishwasher load uses about 2.5 kwh for hot water. Each washing machine load uses about 5 kwh for hot wash/hot rinse cycle and about 1 kwh for warm wash/cold rinse cycle.
Source: Edison Electric Institute

two, and occasional use of power tools and such other appliances as suit the family lifestyle. When the wood stove is not fired up for heating, you might also choose to make use of an energy-efficient microwave oven for much of the cooking.

The average household today consumes about 550 kilowatt-hours of electricity per month, not including those amounts used for electric resistance heating and air conditioning. If you aren't all that knowledgeable when it comes to electricity, it might be useful to relate all electrical demands to the amount of electricity used by a light bulb. A 100-watt bulb, for example, consumes 100 watts of electricity per hour. In ten hours of use, it will consume 1,000 watts—or 1 kwh. So where an appliance serial plate indicates that the device uses 300 watts, that means 300 watts per hour—or the amount consumed in three hours by that 100-watt bulb. This might also be given in amperes (the standard unit for measuring the strength or flow rate of an electric current) and volts (the unit of pressure or electromotive force). Amperes multiplied by volts *equals* watts. An appliance that draws 2.5 amperes at 120 volts would use 300 watts per hour. At today's electric rates, 300 watts per hour (0.3 kwh) cost between 1 and 3 cents.

If you can estimate how many hours per month a particular appliance will be in use, whether a water pump or the TV, you can make a pretty fair approximation of your total electrical energy needs. Adjustments have to be made for those appliances, such as refrigerators, electric frying pans, ovens, and the like, that include thermostats and draw electricity only as needed to maintain a selected temperature. The Florida Power and Light Company figures the actual "running time" for the average air conditioner as 60 percent; the clothes dryer, 50 percent; the refrigerator, 40 percent; the conventional oven, 30 percent; and the hot-water heater, 20 percent.

In preparing your estimate, don't worry about the small stuff: gadgets that scrub teeth, clip whiskers, mix food, or tell time don't consume a lot of electricity. Where you don't know the electrical demands of certain appliances, check the Sears catalog, or a similar one, for equivalent items. It might also be useful to take your electric bills for the past twelve months and base your projection on your family's accustomed kilowatt-hour usage, making allowances for appliances you'll be adding to the electrical load and subtracting for those that will be eliminated. If you're buying new major appliances, pay close attention to energy-efficiency labels. By comparing them, you'll be able to pick the most efficient and economical models. For lighting, consider making much more use of fluorescent fixtures. While fluorescent lighting calls for a higher initial investment, the new, warm-tone fluorescents give about three times as much light as incandescent bulbs of the same wattage. And fluorescents, which now come in a variety of decorator shapes, last from five to twenty-five times longer. When you shop for lighting, remember that the amount of light given off by a light bulb, whether incandescent or fluorescent, is measured in *lumens*, not watts.

Allowance will have to be made, too, for peak energy demands. If you use 500 to 600 kwh in the winter months, and only 300 to 400 kwh in the summer months, you'll still have to provide for the maximum rather than the average monthly need. You'll also have to meet the demands of your peak daily load, including surge power requirements, or reschedule the use of certain appliances so they aren't all drawing electricity at the same time. The Department of Energy figures that the peak demand for an average home without electrical heating is approximately 8 kw. But if load management is practiced, a electrical system that is otherwise marginal could become quite adequate.

HARNESSING THE WIND

There was a time in this country when wind machines were common in most rural areas. Water-pumping windmills were used on virtually every farm by the late 1800s. And in the 1920s and '30s, before the Rural Electrification Administration introduced electrical cooperatives and brought cheap electricity (with a nominal connecting charge) to much of rural America, hundreds of thousands of farm families installed windchargers to power their lights and newfangled, battery-run radios. But it's one thing for a homeowner to lift water or recharge a battery or two, and quite another to convert sufficient wind energy into electricity for all of today's appliances. We appear to be on the verge of a new era in wind energy conversion, but you should know the limitations—and costs—of wind power before you get your hopes up.

WIND ENERGY CONVERSION SYSTEMS (WECS)

To begin with the basics, a wind energy conversion system (WECS), which is what we are primarily concerned with here, is not a windmill. A windmill is a low-speed, high-torque wind machine that uses the wind *directly* for mechanical energy. Most people think of Holland when they think of windmills. But thousands of windmills are still in use on farms and ranches throughout America, pumping or lifting water for irrigation and for livestock. Those clanking, multi-bladed wind machines turn more slowly and can take advantage of winds that are of no use at all to most wind turbine generators.

Generally, you need an average wind speed of 10 miles per hour or greater two or three days a week—an *average* of 12 mph six hours per day should be a minimum figure—to generate useful amounts of electricity by wind power. There's no point even thinking about wind power if you don't have enough wind to spin the rotor at the speeds (typically 150 to 300 rpm before being stepped up by gearing) required for wind energy conversion. Most WECS are designed to put out maximum power in a 25-mph wind, but if you normally have wind conditions of 10 to 15 mph and are half a mile or more from the nearest high line, it's probably to your economic advantage to generate your own electricity rather than purchase it from the power company.

There are many variables that contribute to site wind conditions. It would be easy if you could just look up the wind conditions recorded by the nearest government or airport weather station and apply them to your property. But land formations, trees, bodies of water, and buildings all can influence wind flow patterns and velocities.

You may even have too much of a good thing. We know of a family that built a house on a bluff in Bar Harbor, Maine, thinking the site would be ideal for a wind generator. But the gusty coastal winds damaged two wind turbines in succession, and they abandoned the effort.

Another wind power enthusiast, living in Boynton Beach, Florida, wasn't getting much electricity from the ocean breezes with the 2.5-kw wind machine he put up, so he installed a second one, with a 15-foot-diameter rotor. But both together didn't provide him with enough power to begin to approach electrical self-sufficien-

Opposite: Prevailing directions and mean annual speed of wind in mph. *Source:* Climatic Atlas of the United States

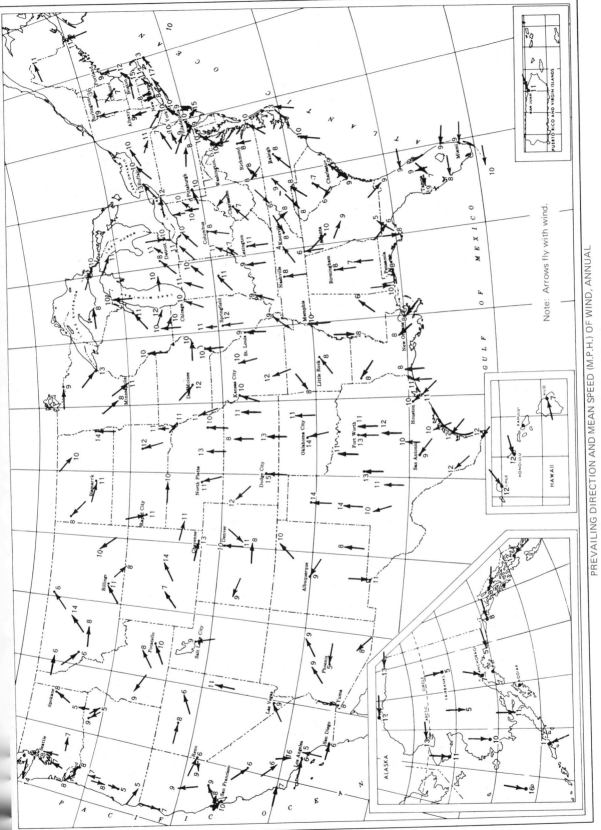

Note: Arrows fly with wind.

PREVAILING DIRECTION AND MEAN SPEED (M.P.H.) OF WIND, ANNUAL

TABLE NINE

ANNUAL PERCENTAGE FREQUENCY OF WIND BY SPEED GROUPS AND THE MEAN SPEED

State and Station	0-3 mph	4-7 mph	8-12 mph	13-18 mph	19-24 mph	25-31 mph	32-38 mph	39-46 mph	47 mph and over	Mean speed mph
ALABAMA										
Birmingham	27	22	30	17	3	1	*	*	*	7.9
Mobile	7	28	38	20	6	1	*	*	*	10.0
Montgomery	31	29	27	12	2	*	*			6.9
ALASKA										
Anchorage	28	35	25	11	2	*	*	*		6.8
Cold Bay	4	9	18	27	21	14	5	2	*	17.4
Fairbanks	40	35	19	5	1	*	*	*		5.2
King Salmon	11	20	30	24	10	4	1	*	*	11.4
ARIZONA										
Phoenix	38	36	20	5	1	*	*	*		5.4
Tucson	18	35	30	14	3	1	*	*		8.1
ARKANSAS										
Little Rock	12	30	39	16	2	-*	*	*		8.7
CALIFORNIA										
Bakersfield	35	30	24	10	1	*	*			5.8
Burbank	52	26	18	4	1	*	*	*		4.5
Fresno	30	41	22	7	1	*	*			6.1
Los Angeles	28	33	27	11	1	*	*			6.8
Oakland	26	28	28	16	2	1	*	*	*	7.5
Sacramento	15	28	31	18	5	1	*	*	*	9.3
San Diego	28	38	28	6	*	*	*			6.3
San Francisco	16	21	26	22	11	3	*	*	*	10.6
COLORADO										
Colorado Springs	9	27	38	19	6	2	*	*	*	10.0
Denver	11	27	34	22	5	2	*	*	*	10.0
CONNECTICUT										
Hartford	13	26	32	24	6	1	*	*	*	9.8
DELAWARE										
Wilmington	15	31	30	19	4	1	*	*	*	8.8
FLORIDA										
Jacksonville	10	33	35	18	3	*	*	*		8.9
Miami	14	30	34	20	2	*	*	*	*	8.8
Orlando	18	28	32	17	4	*	*	*		8.6
Tallahassee	33	36	23	7	*	*				6.1
Tampa	9	31	40	16	2	*	*	*	*	8.8
West Palm Beach	9	22	36	27	6	1	*	*		10.5
GEORGIA										
Atlanta	13	24	36	21	6	1	*	*		9.7
Augusta	36	29	25	9	1	*	*			6.3
Macon	10	26	46	16	2	*	*	*	*	8.9
Savannah	12	34	37	14	3	*	*	*	*	8.4
HAWAII										
Hilo	7	34	43	15	2	*	*			8.7
Honolulu	9	17	27	32	12	2	*	*	*	12.1
IDAHO										
Boise	15	30	32	18	4	1	*	*		8.9
ILLINOIS										
Chicago (O'Hare)	8	22	33	27	8	2	*	*	*	11.2
Chicago (Midway)	7	26	36	25	5	1	*	*	*	10.2
Moline	14	23	32	24	7	2	*	*	*	10.0
Springfield	7	22	28	27	12	3	1	*	*	12.0
INDIANA										
Evansville	19	23	32	21	5	1	*	*		9.1
Fort Wayne	9	23	33	25	8	2	*	*	*	10.9
Indianapolis	9	22	34	26	7	2	*	*	*	10.8
South Bend	7	21	35	30	7	1	*	*		10.9
IOWA										
Des Moines	3	17	38	29	10	3	1	*		12.1
Sioux City	10	20	31	25	10	4	1	*	*	11.7
KANSAS										
Topeka	11	19	30	27	10	2	*	*	*	11.2
Wichita	4	12	30	31	16	5	1	*	*	13.7
KENTUCKY										
Lexington	8	25	39	22	6	1	*	*		10.1
Louisville	17	28	31	20	3	1	*	*		8.8
LOUISIANA										
Baton Rouge	17	29	34	17	3	*	*	*		8.3
Lake Charles	19	31	29	17	4	1	*	*	*	8.5
New Orleans	16	27	32	19	5	1	*	*	*	9.0
Shreveport	12	26	37	21	4	1	*	*	*	9.5
MAINE										
Portland	10	30	33	22	4	1	*	*	*	9.6
MARYLAND										
Baltimore	7	24	39	22	6	2	*	*	*	10.4
MASSACHUSETTS										
Boston	3	12	33	35	12	4	1	*	*	13.3
MICHIGAN										
Detroit (City AP)	8	23	37	26	5	1	*	*	*	10.3
Flint	16	26	32	22	3	1	*	*	*	9.0
Grand Rapids	14	23	32	25	5	1	*	*	*	9.8
MINNESOTA										
Duluth	6	15	33	31	11	4	1	*	*	12.6
Minneapolis	8	21	34	28	9	2	*	*	*	11.2
MISSISSIPPI										
Jackson	33	25	26	14	2	*	*	*		7.1
MISSOURI										
Kansas City	9	29	35	23	5	1	*			9.8
St. Louis	10	29	36	21	3	1	*	*	*	9.3
Springfield	4	13	34	32	13	3	1	*	*	12.9
MONTANA										
Great Falls	7	19	24	24	15	9	3	1	*	13.9
NEBRASKA										
Omaha	12	17	29	28	11	3	*	*		11.6

TABLE NINE

(Continued)

State and Station	0-3 mph	4-7 mph	8-12 mph	13-18 mph	19-24 mph	25-31 mph	32-38 mph	39-46 mph	47 mph and over	Mean speed mph
NEVADA										
Las Vegas	18	26	25	20	8	3	1	*	*	9.7
Reno	52	20	13	10	4	1	*	*	*	5.9
NEW JERSEY										
Newark	11	25	34	24	5	1	*	*	*	9.8
NEW MEXICO										
Albuquerque	17	36	26	13	5	2	*	*	*	8.6
NEW YORK										
Albany	23	24	27	21	4	1	*	*		8.6
Binghamton	11	23	35	25	5	1	*	*	*	10.0
Buffalo	5	17	34	27	13	3	1	*	*	12.4
New York (Kennedy)	6	17	35	28	10	3	*	*	*	12.0
New York (La Guardia)	6	15	30	31	12	4	1	*	*	12.9
Rochester	8	22	34	25	9	2	1	*	*	11.2
Syracuse	14	27	30	23	5	1	*	*	*	9.7
NORTH CAROLINA										
Charlotte	20	32	31	14	2	*	*	*		7.9
Greensboro	20	32	31	14	2	*	*	*		8.0
Raleigh	18	33	34	14	2	*	*	*	*	7.7
Winston-Salem	19	22	33	21	4	1	*	*		9.0
NORTH DAKOTA										
Bismarck	14	20	27	24	12	3	1	*	*	11.2
Fargo	4	13	28	31	15	7	2	*	*	14.4
OHIO										
Akron-Canton	7	25	35	26	5	1	*	*	*	10.4
Cincinnati	11	27	36	22	4	1	*	*	*	9.6
Cleveland	7	18	35	29	9	2	*	*	*	11.6
Columbus	26	23	29	18	4	1	*	*	*	8.2
Dayton	8	25	36	23	6	2	*	*	*	10.3
Youngstown	7	26	36	24	6	1	*	*	*	10.3
OKLAHOMA										
Oklahoma City	2	11	34	34	13	6	1	*	*	14.0
Tulsa	9	24	34	26	7	1	*	*	*	10.6
OREGON										
Medford	47	31	14	6	2	*	*	*	*	4.6
Portland	28	27	25	16	4	1	*	*	*	7.7
Salem	25	32	28	13	2	*	*			7.1
PENNSYLVANIA										
Harrisburg	28	31	25	13	3	1	*	*		7.3
Philadelphia	11	27	35	21	5	1	*	*	*	9.6
Pittsburgh	12	26	34	22	4	1	*	*		9.4
Scranton	11	33	35	18	2	*	*	*		8.8
RHODE ISLAND										
Providence	11	20	32	28	7	2	*	*	*	10.7
SOUTH CAROLINA										
Charleston	12	28	35	19	4	1	*	*		9.2
Columbia	25	35	26	12	2	*	*			7.0
SOUTH DAKOTA										
Huron	10	18	29	29	10	3	1	*	*	11.9
Rapid City	15	22	28	21	10	4	1	*	*	11.0
TENNESSEE										
Chattanooga	39	25	24	11	1	*	*			6.1
Knoxville	29	29	25	12	4	1	*	*	*	7.5
Memphis	14	26	34	20	5	1	*	*		9.4
Nashville	27	31	25	14	2	*	*	*	*	7.2
TEXAS										
Amarillo	5	15	32	32	12	4	1	*	*	12.9
Austin	13	25	34	23	5	1	*	*		9.7
Brownsville	10	17	25	30	14	3	*	*	*	12.3
Corpus Christi	11	16	26	33	12	2	*	*		11.9
Dallas	9	21	32	28	9	1	*	*		11.0
El Paso	10	22	32	22	9	4	1	*	*	11.3
Ft. Worth	4	14	34	34	10	3	*	*		12.5
Galveston	4	13	39	33	10	2	1	*	*	12.5
Houston	6	18	36	28	10	2	*	*		11.8
Laredo	6	15	32	34	12	1	*	*		12.3
Lubbock	4	11	33	34	13	5	1	*	*	13.6
Midland	9	22	38	26	4	1	*	*		10.1
San Antonio	18	23	32	22	4	1	*	*		9.3
Waco	3	14	36	35	10	2	*	*		12.5
Wichita Falls	5	22	41	27	5	1	*	*		10.5
UTAH										
Salt Lake City	12	33	36	14	4	1	*	*	*	8.7
VERMONT										
Burlington	24	24	28	22	2	*	*			8.3
VIRGINIA										
Norfolk	14	23	30	25	6	1	*	*	*	10.2
Richmond	14	37	36	11	1	*	*	*		7.8
Roanoke	31	22	23	17	5	2	*	*		8.3
WASHINGTON										
Seattle-Tacoma AP	13	16	35	26	8	2	*	*	*	10.7
Spokane	17	38	27	14	3	1	*	*		8.1
WASHINGTON, D.C.	11	26	35	22	5	1	*	*	*	9.7
WEST VIRGINIA										
Charleston	29	37	25	8	1	*	*			6.2
WISCONSIN										
Green Bay	8	22	32	26	10	2	*	*	*	11.2
Madison	15	22	30	23	7	2	*	*	*	10.1
Milwaukee	8	17	31	30	11	3	1	*	*	12.1
WYOMING										
Casper	8	16	27	27	13	7	2	*	*	13.3
PACIFIC										
Wake Island	1	6	27	48	17	2	*	*		14.6
PUERTO RICO										
San Juan	15	28	27	25	4	*	*	*	*	9.1

Source: Climatic Atlas of the United States.

cy. He sold them to the Florida Power and Light Company for further study. It's been fairly well established, though, that the wind conditions in Florida, which can be very strong for days and very flat for weeks, are not that favorable for generating electricity through wind power.

It takes an on-site survey to determine whether the prevalent (5 to 12 mph) and energy (13 to 25 mph) winds that pass over your particular bit of real estate do so with sufficient force to warrant investing in a WECS. Such a survey involves setting up an anemometer and measuring the wind velocity several times a day for a couple of months. This could be done with a hand-held anemometer or a pole-mounted electronic wind odometer, but more accurate readings can be obtained with a rented strip-chart recorder, which records wind speeds on a slowly moving strip of graph paper, or a site survey analysis computer, which automatically computes and records the average wind speeds over a period of time. Wind systems distributors such as Enertech and Sencenbaugh Wind Electric can help you select the proper anemometer or anemometry system.

To predict the wind behavior at your location for the entire year, you then need to compare your results with those recorded for the same period of time by the nearest weather station. If your readings correlate, you can then extrapolate the year-round wind conditions by reviewing the recorded average monthly and annual wind data for the area going back several years. Wind data is collected from about six hundred weather stations across the country and can be obtained for specified areas from the National Climatic Center, Environmental Data Service, Federal Building, Asheville, North Carolina 28801.

Do not lose sight of the fact that the *im-*

mediate topography can have a considerable influence on the velocity of the wind. Airport locations generally are purposely chosen to avoid sites where local topography might contribute to high winds. For an excellent guide to finding the best locations for a wind generator, get hold of a copy of *A Siting Handbook for Small Wind Energy Conversion Systems.* The 66-page booklet, if not available in the government publications file of your local library, costs $5.50 and can be ordered from National Technical Information Service, U.S. Department of Commerce, 5285 Port Royal Road, Springfield, Virginia 22151. Using new research on how the wind interacts with land features, the handbook provides guidelines for selecting the best location in any type of terrain.

Once you have confirmed that you do have winds of sufficient monthly average strength to make a WECS effective, it's time to look at a wind generator. A conventional, horizontal-axis wind generator is made up of a two- or three-bladed rotor, a governor, a gearing device, the generator (or, more likely, the alternator, which is merely a generator with the magnetic field in the armature instead of in the coil), and usually a rudder or tail vane to turn the plant into the wind. All of this is pivot-mounted atop a tower anchored firmly in the ground, *never* on the roof of the house, unless you want to shake your teeth, and a whole lot more, loose. Since you'll have to store most, if not all, of the electricity generated, you'll also need a direct-current (DC) storage system, which means a set of heavy-duty, deep-cycle batteries—the sort used in stationary lighting plants—and a voltage regulator, to avoid overcharging the batteries. You'll probably need an inverter, too, to convert the direct current stored in the batteries to the alternating current (AC) that is standard for household use, but we'll get to that later.

A rotor generally does not spin fast enough at wind speeds of less than about 8 mph to generate useful amounts of electricity. But at speeds above 5 mph, the power output of the system increases *eight times* when the wind speed doubles! The output of the generator is determined both by the velocity of the wind and the diameter of the rotor. If you double the diameter of the rotor, you increase the output in watts by a factor of 4.

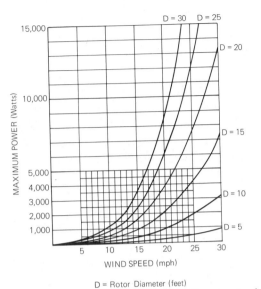

Typical wind power curves. *Department of Energy*

TABLE TEN

WIND GENERATOR POWER OUTPUT IN WATTS*

Rotor Diameter in Feet	Wind Velocity in mph					
	5	10	15	20	25	30
6	5	43	146	345	670	1,170
8	10	77	260	615	1,200	2,070
10	15	120	400	960	1,870	3,240
12	22	175	580	1,380	2,700	4,670
14	29	235	790	1,880	3,670	6,350
16	38	310	1,040	2,460	4,800	8,290
18	49	390	1,310	3,110	6,070	10,500
20	60	480	1,620	3,840	7,500	12,960
25	94	750	2,530	6,000	11,720	20,250

* Assuming efficiency of 50 percent of theoretical maximum.

Table Ten shows the effect of increases in both rotor size and wind velocity. Compare using a 6- and a 12-foot-diameter rotor at an average wind velocity of 15 mph. You'll see that when the blade length is doubled, the output in watts jumps from 146 to 580. Take that 6-foot rotor and see what happens when the wind velocity increases from 10 mph to 20 mph. The output in watts leaps from 43 to 345, or a multiple of 8. The table takes into consideration the several factors that limit the efficiency of a WECS. One is the Betz theorem, which states that the maximum amount of power that can be achieved by an open-air wind plant is 59.26 percent of the kinetic energy contained in the wind passing through the disc area of the rotor. But all you really need to know is that the theoretical maximum amount of power in watts (P) that can be extracted by a wind machine is equal to 0.0024 times the diameter (D) of the rotor squared times the velocity (V) of the wind cubed—and that considerable power is lost in step-up gearing and in the generator itself. So the efficiency (output) of a wind plant comes down to about 50 percent of its theoretical maximum—or:

$$P = 0.0012D^2V^3.$$

One other factor enters into the calculations here. To protect against damage in high winds, rotors have to be "feathered" or otherwise brake themselves to spin no faster in higher winds than they would under the *rated* wind speed for the particular machine. This means that with a wind velocity of 40 mph and a generator wind-rated for 25 mph, the rotor won't spin any faster than it does with a 25-mph wind. A governor in the hub will vary the blade pitch to spill wind, or centrifugal force will extend spoilers to prevent overspeeds. Most machines shut down automatically at destructive wind speeds.

At one time, there were several hundred companies cranking out or distributing wind machines, but REA and World War II put an end to that. By the time the energy crunch of 1973–74 began to encourage the search for alternative sources of energy, there was only one company in the United States devoted to manufacturing WECS, plus three that were producing windmills for pumping water. The off-the-shelf WECS was a 200-watt plant, sold primarily for use in remote weather stations and the like, and hardly capable of producing much more than enough juice to light a backwoods cabin. Systems with greater rated capacities (up to 6 kw) were available from Dunlite of Australia, Elektro of Switzerland, Lubing of West Germany, and Aerowatt of France. But these were expensive, at least so far as most mid-1970s wind power enthusiasts were concerned, and became more so with the fall of the dollar. The alternative was to scour the countryside for surviving generators and wind system components from the pre-World War II years.

Back in the 1930s, the two biggest names in wind power were Wincharger and Jacobs. The Winchargers were the Model T's of the industry, and the Jacobses, the first to use three-bladed rotors, were the Cadillacs. There are hundreds of rebuilt Jacobs wind plants, with rated capacities of 2 kw and 3 kw, serving "homesteaders" today. But your chances of picking one up cheap from a farmer who doesn't know its value are slim. As with the 10-kw wind plants built by Hutter-Allgaier in West Germany between 1961 and 1966, there's a seller's market for these plants.

Wincharger is still in business, as the Winco Division of Dyna Technology, Inc. And Jacobs Wind Electric Company, which didn't manufacture any wind plants for more than two decades, is back with an 8-*kva* machine (it employs an alternator rather than a generator, hence the rating is given in volts-amperes rather than watts). Other companies have entered the market, too, including such major manufacturers as Grumman and Alcoa. The U.S. government has been putting up millions of dollars to spur the development of both large and small WECS, and more companies will be offering wind energy systems in the years ahead.

The range of units available today for farm and home applications goes from 200 watts to 15,000 watts (15 kw). Anything under 1,000 watts isn't going to make much of a contribution toward self-sufficiency unless you give up almost all electrical conveniences. Even at an average monthly wind speed of 14 mph, a 200-watt system can't put out more than about 30 kwh per month, about enough electricity to keep a 100-watt bulb lit for ten hours a day.

The only wind-driven generator currently offered that bears the Wincharger name is a 12-volt, 200-watt DC unit. It is supplied complete with generator; 6-foot-diameter, two-bladed rotor (propeller); control panel with reverse current protection; and a 10-foot, four-leg, angle-iron tower—all for $625. The mini wind plant, the design of which has remained basically unchanged for twenty-five years, includes a brake to be used if the generator is charging the battery at a higher rate than required by the load. A voltage regulator is preferable to a brake and can be had for an additional $75. The only additional pieces of equipment necessary are the batteries to store the charge and the wiring. A minimum 230-ampere-hour battery is recommended. The Wincharger starts charging at 7 mph (cut-in speed) and reaches governing speed in a 23-mph wind. At governing speed, the output is 200 watts. The governor operates by centrifugal force; when wind velocity exceeds 23 mph, flaps automatically open and introduce air drag. The Wincharger, though it is not identified as such, is featured in the Edmund Scientific Company catalog, at about the same price for the complete package.

Three other sources of small WECS (SWECS) rated at 500 watts or less are Enertech, Sencenbaugh, and Aerowatt. We should warn you that Aerowatt systems, which are made in France, are frightfully expensive. Automatic Power, Inc., of Houston, Texas, imports and sells Aerowatt generators in five sizes, from 28 to 4,100 watts, but discourages their use in domestic applications. The big advantage with these particular wind plants is that power generation begins at 6 to 7 mph and reaches full output at 16 mph. Above 16 mph, the regulator functions to maintain a constant rotational speed and power. The 300-watt Aerowatt, at an average wind velocity of 10 mph, produces 1,600 kwh of energy annually—or a little more than 4 kwh per day. It lists for over $10,000, F.O.B. Houston.

Much of the recent interest in WECS has focused on systems in the 1,000-to-3,000-watt range, if only because of availability and pricing—and memory of the virtually indestructible Jacobs 2- and 3-kw models. The Dunlite 2000, which is manufactured in Australia, has done very well here, and is currently available from Enertech in Vermont and Sencenbaugh in California for about $4,100. Dunlites are also sold under the name Quirk's. The line includes a 1,000-watter, the Dunlite 1000. It has a 12-foot rotor and reaches its rated output at 25 mph. Sencenbaugh also offers its own 1,000-watt plant, with 12-

Sencenbaugh Wind Electric's 1,000-watt horizontal-axis upwind plant, with a 12-foot-diameter rotor, generates its rated output in winds of 22 to 23 mph. It is designed for battery-charging applications. *Sencenbaugh Wind Electric*

foot rotor, in either 12V or 24V DC, priced at $2,950 and $3,150, respectively.

Aero-Power Systems has a well-engineered 1,000-watt plant, the Aero-Power SL 1000, priced at about $3,000. The 75-amp, 12V, completely automatic battery-charging system reaches its rated output at 20 mph. Kedco is another name you should know. Based on a three-bladed downwind design, which turns into the wind with the rotor to the rear, the Kedco family of seven wind generators includes SWECS with 12- and 16-foot rotors and power output ratings of 1,200, 1,900, 2,000, and 3,000 watts. Prices range from about $3,300 to $4,500. Swiss-made Elektros, rated at 1,200 and 2,500 watts, are also very highly regarded and can be purchased in the United States from Enertech, Real Gas and Electric Company, and Independent Power Developers.

Almost all the WECS with rated power outputs of 4,000 watts or higher are imports and are system-priced (usually with tower, batteries, inverter, etc.) at anywhere from $14,000 to $42,000. The new Jacobs 8-kva was to be introduced about the time this book went to the printer, but Marcellus Jacobs hadn't yet released pricing details. The 8-kva incorporates a number of new features, including "Inclined Hypoid Gear Drive," which tilts the rotor at a slight angle to take better advantage of the wind. Other features include lifetime sealed oil in the gearbox, and an attention-free alternator mounted vertically in the tower, which eliminates collector rings and brushes. Marcellus Jacobs is as respected in this field as architect Frank Lloyd Wright was in his, and the new Jacobs wind plant, if the price is right, could crowd out a lot of imports.

While much money is going into the development of megawatt wind machines that can compete with conventional power plants, the big daddy as far as the homesteader goes would have to be the Grumman 25. Spinning a 25-foot-diameter rotor, the Grumman 25 develops 15 kw of electricity at 26 mph for DC operations, or 20 kw at 29 mph for synchronous AC. The annual output of the wind plant is

The Kedco family of wind generators is based on a three-bladed, downwind design. It turns into the wind with the rotor at the rear. Blade diameters are either 12 or 16 feet, and rated power ranges from 1,200 to 3,000 watts. A diameter increase from 12 to 16 feet nearly doubles the energy yield. *Kedco, Inc.*

Grumman Energy Systems' three-bladed horizontal-axis downwind machine, with a rotor diameter of 25 feet, is designed to generate 15 kw of electrical power in wind speeds of 26 mph. *Department of Energy*

approximately 40,000 kw. You could light, heat, and cool a Holiday Inn with this one.

If your needs for electricity run somewhere between 400 and 800 kwh per month, you'll find that while the wind may be free, converting it into electricity is far from cheap. The Department of Energy (DOE) is trying to do something about this. Under the Federal Wind Energy Program, a national Small Wind Systems Test Center has been established at Rocky Flats, Colorado, and is being managed for the DOE by the Energy Systems Group of Rockwell International. At Rocky Flats, which is approximately 15 miles northwest of Denver, advanced wind energy systems are being developed by private industry under federal grants to improve the state of the technology and to reduce SWECS costs. Testing of prototype and commercially available 1-kw, 2-kw, and 8-kw systems under natural wind conditions began in 1979. The test center site is on a large flat plains area facing a mountain pass, providing a large variety of wind conditions from gentle breezes to hurricane-force wind storms. Additional subcontractors will be competitively selected to develop 4-kw and 15-kw systems.

Under the Federal Wind Energy Program, a national Small Winds Systems Test Center has been established at Rocky Flats, Colorado, to improve the state of the technology and reduce the costs of wind energy conversion systems. Both commercially available and prototype units for farm and rural home use are being put through extensive testing. The most successful of the new wind machines to emerge from the DOE's Rocky Flats program are expected to be commercialized. *Department of Energy*

The most successful of the new wind machine designs to emerge from the Rocky Flats program are expected to be commercialized in the 1980s. Needs have been identified for low-cost WECS of approximately 8-kw output (in a 20-mph wind) for farm and home use. The goal of the program is to challenge industry to produce an 8-kw wind system at an initial cost to the buyer of $750 per installed kilowatt—or $6,000 (1977 dollars) for the 8-kw wind plant, excluding batteries, inverter, and other secondary components but including the tower. This could be an acceptable price for someone looking for self-sufficiency but not willing to give up very many of the conveniences that normally require an unlimited electrical supply. At an average monthly wind speed of 10 mph, an 8-kw WECS should generate roughly 450 kwh monthly; at 12 mph, 600 kwh; at 14 mph, 750 kwh. This is about seven times the output you might expect with a 1,000-watt WECS.

In addition to the generating system, whether 200 watts or 15 kw, there are a few other essentials that need to be mentioned—and priced. For one, you've got to get that rig up there to expose the rotor to the maximum available wind. This takes a support structure that will place the generator at least 30 feet above any obstruction within a radius of 100 yards, or 40 feet up in the air, whichever is greater. Tower height can be critical even where there are no obstructions. Wind speeds at 30 feet up are 20 to 50 percent stronger than at ground level—and the power output of the generator is several times as great. An additional 2 or 3 mph of wind speed can make all the difference with a WECS. Increasing the height of the tower—up to about 90 feet—is the least expensive way to get more power from the wind.

You could erect a telephone pole, guy it, and park one of the lighter-weight wind generators on a pivot-mount at the top, but the more usual support structures for wind generators are either guyed or self-supporting galvanized steel towers. Guyed towers, with their stretched cables, take up more ground area than tapered, self-supporting towers but are less expensive. Prefabricated, three-legged, self-supporting towers typically cost almost twice as much as guyed towers of the same height. Whereas a self-supporting 40-foot Rohn (the big name in towers) costs around $1,250, a nontapering 40-foot Rohn guyed tower, including top adaptor, base plate, steel guy cables, cable clamps, turnbuckles, and ground anchors, costs from $630 to $740. Rohn guyed towers are shipped preassembled in 10-foot lengths. Figure about $15 per foot for a guyed tower complete with all necessary hardware; $30 per foot for a self-supporting tower. Tubular pole towers, which are sometimes used where guy cables are impractical, are the most expensive of all, costing around $40 per foot.

The best towers are designed to support the weight of the generator and withstand lateral wind loads of 140 mph, plus a generous safety factor. But to survive at all, the base of a guyed tower must be encased in a concrete cube and guy-cable anchors must also be set in concrete. The legs of a self-supporting tower must be set in concrete footings 4 to 5 feet deep.

Before you invest in a WECS, check to see whether local building codes or zoning laws would bar the erection of a tower or limit its height. We know of more than one case where a WECS is sitting in a garage because the owner hasn't been given permission to erect his tower. A WECS has been installed atop a New York City apartment house, however, so there is a precedent for WECS in urban and suburban areas. You aren't likely to encounter any unwaivable restrictions in rural areas other than that the height of the tower must be no greater than the distance from the base to the nearest property line. To avoid large transmission losses with DC current, the distance between the tower and the house ideally should be less than 1,000 feet.

Wind is an intermittent energy source, so some means of storing the energy generated by the spinning rotor is necessary if energy is to be available to the load on demand. If you tapped the generator directly for current, there would be an unsteady output, suitable mostly for resistance heating. There's been a lot of research into the subject, but the DC storage battery, just as it was fifty years ago, remains the most practical means of storing wind-generated energy and stabilizing it for household use.

Any storage battery won't do. Automotive batteries would be a poor investment. Heavy-duty lead-acid batteries that can withstand some 2,000 complete charge/discharge cycles are recommended. These are commonly called standby or houselighting batteries and have a life expectancy of at least ten to twenty years. Generally, you'll need a matched set (do not mix batteries of different ages) that can supply your electrical needs through three or four days of little or no wind. For longer periods, if infrequent, it's usually more economical to add a standby diesel- or gas-driven generator (see pp. 167–174) to charge the batteries, rather than add to the capacity of the battery bank.

Let's say you have a 2-kw WECS and an average monthly generator power output of 160 kwh—or about 5 kwh per day of electricity. If you are dependent on that 5 kwh, you'll have to install a bank of batteries with the capacity to deliver 5 kwh daily for three or four windless days—or a total backup of 15,000 to 20,000 watts. Whether for 12V DC or 115V AC, that's about $1,200 to $1,600 worth of batteries, at $80 per kilowatt-hour. If you have a generator with a monthly power output closer to 500 kwh and decide you need battery storage to cover a full week, you're talking about $7,500 to $10,000 worth of batteries. But then, if you can store a week's worth of power, you might not need an auxiliary engine to charge the batteries during periods of inadequate wind.

Storage batteries are bought in ampere-hour capacities at a given discharge rate (usually 8, 10, or 20 amps per hour) and are series-wired to produce the required higher voltage. For 20,000 watts and 115V current, you might series-wire 19 6V 180-amp-hour batteries. This would give 114 volts multiplied by 180 amperes for 20,520 watts. Voltages are underrated, so there's some leeway here. If you have a 12V generator and can run everything off 12V current (as you might with 12V DC appliances designed for use in recreational vehicles), you would need an equivalent amp-hour bank of 12V batteries wired in parallel.

The minimum storage capacity of the batteries in amp-hours should be seven times the maximum current (in amps) from the generator, or no more than 14 amps from the generator for every 100 amp-hours of storage. With a 115V 2-kw wind generator, the maximum current from the generator would be 17.3 amps. In this case, the minimum storage capacity for 115V service should be more than 121 amp-hours. With 180-amp-hour batteries, we are comfortably above that, and there's little danger that the batteries would be charged too rapidly.

Batteries need to be stored off the floor, on wood or steel racks, in a clean, dry location. Good ventilation is essential because in the electrochemical process batteries give off hydrogen, which can be explosive if it's not carried away. The preferred storage facility would be a shed adjacent to the house. In cold climates, it may be necessary to heat the storage facility, since batteries lose efficiency the colder it gets.

Whether you have a generator or an alternator at the top of your tower, the current that comes through the slip-ring commutators and down the cable to the battery bank is direct current. Alternators produce alternating current, but this is rectified to steady DC by diodes before it's drawn off. Alternating current cannot be stored. So how do you get the steadily pulsating, 60-cycle, 115V AC required for most standard household appliances from a bank of storage batteries? You lay out more money—for a DC-to-AC inverter. Alternating current must be made as it is used, and an inverter, either mechanical or solid state, produces 60-cycle, 115V AC on demand from almost any DC voltage.

A rotary or mechanical inverter employs a DC motor that runs at constant speed off the battery and drives an alternator on a common driveshaft to produce 115V AC. Unfortunately, the efficiency of a rotary inverter is only about 60 percent. Like the fat kid behind the candy counter, it eats up a lot of the inventory. A disproportionate amount of power is consumed by the inverter itself, even at idling current, when no appliance is drawing power. A 250-watt rotary inverter, for example, draws 100 watts at no load. Because of their inefficiency, rotary inverters are used mostly with low-wattage loads. For 12V or 115V systems, the largest rotary inverter recommended would be 300 or

500 watts. Inverters with these capacities cost about $125 to $250.

For bigger loads and higher operating efficiencies, electronic solid-state inverters are recommended. With efficiencies of 85 to 95 percent and a very small draw under no-load conditions, these inverters, which are silent, can be quite expensive. For continuous output capacities of 2,000 watts, expect to pay about $3,500 for the inverter.

For convenience, the ideal would be to have an inverter that permits you to run all of your appliances on 115V AC and provides a reserve to meet high starting currents; however, it could be much more economical to use small rotary inverters for individual appliances or outlets, switching on the particular inverter only when AC is needed. The efficiency of the inverter is highest when near full output.

When you start pricing inverters, you may have second thoughts as to what you really require in the way of electrical conveniences. You may settle the inverter question by buying only 12V or 115V appliances that can be run on direct current. As mentioned earlier, many such items are being manufactured for use in recreational vehicles, and a secondary market is developing for everything from 12V DC fluorescent lighting to compact refrigerators that can operate off 12V DC, 115V AC, or LP gas. Incandescent lights and small appliances and portable power tools with "universal" motors can run on either AC or DC. Appliances with simple resistive heating elements, such as irons, toasters, and coffee makers, can be used with DC. If you can live without a complex stereo, an electric clock, and the few other appliances that require a pulsating current, you just might get by without an inverter. Another resolution to the AC/DC problem would be to wire the house for both AC *and* DC current. Just don't plug an AC appliance into a live DC outlet. You'll total the appliance!

There is another type of inverter, called a synchronous inverter, or line commutated inverter, that should be mentioned. It has been getting a lot of attention because it is used in conjunction with power supplied by a utility for a reference voltage signal. In theory, if the wind is in your favor, you "sell" power (the meter runs backward) to the utility whenever your generator is producing more power than you require at the moment. You draw "make-up" power from the utility only when your WECS isn't providing sufficient power. The system eliminates the need for battery storage, but it doesn't fit into our philosophy of self-sufficiency.

If commercial power *is* available without having to pay thousands of dollars to have it brought to your property, by all means hook up. With an energy-efficient house, it easily could prove to be cheaper and is certainly more convenient than producing your own power with generating and ancillary equipment that calls for a sizable capital investment and depends on the vagaries of the wind. We can't, however, recommend investing in a WECS *and* tying into the power grid. Even with escalating electric rates, the payback period for a suitably sized wind generator, tower, and synchronous inverter could be a long one. If the utility permits the mixing of power to meet the homeowner's needs, and opposes allowing the meter to run backward, a not infrequent condition of the agreement, the payback period becomes even longer.

WINDMILLS

The multi-vane fan-type farm windmill comes closer to the self-sufficiency ideal than a wind generator with all its ancillary equipment. All a windmill needs is a bit of wind, and an oil change once a year. But then, you can't produce electricity with a windmill. It's good for just one thing—converting wind energy into mechanical energy.

Historically, windmills have provided the muscle for grinding grain, cutting feed, sawing wood, and pumping water. The only application that will be considered here is water-pumping. Windmills are still widely used on farms and ranches to operate pumping cylinders in wells and other water sources. Gears convert the rotary motion developed by the "sails" into up-and-down pumping motion. The stroke is adjustable: longer stroke, more water; shorter stroke, more power.

The direct pumping of water into a storage tank or cistern by wind energy is more convenient than running a diesel- or gas-driven engine for the same purpose, and—where large amounts of water are required—more practical than first generating electricity to be used to operate a pump. But unless you need more than the 300 or so gallons of water a day required by the average family, you might do better economically to consider a small electric pump and some of the other alternatives covered in Section One.

Fifty years ago you could buy a 10-foot-diameter Peerless windmill from Sears for around $50 and a 50-foot tower for less than $80. Today an equivalent package costs at least $2,500. Nobody is giving away windmills. For a 6-foot wheel, the smallest size offered by America's three surviving windmill manufacturers—Aermotor, Dempster, and Heller-Aller, the youngest of which has been in business for more than ninety years—you'll pay at least $500. Add another $1,100 for a 40-foot tower. Wheel sizes run from 6 to 16 feet. For a 16-footer, you'd pay over $5,000.

As with wind turbines, the wheel of the wind pump should be up where it can catch the wind from any direction. The usual recommendation is at least 15 feet above all wind obstructions within a radius of 400 feet. Since the windmill must be directly over the well, it is essential to find water at a site that's also suitable for the windmill.

With a 15-to-20-mph wind, a windmill with a 6-foot wheel typically can pump 105 gallons of water per hour from a depth of 130 feet and 900 gallons per hour from 17 feet. Storage capacity should be such that the windmill can take advantage of long pumping periods and keep you supplied through a week of no wind. For backup, a force pump might be a good

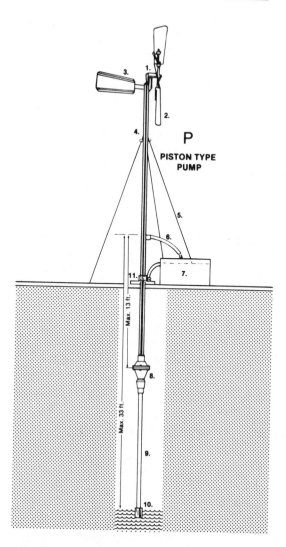

P

PISTON TYPE PUMP

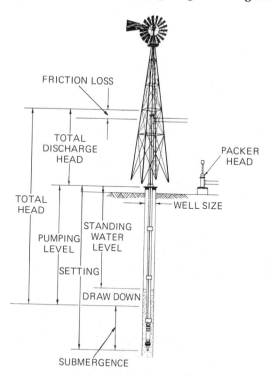

Typical windmill pumping installation. *Dempster Industries, Inc.*

Sparco piston-type wind-powered water pump is a simplified version of a traditional water-pumping windmill. Cost of the imported pump, which can lift over 30 gallons per hour whenever winds reach 7 mph, is around $400. It's of no use, however, unless you can find a good source of water at less than 33 feet. System parts, as noted: (1) ball bearing housing and crankshaft; (2) 50-inch rotor assembly with self-feathering blades; (3) tail vane; (4) guy wire hooks; (5) guy wires; (6) pump outlet; (7) water tank (not included); (8) pump housing; (9) ½-inch intake pipe (not included); (10) foot valve; (11) adjustable base plate with bearing-fitted sleeve. *Enertech Corp.*

idea if your supply isn't calculated to last more than a few days.

Unless you can use as much water as you pump, perhaps for irrigation, you'll also need a windmill regulator (cost: about $100), which pulls the wheel out of the wind when the storage tank is full and throws it back into the wind when the water level drops 5 inches. Most smaller wheels will start under full loads in light breezes, but windmills generally prefer winds of 8 mph or better. They are engineered to turn out of winds that are too strong.

With all the research underway on various aspects of wind energy and wind energy conversion, you might want to keep abreast of the developing technology. There are a number of publications covering the subject. One that we can recommend is *Wind Power Digest,* published by the American Wind Energy Association, 54468 CR 31, Bristol, Indiana 46507. A one-year subscription, four quarterly issues, costs $6. Another organization that offers information on wind energy is the Wind Energy Society of America, 1700 East Walnut Street, Pasadena, California 91106.

Home-built wind generators haven't been too successful, but if you want to investigate the possibilities of building a low-cost wind pump, write to Brace Research Institute, Publications Department, Macdonald College of McGill University, Ste. Anne de Bellevue, Quebec, Canada H9X 1CO. Request the list of BRI publications on wind power.

For $10 per year, you can subscribe to the bimonthly *Alternative Sources of Energy* (Route 2, Milaca, Minnesota 56353), which has given a lot of coverage to home-builts, much of which is collected in the large-format paperback of the same name, *Alternative Sources of Energy,* published in 1974 (see Overviews, under For Further Reading). ASE No. 24 (February 1977) is a special issue on wind power.

INDEPENDENT WATER POWER

The popular concept of the harnessing of water power for individual use is an old-fashioned paddle wheel churning slowly at the side of a fieldstone cottage or mill. The lumbering waterwheel, long used to power grist- and sawmills, goes back to biblical times and represents one of the earliest forms of applied mechanics. But you'd have to look pretty far to find anyone building mill wheels today. They're not practicable when it comes to generating electricity.

The earliest waterwheels were undershot wheels, which means that the paddled wheel dipped down into the water and the kinetic energy of the flow caused the wheel to turn. Later, the overshot wheel was introduced, with water conveyed to the wheel by a wooden or metal sluice at a slightly higher elevation than the wheel. The weight of the water falling into the troughs of the revolving wheel, as well as the kinetic force of the flow, boosted the wheel's efficiency. But even the best of these designs takes such enormous stepping-up, with belts, pulleys, and gears, to approach the shaft speed required by a generator that they almost never are used to generate electricity.

That's about all that needs to be said about old-fashioned waterwheels. We're going to be talking almost exclusively about impulse turbines and will not burden you with details on passé water power systems. With an impulse turbine less than 10 inches in diameter, spun at high speeds by a continuous stream of water jetted through a nozzle less than 2 inches in diameter, it's possible to generate more electricity than even most all-electric homes require. You don't necessarily need a dam or swift-flowing stream, which are essential with most other large- and small-scale hydroelectric plants. The key here is *head*—the difference in elevation between the water source that is tapped to drive the turbine and the turbine itself. The essential ingredient for an impulse-turbine system is a spring, stream, brook, or other dependable body of water at a higher elevation than the power house. The higher the head, the lower the development cost.

Like air pressure, an elevation of head produces the same pressure per square inch (psi, with *p* standing for pounds) no matter the diameter of the column. One foot of head equals .433 psi, whether that's a 2-inch-diameter column of water 1 foot high, or a 1-foot cube of water. Thus, 2 feet of head equals .866 psi; 10 feet, 4.33 psi; 20 feet, 8.66 psi; 100 feet, 43.31 psi. It is this pressure, forcing a constant jet of water through a narrow orifice, that drives the turbine.

There's a simple formula for calculating the theoretical mechanical power that can be obtained with a fall of water: The fall in feet multiplied by the rate of flow in cubic feet per second (cfs), with the product divided by 11, gives the result in horsepower. Take a head of 75 feet and a flow rate of 1.0 cfs and divide by 11 and you get 6.8 hp. Since 1 hp is the equivalent of 746 watts, multiplying 6.8 times 746 gives us 5,072.8 watts, or 5 kw. Allowing for conversion efficiency losses, a more realistic figure is 3.25 kw—which still isn't a bad output, since most individual water power systems, unlike wind

TABLE ELEVEN

HORSEPOWER DUE TO CERTAIN HEAD OF WATER

The table gives the horsepower of 1 cubic foot of water per minute, and is based on an efficiency of 85 percent.

Heads in Feet	Horsepower	Heads in Feet	Horsepower
1	0.0016	250	0.402
10	0.0161	300	0.483
20	0.0322	350	0.563
30	0.0483	400	0.644
40	0.0644	450	0.724
50	0.0805	500	0.805
60	0.0966	600	0.966
70	0.1127	700	1.127
80	0.1288	800	1.288
90	0.1449	900	1.449
100	0.1610	1,000	1.610
120	0.1932	1,200	1.932
140	0.2254	1,400	2.254
160	0.2576	1,600	2.576
180	0.290	1,800	2.898
200	0.322	2,000	3.220

Source: Small Hydroelectric Systems & Equipment

generators, can produce power continuously.

It's generally not practical (or economical) to seriously consider small water power applications except where heads of 50 feet or more are naturally available. A meandering stream and flat land won't do. A high mountain spring, a swiftly falling stream, or a sizable body of water at a considerably higher elevation than the proposed site for the power plant is needed. New England, the Northwest, and parts of Appalachia, where mountain streams abound, are areas where small-scale hydroelectric systems are on the increase.

If you don't have access to a surveyor's transit to measure head and estimate the power potential, you can improvise. You'll need a long board, a stake calibrated in inches, and a carpenter's level. Starting at the elevation at which you plan to tap the water source, set one end of the board on the ground, raise the free end against the perpendicular stake, establish that the board is level, and record the height at the stake. From the stake, repeat the process down the slope until you reach the level where the power plant is to be located. Total the elevation measurements to get the head. You needn't be concerned with horizontal distance for head determination.

There are several ways to measure flow. At this point, however, all you really need to know is that the same horsepower (without taking into account pipe losses due to friction) is developed with a flow of 15 gallons per minute (gpm) and 300 feet of head, 30 gpm and 150 feet of head, and 60 gpm and 75 feet of head.

Water is neither consumed nor altered in generating electricity. All the water that passes through the power plant will have to be discharged into a tailrace and allowed to continue on its way. Usually, the power plant is located where the water can easily be returned at some lower point to the flow from which it is drawn. This is ecologically sound and at the same time does not interfere with the water rights of landowners farther downstream.

There are high- and low-head turbine systems. Pelton and Pelton-type wheels, the most economical impulse turbines, are not used where the head is less than 40 feet. Another type of impulse turbine, the Michell, or Banki, can be used with heads of 15 to 40 feet. Still another class of turbines, known as reaction turbines, can be used with heads as low as 3 feet.

But let's follow through with a Pelton wheel. These wheels, which are capable of 80 to 90 percent efficiency, are available for independent water power systems in sizes ranging from 4 to about 40 inches in diameter. A typical Pelton wheel, or "runner," made of bronze, steel, or aluminum, has spoon-shaped deflector buckets mounted around the periphery of the wheel, with the buckets usually divided by a center ridge for a double-cup design. The head of water, conducted to the power plant via a pipeline, or penstock, is jetted against the buckets, causing the wheel to spin. The water comes out of the penstock through a nozzle of a diameter smaller than the piping, which, like the nozzle on a garden or fire hose, amplifies the pressure. A gate valve normally is installed just ahead of the nozzle, with another sometimes located nearer the water source, to control water flow for maintenance and power management.

Pelton turbines can be run with as little as 1.5 cfm of water. One system that we have seen in action employs a 15-inch runner and a flow of 10.4 cfm through a half-inch opening to provide $1\frac{1}{2}$ hp (or 1.12 kw) with a head of 50 feet. We've

Pelton-type impulse turbine. Water jets from the nozzle under great pressure and strikes the curved buckets of the runner, causing the wheel to spin at a high speed. The gate valve controls water flow. Concrete housing supports the penstock and provides a bed for the tailwater, which is conducted away from the power house as fast as it enters.

double what it would be using a single jet.

Actually, no two water power systems are identical. They can't be mass produced, but must be designed to take advantage of natural conditions and to meet the power needs of the homeowner. Double the size of the Pelton wheel and the diameter of the jet, and it develops four times the power and uses four times the water.

Do not underestimate the flow of water required with some combinations. One cubic foot per second is 86,400 cubic feet of water per day. That's a *lot* of water—enough to fill a 100-by-100-foot tank to a depth of 8.64 feet. But again, the greater the head, the less water required.

With Pelton systems, both the buckets and the nozzle will wear down and need to be replaced sooner or later—sooner, if the water contains more than a little grit. But the Pelton wheel and the nozzle are two of the least expensive components of

also looked over a 2-kw installation that uses two jets with twin Peltons and requires even less water. The diameter of the runner is half and its speed virtually

TABLE TWELVE

PELTON WHEEL POWER TABLES

HEAD OF WATER (in feet)	WATER FLOW GAL/MIN	RPM	HORSEPOWER	WATTS	KWH PER MONTH
3/8-inch Jet——4.5-inch Wheel					
50	20	1,320	0.20	100	72
100	28	1,877	0.56	280	202
250	44	2,969	2.20	1,100	792
400	56	3,755	4.50	2,250	1,620
5/8-inch Jet——9-inch Wheel					
50	54	664	0.55	275	198
100	77	938	1.60	800	576
200	108	1,328	4.40	2,200	1,584
500	176	2,099	17.50	8,750	6,300
1 1/8-inch Jet——18-inch Wheel					
50	180	332	1.60	800	576
150	306	575	10.00	5,000	3,600
400	504	939	43.00	21,500	15,480

Source: Short Stoppers Electric

The Pelton wheel, housed, is at left; the generator, at right. The rpms delivered to the generator can be stepped up by using a large drive wheel, as shown here.
Short Stoppers Electric

an independent water power system. A Pelton wheel typically costs from $150 to $250. The alternator or DC generator, to convert mechanical energy to electrical energy, is the expensive item; it can run to a couple of thousand dollars with a power plant designed to produce 5 to 8 kw. If you want 115V AC household current, you'll also have to include an inverter in your energy budget. Or, you could incorporate a governor to control turbine speed and generate AC direct to load. Some systems also go the WECS route and include a bank of batteries for the storage of electricity.

Rather than sizing the turbine and generator to meet peak demands, Independent Power Developers (I.P.D.) finds it more economical to scale down the system and incorporate a battery bank as a power reservoir. When power demand exceeds the generator output, power is drawn from the battery bank. When power demand falls below generator output, the excess power is used to charge the batteries.

An I.P.D. hydroelectric power system is capable of using all the power produced.

The high-head system uses a 4-inch Pelton-type impulse turbine capable of 80 percent efficiency and a maximum of 3 hp at 3,500 rpm, given the optimum hydraulic conditions. The runner, which is cast aluminum, is coated with epoxy to minimize wear from impact.

I.P.D. high-head small-flow systems can be packaged for monthly power outputs of 200, 500, 1,200, and 6,000 kwh. The component battery banks consist of six batteries per 3 kw of peak system output. I.P.D. systems include turbine, generator, batteries, inverter, and all intersystem electrical hookups. Site preparation is normally limited to preparing a simple inlet arrangement, installing the inlet and discharge pipes, and constructing a small enclosure to house the power plant. Figure about $1 to $1.25 per peak watt for an I.P.D. high-head outfit.

To bring the water from the higher elevation to the power plant, most designers of independent water power systems recommend the use of class-B PVC piping. Less pressure is lost due to friction with PVC than with steel, iron, or concrete pipe. It's also much easier to handle.

Michell (or Banki) impulse turbines deliver water to the runner either from a vertical flow, as shown here, or a horizontal one. The runner is much broader than with Pelton wheels and the water is delivered in a wide flow, which means the turbine requires a considerably greater flow of water than the typical Pelton turbine.
Short Stoppers Electric

Water has to be siphoned into the pipe at the supply source. With a sizable stream, it's usually advisable to divert the flow from the main body before attempting to draw off water. This can be done by maximizing a natural obstruction, such as a large boulder or a spit of land, to form a basin. This is especially recommended if settling is required. The intake of the pipe, fitted with a wide, screened mouth, would then be floated just below the surface. A trashrake, or iron grating, would also be required to keep leaves and other waterborne debris from clogging the intake. During the fall, and with spring runoffs, daily maintenance is sometimes called for to remove debris from the trashrake and intake, so as not to reduce the flow that drives the runner.

In an area where the water source is subject to severe seasonal fluctuations, it may be necessary to install a dam of some sort to provide a reservoir. But the installation of a dam usually requires permits and close state supervision. If the dam is to be more than 5 feet high, employment

of a qualified engineer is required by law in most states. If damming *is* going to be necessary, you might do better to investigate the other alternatives for producing your own power.

A Michell or Banki impulse turbine works with less head than a Pelton wheel. The normal range for a Banki manufactured by Ossberger Turbinenfabrik of Bayern, Germany—source of most of the Bankies in this country—is 15 to 40 feet of head. However, the turbine, with the runner measuring from 1 to 3 feet in diameter, requires a considerably higher flow of water—a flow of 0.5 to 250 cfs. With the Banki turbine, water passes through the runner twice, in a narrow jet, before being discharged into the tailrace.

Reaction turbines, which are vertical-axis turbines, with a propeller-type runner, operate with the runner submerged at all times. The rotary speed is approximately that of the incoming water. James Leffel & Co., the major source of reaction turbines in this country, builds mostly larger turbines for community and commercial/industrial power needs, but does include Hoppes units, capable of developing from 0.5 to 10 kw. The 0.5-kw (DC only) unit works with a head of from 8 to 12 feet and requires from 68 to 104 cfm. The 10-kw unit works with 12 to 25 feet of head and a flow of 480 to 980 cfm.

Too few readers will have the site and flow potential for developing water power beyond the capacities available with Pelton turbines to warrant our going deeper into hydraulics, the building of dams, or the measurement of flow here. To those who wish to pursue the subject, we would recommend reading Gil Masters, on "Electricity from a Stream," in *Other Homes and Garbage*; Robin Saunders, on "Harnessing the Power of Water," in *Energy Primer: Solar, Water, Wind, and Biofuels*; and E. F. Lindsley's article, "Water Power for Your Home," in the May 1977 issue of *Popular Science*. Find out as much as you can on the subject *before* contacting any of the companies mentioned.

The Department of Energy may get around to supporting the development of individual water power systems someday, but at the present time there are only a handful of mostly very small companies concerned with this area of energy. Chances are, you won't even find a heading for the subject in your Yellow Pages. The individuals behind such companies as Independent Power Developers, Short Stoppers Electric, and Small Hydroelectric Systems & Equipment are dedicated to the development of small water power systems, but they're also overburdened by the correspondence that comes in whenever they are listed as sources of water power hardware and specifics. Give them a break and do some further research in the sources noted above and listed in the bibliography under Harnessing Water Power. If you do send a request for more

detailed information, include a couple of dollars to help with the costs of printing and mailing the catalog or information package.

ENGINE-DRIVEN POWER PLANTS

Looking for ways to increase its sales of enameled-iron bathtubs and sinks back in the post-World War I era, one of this country's largest (then and now) manufacturers of plumbing fixtures saw a *big* potential market in sales to farm families. But there was a slight hitch. At the time, few farmhouses boasted running water. So in 1920 the Kohler Company developed The Kohler Automatic Power & Light Plant, a 1,500-watt, four-cylinder forerunner of today's self-contained electric generator sets, to give the farmer electricity to operate not only a few lights but a pump that would bring running water into the home and, along with it, the convenience of indoor plumbing. This fully automatic generator was the first to deliver current (110V DC) directly to the line.

In those early days, electric plants were called light plants, and, until the advent of The Kohler Automatic, included a storage battery (usually 32V), with small electrical loads operated directly from the battery. The cruder, ruder engines of the period could not be run for long periods without risking a breakdown, and most light plants were operated only a few hours at a time, a day or two each week, to recharge the battery. While engine maintenance is still a problem, today's plants do away with the storage battery and gener-

Standby emergency and stationary power plants designed to withstand continuous operation usually are installed on a concrete pad and protected by housing that also serves to reduce the noise level.
Generac

ate only the amount of electricity actually used, drawn directly from the generator (or alternator).

Although modern electric plants, more appropriately known as power plants, are much more efficient than their precursors, the cost of the fuel essential to their operation has increased dramatically. With the soaring costs of gasoline, diesel oil, and LP gas, and the constant threat of interruptions in their delivery, we don't recommend dependence on engine-driven generators in prime power applications. If there are other alternatives, we would employ an engine-driven power plant in a standby emergency or auxiliary power capacity only.

Any engine-driven power plant used more than occasionally is going to run up big fuel bills. Take a 3,000-watt, gasoline-powered, extended-run alternator (cost: around $1,000) that produces 115/230V AC and is used as a primary source of power. The approximate fuel consumption would run from .34 gallons per hour (gph) at quarter-load to .45 gph at full-

load. At a minimum, you'd be paying $300 per month (based on $1-per-gallon gasoline) for 540 kwh of electricity, or better than 50 cents per kilowatt-hour. Even a 1,500-watt standby generator, to be used only during power failures or other temporary shutdowns of your prime power source, to keep the freezer, sump pump, and a few lights going until normal power is restored, can gulp down as much as $5 worth of fuel between sundown and sunup.

Power plants designed for home standby or auxiliary power use are mostly the so-called portable units, with wattage ratings ranging from 400 to about 5,500 watts. They generally offer the convenience of power at any location. Most of the true portables, however, are under 3,500 watts, if you put a 75-pound ceiling on portability. Larger-wattage units do come with wheels or a carriage, but when the power plant weighs several hundred pounds, portability is much more limited than it is with a compact unit that you can pick up without risking a hernia. Self-contained power plants designed to with-stand continuous operation are more often referred to as stationary models. Meeting the total electrical needs of a typical, non-energy-efficient, suburban tract home, including air conditioners and other high-wattage appliances, could call for an 8-kw stationary generator. The unit itself would cost about $3,500. But that's only the down payment, so to speak. An 8-kw stationary generator consumes up to 1½ gallons of fuel per hour. To provide continuous power, it would be running round the clock. Can you afford such a luxury?

Engine-driven power plants come in hundreds of sizes, with rated capacities up to 1,000 kw. But we're not interested here in the big bruisers designed to provide standby power for hospitals and jails and the like. Our interest is in the lower end, units of generally under 10 kw. For convenience, we'll describe these as small (under 3,500 watts), medium (between 3,500 and 7,500 watts), and large (7,500 watts and up).

Most of the generator sets manufac-tured by such companies as McCulloch, Honda, and Homelite fall into the small category. Typically, these power plants are based on a gasoline-powered, one-cyl-inder, four-cycle engine that can't be run more than two to four hours without re-fueling and being topped off with oil. Prices range from under $400 for Honda's 400-watt plant and McCulloch's 1,500-watt (4-hp) Mite-E-Lite generator (which has fewer moving parts than conventional generators) to over $600 for McCulloch's 3,300-watt (8-hp) Mite-E-Lite and about $1,000 for Honda's 3,500-watter.

Although few generator sets with rated capacities under 3,500 watts are capable of supporting home electrical needs on any-thing beyond a very limited basis, several companies do offer at least one model de-signed for extended, if not prime power, use in remote locations. Winco has 2,000- and 3,000-watt "heavy-duty" models. The company also produces a "basic" and a "high-performance" series. Sears sells a "long-run" 3,000-watt plant (around $750) that, using an auxiliary fuel-and-oil

Net weight of Unigen handle-equipped 1,200-watt generator is 65 pounds. Approximate fuel consumption of this Lightning Alternator Series 10-amp, 115V AC portable is .28 gallons per hour at full-load, .20 at quarter-load. Start is recoil. List price: around $425. *Unigen, Inc.*

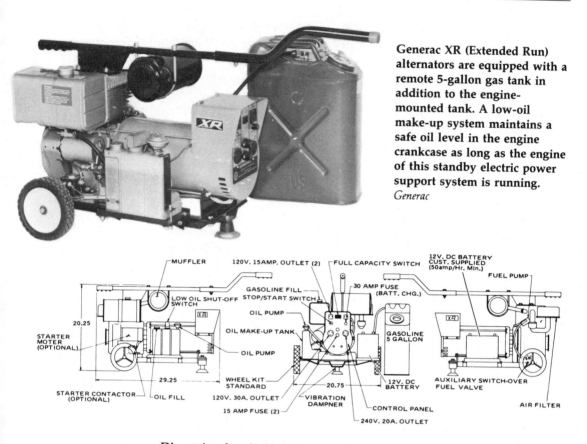

Generac XR (Extended Run) alternators are equipped with a remote 5-gallon gas tank in addition to the engine-mounted tank. A low-oil make-up system maintains a safe oil level in the engine crankcase as long as the engine of this standby electric power support system is running. *Generac*

Dimensional outline of Generac XR alternator. *Generac*

system, can run up to twenty-four hours without refueling. Generac's 3,000-watt XR (Extended Run) Alternator (about $815) is "designed for hours of unattended operation." And Onan's electric generator sets include a 2,500-watter rated for "continuous service." Unlike most of the portables, it runs at 1,800 rather than 3,600 rpm.

For alternating current, the rotor must revolve at a multiple of 60 rpm. For reasons we won't go into here, the common speed of most generators designed for standby or very limited duty is 3,600 rpm. Stationary power plants and smaller models designed for extended use generally run at 1,800 rpm. The slower-speed models cost more initially but offer a number

of advantages, including less engine wear, less fuel consumption, and less noise. The noise problem is something you should give serious consideration to before you commit yourself to the purchase of an engine-driven power plant. Some of these units, particularly the smaller, single-cylinder models, can be violently noisy.

Moving up to power plants with rated capacities of between 3,500 and 7,500 watts, we find there are all sorts of options, from automatic idle controls to a choice of manual, electric, or remote start. The "add-ons" all cost money. An LP-gas conversion for Unigen's 5,500-watt Lightning Alternator costs $143. Automatic idling control for the $1,200-plus unit costs $107. Electric starting typically adds

Generac "G" series portable alternators are available in capacities ranging from 1,350 to 5,000 watts. Net weights: 71 to 163 pounds. Spring mounts eliminate "walking" when unit is in use. A wheel kit is offered as an option.
Generac

TABLE THIRTEEN

GENERAC'S 3,000-WATT XR ALTERNATOR

Model No.	Weight (pounds)	Height	Width (inches)	Length	Starting	Wattage
6898	180	20¼	20¾	29¼	Manual	3750
6899	180	20¼	20¾	29¼	Electric	3750
8224	170	20¼	20¾	29¼	Manual	3000

at least $100 to the price of a generator set and doesn't necessarily include the cost of the 12V battery it requires.

Representative medium-size power plants and their prices (in 1980 dollars) include Generac's "G" series of portable alternators with a 5,000-watt (11-hp) model at $930; Generac also offers a 7,000-watt (16-hp) XR Alternator at $1,699. Kohler's recently introduced 5,000-watt "multiuse" wheelabout lists for $1,390 with electric start. Sears offers a "long-run" 7,000-watt power plant that puts out "enough power to operate all the appliances in most homes at the same time" for $1,600. Homelite's new 5,000-watt standby electric generator comes in a lockable, weatherproof box that is installed on a precast

concrete pad outside the house. The engine tank holds 5 gallons of fuel—enough for eight hours of average use. The wiring involved in hooking up the generator to serve as a standby to electrical power from a utility is pretty tricky and should be done by a licensed electrician. The unit costs $2,300.

Most generator sets designed to run on diesel oil come under the "large" heading, with only a small handful that might reasonably be considered for home duty. Diesel engines cost considerably more than gasoline engines. They have to be larger and of heavyweight construction because of the extremely high combustion pressures. But with the diesel's fewer moving parts, they wear well and require less maintenance. There's also an advantage in the higher BTU content of diesel oil as compared to gasoline. Until mid-1979, the lower cost of diesel fuel usually offset the higher initial cost of the diesel engine, but the price of diesel oil has since climbed closer to the price of gasoline and much of that advantage has been lost.

Onan, a major manufacturer of diesels, leads off its long parade of diesel generator sets with air-cooled, four-cycle, 3,000- and 6,000-watters. Both models run at 1,800 rpm. The smaller unit has a single-cylinder engine; the larger one, two cylinders. Kohler has air-cooled diesels rated at 4, 8.5, and 12 kw, and two liquid-cooled units that, at 10 and 12.5 kw, represent our upper limit in stationary power plants for home use. Winco's diesels include air-cooled models rated at 4, 8, and 12.5 kw. Horsepowers of the Winco diesels are 6, 12, and 18, respectively.

Air cooling is standard with generator sets below 15 kw. As a rule, larger units are equipped with a liquid system for maximum cooling protection. The two Kohler units are exceptions. Another exception is a nondiesel 8-kw Generac. This liquid-cooled stationary plant, priced at over $3,500, runs on gasoline or, optionally, LP or natural gas.

The big standby plants that hospitals and other institutions depend upon in an emergency run on the cheapest fuel available. In most urban and suburban areas, that means natural gas. In a remote area, the alternative with a *gas* engine would be LP or bottled gas, which is considerably more expensive than natural gas. Using a propane-powered generator to supply electricity for the home, however, except in standby situations, generally requires too much maintenance to be practical. Gas generators are also slightly more expensive than gasoline models. Unless you're using LP gas in some other application (such as to provide hot water or to fuel the cookstove) and thus normally keep a good supply of the fuel on hand, we don't recommend the purchase of a gas generator.

Virtually all of the electric generator

TABLE FOURTEEN

SIZING THE POWER PLANT

Will run at one time	Wattage						
	1800	2200	2600	3000	3750	4500	7000
1/3-hp furnace fan	X	X	X	X	X	X	X
Houselights	X	X	X	X	X	X	X
Refrigerator	X	X	X	X	X	X	X
1/3-hp sump pump		X	X	X	X	X	X
Freezer			X	X	X	X	X
Television				X	X	X	X
Automatic washer					X	X	X
Electric stove (one element)						X	X
1/2-hp submersible pump							X

Source: Sears, Roebuck & Co.

sets we've been describing produce alternating current, which is fed directly to the line to which lights, motors, and appliances are connected. The generator must be run anytime electricity is needed. While AC plants are the most widely used, there are also DC plants and battery-charging (DC) plants. Like AC plants, the DCs, with 115V or 230V capability, feed electricity directly to the line, but are used mostly for lighting and to operate power tools at construction sites. On account of DC line losses, AC would be preferred where the current must be carried more than 300 feet.

Some AC generators include DC-battery-charging capability, but where you are purchasing an engine-driven generator as a backup or auxiliary system to charge a bank of batteries employed with a wind energy conversion system, let's say, you should go to a pure-and-simple battery-charging plant. These units, operated only to charge batteries, or to provide additional electricity for heavy loads, come in 12V, 24V, 32V, and 110V capacities.

Make a careful assessment of your requirements before investing in a generator. For primary power, list the total wattage of all lights, tools, and appliances that must be operated at the same time. For standby emergency use, the power needs should be based on a slowed-down household, with the use of electricity rationed, if possible, to less than 2,500 watts. The usual recommendation is to select a unit with a 25 percent higher rating than the combined wattage of all *essential* appliances. But this can lead to trouble if you don't take the surge requirements of major appliances into consideration.

The larger electric motors require a great deal more starting current than operating current—usually at least twice the nameplate figure for power requirements.

And while most generators have a built-in surge capacity of 20 to 100 percent or more, if you try to accommodate several motors or large appliances at the same time, you may find you require a far more expensive setup than you bargained for. The way to get around this is to stagger the use of heavy-load appliances. Supply power to various appliances in cycles to avoid overloading the generator. In an emergency situation, with your main power out, you might run the freezer for a while and then shut it off to allow the water pump, furnace controls, or some other appliance to function just long enough to meet your immediate needs.

With a generator that is to be used as your primary source of power, you'll require a larger fuel-feed system, most likely including an underground tank for fuel storage. Distillate fuels should not be stored indoors. A few other words of caution: Never try to start a portable generator with an electrical load on the unit, and never fill the gas tank while the engine is operating.

The installation of a dependable power package takes some thought. You can't very well install a gasoline-driven plant in an unventilated basement or other indoor area, because of the carbon monoxide in the exhaust gases. Any generator needs a well-ventilated area. Nor do you want to locate a standby, and certainly not a primary power generator, near a sleeping area, unless you're insensitive to noise. If the generator is intended solely for standby emergency duty, the unit could be permanently connected to the house circuitry. However, most owners find other uses for their generators. With portability, you have electric power anywhere you want to go—to saw wood in the back lot or to trim hedges or edge the lawn—without dragging "miles" of extension cord.

Onan's 5-kw home standby electric sets are available in dolly-mounted portable and self-contained stationary models. A load transfer switch, installed between the home's watt-hour meter and meter box, permits electric power from the generator set to enter existing house wiring. Approval by the local utility is required. *Onan Corp.*

For standby, whether permanently connected or rolled out and plugged in for emergencies, you'll need a load-transfer switching system, either manually operated or automatic, if the backup power is to be fed into the existing household circuit. Standby electric transfer systems that back up power from a utility are not cheap. The Sears catalogue lists a 100-amp transfer system at $250, a 200-amp system at $455.

A major problem with standby generators is that few owners give them the tender loving care that is required if they are to come through in an emergency. While the generator may sit idle for months on end, maintenance cannot be ignored. Preventative care is a must. It's good practice to drain all gasoline out of the engine tank and run the carburetor dry if the unit is to remain idle for more than 3 or 4 weeks. Almost all generators need some overhaul after a month of use, and a complete overhaul—with carbon removed, valves ground, and worn parts replaced—with every thousand hours of use.

For portable and standby emergency power applications, our recommendation would be for a gasoline-powered plant. Choose the lightest weight, lowest cost plant that meets your scaled-down needs. For primary power, to operate many continuous hours, or as your main source of electricity, consider a diesel plant in the range of 3 to 8 kw, but only if there is no other reasonable primary power alternative.

FUEL CELLS

The first crude fuel cell was developed more than 140 years ago by Sir William Grove, a British scientist. Sir William's fuel cell combined oxygen and hydrogen to produce water and a little electricity. More recently, fuel cells played an important role in getting man to the moon and in explorations of the lunar surface. Carried aboard spacecraft and lunar rovers in the compressed liquid state, oxygen and hydrogen were combined in fuel cells to produce electricity as needed—with a useful supply of pure water as the byproduct.

Fuel cells convert chemical energy into electrical energy by a process that is the reverse of the electrolysis of water. Pass an electric current through a liquid electrolyte (in this case water with an additive to make it conductive) between two electrodes, and hydrogen gas is generated at the anode (positive electrode), oxygen at the cathode (negative electrode). In a fuel cell, the reaction is reversed. Oxygen and hydrogen are fed into permeable electrodes, and an electric current flows between the two terminals.

Several years ago, when natural gas was only about 20 percent as expensive to distribute as electricity, a nonprofit consortium of gas and electric companies in the United States, Canada, and Japan poured a lot of money into the development of a fuel cell that would take hydrogen from natural gas, oxygen from the air, and, in the process of combining the two, produce electricity from the motion of the hydrogen and oxygen electrons. While the output is direct current, which requires an inverter for most household applications, the beauty of such a fuel cell is that there are no moving parts and it is virtually nonpolluting, the only emissions being carbon dioxide, water, and heat. Also noteworthy, it supplies electricity only as needed and, as demonstrated by field-tested 12-kw prototypes, is able to provide power almost instantaneously to meet load demands.

The idea was that a single fuel, natural gas, would meet the total energy needs of the home, supplying all power for heating, cooling, lighting, and the operation of appliances. Fuel cells that depend on natural gas are still under development, but just when the cost had been brought down to below $400 per peak kilowatt, from $1,200 per kilowatt a few years earlier, the energy crunch led to moratoriums on new gas tap-ins and took the lid off the price of natural gas.

Rather than fuel cells that combine hydrogen and oxygen to produce electricity, the emphasis today is on turning water into cheap fuel, by first dissociating water into hydrogen and oxygen and then using the hydrogen as a fuel for heating or for driving an internal-combustion engine. (The oxygen is allowed to escape.) Ordinarily, electricity is employed to dissociate water into its two chemical components, but researchers at Purdue University and California Institute of Technology have demonstrated that water molecules can be split into oxygen and hydrogen by collecting and focusing sunlight onto electrodes in water-filled electrochemical cells. The Purdue process, which combines chlorophyll—nature's water-splitter—with platinum for the electrode/catalyst, is an expensive one. The Caltech process is also costly, calling for chemical compounds containing rhodium. Exposed to sunlight, the rhodium compound interacts with hydrogen in water to produce hydrogen gas.

The freeing of hydrogen from water by

sunlight, with less expensive substitutes for platinum already introduced by industry researchers, would seem to be an important breakthrough. It could be the key to the practical development of the long-heralded "little black box," which would be self-sustaining and could be used to power everything from a houseful of appliances to the family car.

Hydrogen may even power spacecraft someday, but for our down-to-earth purposes of self-sufficiency, the most practical system for generating electricity in a remote area today, based on hydrogen as a power storage medium, would seem to be one that incorporates a wind generator to supply the current for the electrolysis of water to produce the hydrogen. The electrolytic process is fairly simple and can operate with the fluctuating current of a DC wind generator—for more efficient storage of energy from the wind. The hydrogen is drawn upon as needed to generate a constant output of electricity, either by recombining it electrolytically with oxygen to generate power when the wind is down, or by using the hydrogen

to fuel a gas-turbine generator. Either system replaces the less efficient battery bank used in more common, and usually larger and more expensive, wind energy conversion systems. Hydrogen from storage can also be used in the home directly as a fuel for cooking and heating.

To make a hydrogen-based energy system practicable requires a hydrogen generator, unless you choose to buy your hydrogen in pressurized cylinders from a commercial source. Jack Couper, a Denver, Colorado, inventor, found the way to energy independence with a hydrogen generator about the size of a suitcase. Manufactured by Teledyne Energy Systems, the generator produces 50 cubic feet of hydrogen gas a day, which Couper uses primarily for heating. The electricity required to break down water and produce hydrogen and oxygen is produced by a small wind generator and a modest array of photovoltaic cells, with the electricity stored in a 12V battery system. The hydrogen is stored in a pressurized tank and tapped when needed.

Since hydrogen has higher heating val-

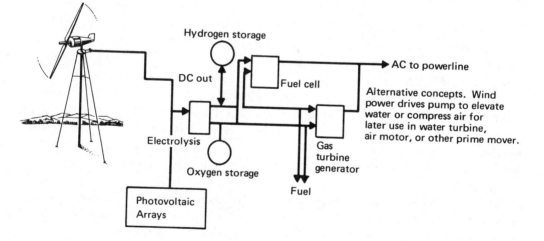

Fuel-cell system permits more efficient storage and use of energy from the wind. Photovoltaic array (solar cells) could supplement the input required by the electrolyzer during periods of low wind. *Source:* Wind Machines

Teledyne ElectraCell hydrogen gas generators are designed to provide a reliable source of high-purity gas. Base price, depending on model and voltage, runs from about $2,000 to $2,600. An automatic water supply system is a $200 to $275 option.
Teledyne Energy Systems

ue than natural gas, Couper found it took much less of it, on a weight basis, to keep the house warm. With water the only by-product from the burning of hydrogen, Couper also found he could eliminate a flue, or chimney, one of the biggest wasters of home-heating energy. Electricity not used in Jack Couper's power system to generate hydrogen is converted to 120V AC for household lighting. The hydrogen generator cost $2,500.

With sufficient demand and large-scale production, hydrogen could become one of the least expensive of all fuels. A "curse," however, has been hanging over hydrogen since 1937, when the dirigible *Hindenburg* met its fiery end. The *"Hindenburg* syndrome" makes an awful lot of homeowners reluctant to have any part of hydrogen as a domestic fuel. But while hydrogen as a compressed gas, or in liquid form under refrigeration, must be regarded as a potential hazard, hydrogen stored in a metal hydride appears to be quite safe.

Hydrides are materials, such as chips of iron-titanium, that have a pronounced affinity for hydrogen. They soak it up like a sponge, and release it as needed when sufficient heat is applied to the container. The safety of hydrogen-loaded hydrides has been proven on an Army firing range. Armor-piercing incendiary bullets could not cause the hydrogen-charged canisters put to the ultimate test to emit anything more than a small, self-extinguishing flame.

SOLAR CELLS

If Department of Energy goals are met, the greatest boon to the self-sufficient house could come during the 1980s with the mass production of solar cells priced to sell at 50 cents or less per peak watt. These will be close cousins to the high-quality, largely handcrafted cells that power spy-in-the-sky cameras, TV-signal relays, and the other wondrous electronic

Installed at a temporary trail construction camp on a wilderness archipelago in northern Lake Superior, about as removed from civilization as the dark side of the moon, this 200-watt photovoltaic array was used with battery storage to run a refrigerator as one of a series of experiments developed by NASA to test applications in which P/V systems are, or soon will be, cost effective. *NASA*

devices carried by satellites orbiting the earth or hurtling through space toward some far-distant rendezvous. Where solar cells for the Vanguard satellite (1958) cost $2,000 per peak watt, the price was down to about $125 by 1971, and terrestrial spin-offs were available to the consumer at $7 per peak watt by the end of 1979.

A solar cell, or photovoltaic power system, converts sunlight directly into electrical energy. First demonstrated in 1954 by the same Bell Laboratories team of engineers and scientists that had produced the transistor, the cell, typically disc-shaped and about 3 inches in diameter, essentially is a thin wafer of silicon or other

Silicon Solar Cell

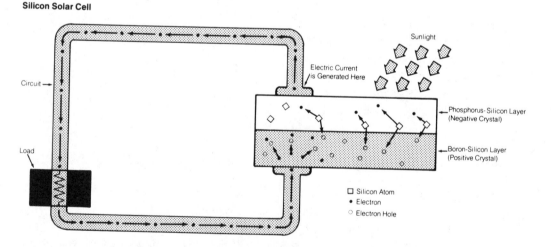

Diagram of a silicon solar cell. The cell is composed of a phosphorus-silicon (negative or n-type) layer and a boron-silicon (positive or p-type) layer, which are connected to a circuit. When sunlight (photons) strikes the crystal, electrons are pushed out of some atoms, leaving "holes." The electrons move to the n-type layer and then through the circuit, where they generate an electric current. The electrons then enter the p-type layer, where they recombine with the holes. *Department of Energy*

transparent, high-purity, semiconductor material, with a "positive" and a "negative" layer and electrical connections. When sunlight strikes the p-n junction between the two layers, a continuous stream of electrons is dislodged, migrating upward and out through an electrical circuit, producing a current.

Normally, a number of solar cells are interconnected in series-parallel combinations to build up the voltage to a useful level, and the power to about 10 watts per square foot of module. Solar cell modules are the building blocks of solar electric systems. They are simple, with no moving parts, and their operation produces no noise, no fumes, and no waste products. They have virtually no impact on the environment, and there is never any need for fuel resupply. For terrestrial applications, solar cell modules are sealed under glass or a clear plastic to protect them from the elements and minimize maintenance. Most modules are made to be self-cleaning.

Solar cells respond to a broad range of light wavelengths and will produce a significant output of electrical energy even on cloudy days. Link enough solar cell modules together and you can generate sufficient energy to meet the electrical needs of any household. However, until the cost of solar cells is brought down to $2 or less per peak watt (terrestrially, the wattage delivered at noon on a clear day), a solar electric system designed to make the average home power independent will remain beyond the means of most families. For a draw of up to 750 kwh of electricity per month, a 5,000-watt array of solar cells is needed. With an average of five hours of full sunlight per day, you'd then have 25 kwh daily (average) to meet your electrical needs, provided you stored the excess electricity not required by the load or generated through the longer periods of sunshine. At $2 per peak watt, that's $10,000 for the solar cells alone.

The current generated by solar cells is DC. There are alternatives, as discussed under wind energy conversion systems, but if you require conventional 115V household current, you'll have to include storage batteries and an inverter in the delivery system. And unless you have access to power from a utility to meet your electrical requirements after dark and furnish power to the load on sunless days, you'll likely need a sizable bank of batteries. Figure up to $10,000 for the balance of the system, including the batteries; a battery voltage regulator, which allows only as much current to flow into the batteries as is needed to maintain a full state of charge; and the inverter. Most systems are designed to use lead-acid or nickel-cadmium batteries, with blocking diodes incorporated into the system to prevent the batteries from discharging into the array at night.

All of these components, in theory, should be good for at least twenty years. With the operating costs almost zero, you'd be paying, at the $2 per peak watt cost of the solar cells, approximately $1,000 a year for electricity on a twenty-year basis. At 50 cents per peak watt, the cost would come down to $625 per year for up to 750 kwh per month—or about 7 cents per kwh.

While that "rate" might look good to you, utility company money managers might point out that you have to figure that the same $20,000, if invested in high-grade bonds or Treasury notes, might easily give you a safe (but taxable) return of at least $2,000 a year. If it takes a bank loan or a bigger mortgage to finance the electrical generating system, the kilowatt-hour cost could run quite a bit higher. But we don't want to get into the complexities of "true costs" here. Our subject is solar cells and their potential for use in remote and other locations to achieve power independence where the apparent costs of providing conventional power are prohibitive.

Getting back to basics, each square foot of earth is flooded by enough solar energy to keep a 100-watt bulb glowing an average of five hours per day, if all that energy could be converted into electricity. (If you want a finite figure for the energy available in your location, refer to the Annual Mean Daily Solar Radiation map on page 91. To convert BTUs per square foot to watts, simply multiply by 0.2931. For the average *hourly* rate, divide by 5.) But, you may recall, a few paragraphs back we indicated that solar cells could produce about 10 watts of power per square foot of module. That's because (1) the circular shape of most cells means that at least one-fourth of the area is not covered by cells, and (2) the average conversion efficiency of the solar cell, at this writing, is around 13 percent.

The theoretical conversion efficiency of the solar cell is 22 percent. So, if square solar cells can be produced (they can) and the conversion efficiency can be further improved (back in the 1960s it was only 2 percent), we may someday see solar cells capable of producing 20 watts of electricity per square foot of module, which would effectively reduce the expanse of solar array needed by 50 percent. Chances are we'll see solar cells producing a lot more than 20 watts per square foot of module. One of the major areas of solar cell research and development is directed toward optical concentrators that can boost the power of an individual solar cell.

The Department of Energy has made the $1.5 billion, ten-year Solar Photovoltaic Conversion Program (authorized by Congress in 1978) one of its highest priorities. Tens of millions of dollars have been allotted for research efforts under the Low-Cost Silicon Solar Array Project being administered by Caltech's Jet Propulsion Laboratory, a NASA contract facility in Pasadena, California. Sandia Laboratories, in Albuquerque, New Mexico, another prime contractor to the DOE, is leading the development of solar arrays, which concentrate sunlight onto solar cells as a means of reducing the overall cost of photovoltaic power systems. In 1978, using a simple plastic lens for an optical concentrator, Sandia developed a solar cell that can produce 7.4 watts of power in full sunlight, although it is only about 2 inches in diameter. The lens intensifies the solar radiation on the cell surface fifty times, which in turn increases the electrical output of the cell by a comparable amount. With optical concentrators, considerable heat is also generated. Modules are being designed to be mounted on water-circulating heat collectors. In addition to generating electricity, an array of such cells could then also heat water for the domestic hot-water supply and space heating.

It's not just the U.S. government that is vigorously pursuing the development of low-cost solar arrays. Such major corporations as Exxon, Mobil, Atlantic Richfield, Shell, Motorola, and Texas Instruments have multi-million-dollar solar cell research and development programs under way, and the rivalry and secrecy are intense between these companies; they see the great potential of solar energy not in solar heat-collecting systems but in the use of the sun to generate electricity at reasonable cost anywhere in the world. Other major companies are concentrating on bringing in low-cost, high-efficiency batteries and the other components that will be needed to make solar cells an everyday, anywhere practicality.

You can buy solar cell modules in many shapes and sizes from over a dozen companies today, including Solarex Corporation, Solar Power Corporation, Sensor Technology, Inc., and Solar Energy Products, Inc. But until the price comes down, we wouldn't consider solar cells except for those remote applications where power requirements are relatively modest and there's no other practical alternative.

In the near future, the anticipated reduction in solar cell prices will give solar arrays a cost advantage over small fossil-fueled electric generators. By the late 1980s, according to Russell W. Peterson, director of the government's Office of Technology Assessment, photovoltaic electricity could be produced for from 4 to 10 cents per kilowatt-hour—and compete with centrally generated electricity.

FOR FURTHER READING

We've written extensively on many of the subject areas covered in this book during the past ten years and will not burden you with citations of every book, magazine article, interview, workshop session, or manufacturer's fact sheet that may or may not have contributed to our particular knowledge of a subject. Rather than an extended bibliography including outdated material, we've chosen primarily to list recently published books and reports that supersede earlier works and that we believe would be useful to the reader.

You'll note that many of our references are to materials produced by, or under contract to, various federal agencies. All "S/N" listings are available from the Superintendent of Documents, U.S. Government Printing Office, Washington, D.C. 20402. All "NTIS" listings (the more technical reports) are available from the National Technical Information Service, U.S. Department of Commerce, 5285 Port Royal Road, Springfield, Virginia 22161. If you order anything from the GPO or NTIS by mail, there is a $1 minimum. Be sure to list the publication stock number.

If the library that you use is one of the more than twelve hundred included in the expanding Federal Depository Library System, you may find that many of the reports published by the government are available in the Federal Documents Section. Many state capital, large city, and college and university libraries are part of the Federal Depository Library System. For an up-to-date "List of Depository Libraries," write to the Superintendent of Documents at the above address.

The following subject bibliographies, obtainable from the Superintendent of Documents, might also prove useful: SB-009, *Solar Energy*; SB-050, *Water Pollution and Water Resources*; SB-134, *Sanitation and Sewage*; SB-215, *Architecture*; and SB-280, *Housing, Urban and Rural Development*. Subject bibliographies, which are free, are updated periodically to include new listings and reflect any price changes.

The National Solar Heating and Cooling Information Center also has compiled a number of useful bibliographies, including: *Passive Solar Energy Designs and Systems*, *Underground Houses, Solar Greenhouse Bibliog-*

raphy and List of Plans, and Energy Conservation in Building. To receive any of these bibliographies, as well as other information on passive and active solar systems, write to the National Solar Heating and Cooling Information Center, Box 1607, Rockville, Maryland 20850.

We've inserted an asterisk next to those books and other publications that have our highest recommendation.

OVERVIEWS

Alternative Sources of Energy: Practical Technology and Philosophy for a Decentralized Society. Sandy Eccli, ed., 1974, 279 pages, $7.95. The Seabury Press, 815 Second Avenue, New York, New York 10017.

The Autonomous House: Design and Planning for Self-Sufficiency. Brenda and Robert Vale, 1975, 224 pages, $4.95. Universe Books, 381 Park Avenue South, New York, New York 10016.

*Building for Self-Sufficiency. Robin Clarke, 1977, 296 pages, $5.95. Universe Books, 381 Park Avenue South, New York, New York 10016.

Build Your Own Low-Cost Log Home. Roger Hard, 1977, 200 pages, $6.95. Garden Way Publishing, Charlotte, Vermont 05445.

The Complete Kit House Catalog. Frank Coffee, 1979, 176 pages, $6.95. Wallaby Books, Pocket Books, 1230 Avenue of the Americas, New York, New York 10020.

*Design for a Limited Planet: Living with Natural Energy. Norma Skura and Jon Naar, 1976, 216 pages, $5.95. Ballantine Books, Inc., 201 East 50th Street, New York, New York 10022.

The Energy-Efficient Home: A Manual for Saving Fuel and Using Solar, Wood and Wind Power. Steven Robinson with Fred S. Dubin, 1978, 158 pages, $4.95. The New American Library, Inc., 1301 Avenue of the Americas, New York, New York 10019.

*Energy Primer: Solar, Water, Wind, and Biofuels. Richard Merrill and Thomas Gage, eds., 1978 rev. ed., 256 pages, $7.95. Dell Publishing Co., Inc., 1 Dag Hammerskjold Plaza, New York, New York 10017.

Home Energy How-To. A. J. Hand, 1977, 258 pages, $9.95. Harper & Row, 10 East 53rd Street, New York, New York 10022.

Low-Cost Energy-Efficient Shelter for the Owner and Builder. Eugene Eccli, ed., 1976, 408 pages, $5.95. Rodale Press, Inc., Emmaus, Pennsylvania 18049.

New Low-Cost Sources of Energy for the Home. Peter Clegg, 1978 rev. ed., 251 pages, $7.95. Garden Way Publishing, Charlotte, Vermont 05445.

The New Pioneer's Handbook: Getting Back to the Land in an Energy-Scarce World. James Bohlen, 1975, 278 pages, $4.95. Schocken Books, 200 Madison Avenue, New York, New York 10016.

*Other Homes and Garbage: Designs for Self-Sufficient Living. Jim Leckie, Gil Masters, Harry Whitehouse, Lily Young, 1975, 302 pages, $9.95. Sierra Club Books, 530 Bush Street, San Francisco, California 94108.

*Producing Your Own Power: How to Make Nature's Energy Sources Work for You. Carol Hupping Stoner, ed., 1975, 322 pages, $3.95. Vintage Books, Random House, Inc., 201 East 50th Street, New York, New York 10022.

INTRODUCTION

NASA Tech House. National Aeronautics and Space Administration, 1977, 19 pages, $1.10. S/N 033-000-00704-3.

Ouroboros South Project: Summary & Energy Bibliography. R. Scott Getty, 1979, 17 pages, $2.50. Ouroboros South Project, 320 Wesbrook Hall, 77 Pleasant Street S.E., University of Minnesota, Minneapolis, Minnesota 55455.

INDIVIDUAL WATER SUPPLY SYSTEMS

Ground Water and Wells. UOP-Johnson Division, 1972, 440 pages, $10. Universal Oil Products Corp., Box 3118, St. Paul, Minnesota 55165.

Ground Water Manual. USDI, Bureau of Reclamation, 1977, 480 pages, $9.25. S/N 024-003-00106-6.

*Manual of Individual Water Supply Systems. EPA, Water Supply Division, 1977, 155 pages, $2.45. S/N 055-001-00626-8.

*Planning for an Individual Water System. Publication No. 600, 1973, 156 pages, $6.95. American Association for Vocational Instructional Materials, Engineering Center, Athens, Georgia 30602.

Ponds for Water Supply and Recreation. USDA, Soil Conservation Service, 1976, 55 pages, $1.25. S/N 001-000-01137-5.

A Primer on Ground Water. U.S. Geological Survey, 1976, 32 pages, $ .95. S/N 024-001-00004-1.

A Primer on Water. U.S. Geological Survey, 1977, 50 pages, $1.50. S/N 024-001-00003-2.

Treating Farmstead and Rural Home Water Sys- tems. USDA, Science and Education Administration, 1977, 16 pages, $ .35. S/N 001-000-03558-4.

Water Dowsing. U.S. Geological Survey, 1977, 15 pages, $1. S/N 024-001-02998-7.

Water Supply Sources for the Farmstead and Rural Home. USDA, Farmers' Bulletin No. 2237, 1978, 18 pages, $ .35. S/N 001-000-01527-3.

*Water Systems Handbook. Water Systems Council, 1977, 100 pages, $4.50. Water Systems Council, 221 North LaSalle Street, Chicago, Illinois 60601.

Water Well Manual. U.P. Gibson and R.D. Singer, 1971, 156 pages, $6. Premier Press, Box 4428, Berkeley, California 94704.

What You Need to Know About Wells & Water Systems. Water Systems Council, 1975, 32 pages, $ .50. Water Systems Council, 221 North LaSalle Street, Chicago, Illinois 60601.

BEYOND THE SEWER LINES

*Goodbye to the Flush Toilet: Water-Saving Alternatives to Cesspools, Septic Tanks, and Sewers. Carol Hupping Stoner, ed., 1977, 285 pages, $6.95. Rodale Press, Inc., Emmaus, Pennsylvania 18049.

Individual Aerobic Wastewater Treatment Plants. NSF Standard Number 40, revised 1978, 56 pages, $ .50. The National Sanitation Foundation, NSF Building, Ann Arbor, Michigan 48105.

Proceedings of NSF/EPA National Conference on Individual Onsite Wastewater Systems. NSF/EPA, 1979, $22.50. Ann Arbor Science Publishers, Inc., Box 1425, Ann Arbor, Michigan 48106.

Septic Tank Care. U.S. Public Health Service, 1978, 6 pages, $ .60. S/N 017-002-00068-6.

Septic Tank Practices: A Primer for Home Sewage Systems. Peter Warshall, 1978, 156 pages, $3.95. Anchor Press, Doubleday & Co., 245 Park Avenue, New York, New York 10017.

Soils and Septic Tanks. USDA, Soil Conservation Service, 1972, 12 pages, $ .35. S/N 001-000-02914-2.

Stop the Five-Gallon Flush: A Survey of Alternative Waste Disposal Systems. McGill University, 1976, 60 pages, $4. Minimum Cost Housing Studies Group, School of Architecture, McGill University, Montreal, Canada.

Wastewater Recycle/Reuse and Water Conservation Systems. NSF Standard Number 41, 1978, 54 pages, $ .75. The National Sanitation Foundation, NSF Building, Ann Arbor, Michigan 48105.

The Waterless Toilet: Is It Right for You? Ron Poitres, 1978, 31 pages, $1. Garden Way Publishing, Charlotte, Vermont 05445.

Water Treatment and Sanitation: A Handbook of Simple Methods for Rural Areas in Developing Countries. H.T. Mann and D. Williamson, 1977 rev. ed., 90 pages, $5.50. Intermediate Tech Publications.

HEATING AND COOLING

INSULATION

Energy Saving Homes: The Arkansas Story. Owens-Corning Fiberglas Corp., 1977, 50 pages. Owens-Corning Fiberglas Corp., Insulation Operating Division, Fiberglas Tower, Toledo, Ohio 43659.

Guide to Constructing an Energy Efficient Home. Owens-Corning Fiberglas Corp., 1978, 86 pages. Owens-Corning Fiberglas Corp.,

Insulation Operating Division, Fiberglas Tower, Toledo, Ohio 43659.

How to Save Money Insulating Your Home. MIMA, revised 1979, 24 pages, $ .30. Mineral Insulation Manufacturers Association, Inc., 382 Springfield Avenue, Summit, New Jersey 07901.

Insulation Manual. MIMA, 1979, 160 pages, $10. Mineral Insulation Manufacturers Association, Inc., 382 Springfield Avenue, Summit, New Jersey 07901.

In the Bank . . . Or Up the Chimney? HUD, 1977 rev. ed., 77 pages, $1.70. S/N 023-000-00411-9.

VENTILATION

The Handbook of Moving Air. American Ventilation Association, 1977, 60 pages. American Ventilation Association, Box 7464, Houston, Texas 77008.

Principles of Attic Ventilation. Air Vent, Inc., 1978, 24 pages, $3. Air Vent, Inc., 6907 North Knoxville Avenue, Peoria, Illinois 61614.

PASSIVE SOLAR HEATING

The First Passive Solar Home Awards. HUD, Office of Policy Development and Research, 1979, 226 pages, $5.50. S/N 023-000-00517-4.

Passive Design Ideas for the Energy-Conscious Architect. A National Solar Heating and Cooling Information Center Publication, 1978, 52 pages. National Solar Heating and Cooling Information Center, Box 1607, Rockville, Maryland 20850.

The Passive Solar Energy Book. Ed Mazria, 1979, 400 pages, $10.95. Rodale Press, Inc., Emmaus, Pennsylvania 18049.

Solar Dwelling Design Concepts. HUD, Office of Policy Development and Research,

1976, 146 pages, $2.30. S/N 023-000-00334-1.

A Survey of Passive Solar Buildings. HUD, Office of Policy Development and Research, 1978, 176 pages, $3.75. S/N 023-000-00437-2.

Thermal Storage Wall Design Manual. New Mexico Solar Energy Association, 1979, 40 pages, $4. New Mexico Solar Energy Association, Box 2004, Santa Fe, New Mexico 87501.

EARTH-SHELTERED HOUSES

Alternatives in Energy Conservation: The Use of Earth-Covered Buildings. National Science Foundation, 1976, 354 pages, $3.25. S/N 038-000-00286-4.

Earth-Sheltered Housing Design: Guidelines, Examples and References. The Underground Space Center, 1978, 300 pages, $11. The Underground Space Center, University of Minnesota, 221 Church Street S.E., Minneapolis, Minnesota 55455.

ACTIVE SOLAR HEATING

Building the Solar Home: Some Early Lessons Learned. HUD, Office of Policy Development and Research, 1978, 36 pages, $1.70. S/N 023-000-00455-1.

Buying Solar. HEW, Office of Consumer Affairs, 1976, 72 pages, $1.85. S/N 041-018-00120-4.

Climatic Atlas of the United States. U.S. Department of Commerce, 1977, 80 pages, $6. U.S. Department of Commerce, NOAA, National Climatic Center, Federal Building, Asheville, North Carolina 28801.

Homeowner's Guide to Solar Heating. Holly Lyman Antolini, ed., 1978, 96 pages, $2.95. Sunset Books, Lane Publishing Co., Menlo Park, California 94025.

HUD Intermediate Minimum Property Standards Supplement: Solar Heating and Domestic Hot Water Systems. HUD Document No. 4930.2, 1977, $12. Superintendent of Documents.

Performance Testing of a Residential Solar Climate Control System Using a Water Trickle Collector and a Water-Rockbed Thermal Storage During a Winter Period. DOE, Report # HCP/M-2284, 1979, $8. NTIS.

Proceedings of the Department of Energy's Solar Update. DOE, 1978, 226 pages, $4.25. S/N 061-000-00103-4.

Proceedings of the Solar Energy Consumer Protection Workshop: Opening and Final Plenary Sessions; May 3–6, 1978; Atlanta, Georgia. DOE, 1979, 214 pages, $9.25. NTIS.

Solar Heating and Cooling Demonstration Program: A Descriptive Summary of HUD Cycle 2 Solar Residential Projects. HUD, Office of Policy Development and Research, 1977, 103 pages, $2.35. S/N 023-000-00389-9.

The Solar Home Book. Bruce Anderson with Michael Riordan, 1976, 297 pages, $8.50. Cheshire Books, Church Hill, Harrisville, New Hampshire 03450.

Solar Hot Water and Your Home. A National Solar Heating and Cooling Information Center Publication, 1978, 14 pages. National Solar Heating and Cooling Information Center, Box 1607, Rockville, Maryland 20850.

HEAT PUMPS

A Ground Water Heat Pump Anthology. National Water Wells Association, 1978, 52 pages. National Water Wells Association, 500 West Wilson Bridge Road, Worthington, Ohio 43085.

Ground Water Heat Pumps. National Water Well Association, 1978, 12 pages, $.50. National Water Well Association, 500

West Wilson Bridge Road, Worthington, Ohio 43085.

Heat Pump Technology: A Survey of Technical Developments, Market Prospects and Research Needs. DOE, 1978, 464 pages, $6.25. S/N 061-000-00092-5.

WOOD BURNING

The Complete Book of Heating with Wood. Larry Gay, 1974, 128 pages, $3.50. Garden Way Publishing, Charlotte, Vermont 05445.

Home Heating: Systems . . . Fuels . . . Controls. USDA, Farmers' Bulletin No. 2235, 1977 rev. ed., 22 pages, $1.10. S/N 001-000-03470-7.

Jøtul Resource Book on the Art of Heating with Wood. Kristia Associates, 1976, rev. ed., 64 pages, $1. Kristia Associates, Box 1118, Portland, Maine 04104.

The Woodburner's Encyclopedia. Jay Shelton and Andrew Shapiro, 1976, 155 pages, $7.95. Vermont Crossroads Press, Waitsfield, Vermont 05673.

Wood Furnaces & Boilers. Larry Gay, 1978, 32 pages, $1. Garden Way Publishing, Charlotte, Vermont 05445.

*Wood Heat. John Vivian, 1978 rev. ed., 428 pages, $7.95. Rodale Press, Inc., Emmaus, Pennsylvania 18049.

GENERATING YOUR OWN ELECTRICITY

HARNESSING THE WIND

Federal Wind Energy Program, Summary Report, January 1978. DOE, 1978, 71 pages. S/N 061-000-00050-0.

*A Guide to Commercially Available Wind Machines. Rocky Flats Plant, prepared with the assistance of the American Wind Energy Association, Report #RFP-2836/3533/78/3, 1979, 121 pages, $7.25. NTIS.

Harnessing the Wind for Home Energy. Dermot McGuigan, 1978, 134 pages, $4.95. Garden Way Publishing, Charlotte, Vermont 05445.

Is the Wind a Practical Source of Energy for You? Rockwell International Energy Systems Group, 1979, 8 pages. Rockwell International, Rocky Flats Plant, Energy Systems Group, Box 464, Golden, Colorado 80401.

Proceedings of the Second Workshop on Wind Energy Conversion Systems. NSF/ERDA, 1975, 601 pages, $10. S/N 038-000-00258-9.

*Sencenbaugh Wind Electric Catalog (1078). James Sencenbaugh, 1978, 48 pages, $2. Sencenbaugh Wind Electric Company, Box 11174, Palo Alto, California 94306.

Wind and Windspinners: A Nuts 'n Bolts Approach to Wind-Electric Systems. Michael Hackleman, 1974, 115 pages, $7.95. Earthmind/Peace Press, 4844 Hirsh Road, Mariposa, California 95338.

Wind Energy Conversion. U.S. Department of Energy, 1977, 39 pages, $1.60. S/N 060-000-00061-1.

*Wind Energy Conversion Systems: Proceedings of a Workshop Held in Washington, D.C., June 11–13, 1973. National Science Foundation, PB-231-341, 1973, 258 pages, $8.50. NTIS.

Wind Machines. National Science Foundation, 1976, 77 pages, $2.25. S/N 038-000-00272-4.

Windmill Power for City People. CSA, 1977, 65 pages, $2.60. S/N 059-000-00001-2.

*Wind Power for Farms, Homes and Small Industry. J. Park and D. Schwind, Report #RFP-2841/1270/78/4, 1979, 230 pages, $9.50. NTIS.

Wind Power for Your Home: How to Make the

Wind's Energy Work for You. George Sullivan, 1978, 127 pages, $4.95. Cornerstone Library, Simon & Schuster, Inc., 1230 Avenue of the Americas, New York, New York 10020.

HARNESSING WATER POWER

Harnessing Water Power for Home Energy. Dermot McGuigan, 1978, 101 pages, $4.95. Garden Way Publishing, Charlotte, Vermont 05445.

Low-Cost Development of Small Water Power Sites. Hans W. Hamm, 1967, 50 pages, $2.50. Volunteers in Technical Assistance, 3706 Rhode Island Avenue, Mt. Rainier, Maryland 20822.

FUEL CELLS

Hydrogen Technology for Energy. David A. Mathis, 1977, 286 pages, $32. Noyes Data Corp., Noyes Building, Park Ridge, New Jersey 07656.

Wind Powered Hydrogen Electric Systems for Farm and Rural Use. Institute of Gas Technology, Report #AER-75-00772, 1975, 158 pages, $8. NTIS.

SOLAR CELLS

Converting Solar Energy into Electricity. DOE, Division of Solar Energy, 1976, 36 pages, $1.10. S/N 052-070-03525-1.

Photovoltaic Program: Program Summary. DOE, Division of Solar Energy, 1978, 221 pages, $4.

The Solarex Guide to Solar Electricity. Solarex Technical Staff, 1979, 143 pages, $5.95. Solarex Corp., 1335 Piccard Drive, Rockville, Maryland 20850.

PRODUCT SOURCE LIST

Aermotor, Box 1364, Conway, Arkansas 72032

Aero-Power Systems, Inc., 2398 4th Street, Berkeley, California 94710

Air Vent, Inc., 6907 North Knoxville Avenue, Peoria, Illinois 61614

Aladdin Industries, Inc., Kerosene Lamp Division, Nashville, Tennessee 37210

Alcoa Building Products, Inc., Suite 1200, 2 Allegheny Center, Pittsburgh, Pennsylvania 15212

Allied Water Corp., Pier 5, San Francisco, California 94111

AMC Cuno Division, 400 Research Parkway, Meriden, Connecticut 06450

Aquappliances, Inc., 135 Sunshine Lane, San Marcos, California 92069

Aquasaver, Inc., 7902 Belair Road, Baltimore, Maryland 21236

(Aquaspring) New Medical Techniques, Inc., Masons Island Road, Box 429, Mystic, Connecticut 06355

Arkla Industries, Inc., Box 534, Evansville, Indiana 47704

The Ashley Heater Co., 1604 17th Avenue S.W., Box 730, Sheffield, Alabama 35660

Automatic Power, Inc., Box 18738, Houston, Texas 77023

Bellway Manufacturing Co., Grafton, Vermont 05146

The Big Outdoors People, Inc., 26600 Fallbrook Avenue, Wyoming, Minnesota 55092

(Canadian Step-Stove) New Hampshire Stove Co., RFD 1, Brentwood, New Hampshire 03833

(Carousel Toilets) Enviroscope, Inc., Box 2933, Newport Beach, California 92663

Carrier Air Conditioning, Carrier Parkway, Syracuse, New York 13221

The Cawley Stove Co., Inc., 27 North Washington Street, Boyertown, Pennsylvania 19512

CertainTeed Corp., Shelter Material Group, Box 860, Valley Forge, Pennsylvania 19482

Charmaster Products, Inc., 2307 Highway 2 West, Grand Rapids, Minnesota 55744

Clivus Multrum U.S.A., Inc., 14A Eliot Street, Cambridge, Massachusetts 02138

Coldstar Corp., 29240 Phillips Street, Box 1665, Elkhart, Indiana 46514

The Coleman Company, Inc., 250 North St. Francis, Wichita, Kansas 67201

Cromaglass Corp., Box 3215, Williamsport, Pennsylvania 17701

Jim Cullen Enterprises, Box 732, Laytonville, California 95454

Culligan U.S.A., Northbrook, Illinois 60062

Sam Daniels Co., Box 868, Montpelier, Vermont 05602

Daystar Corp., 90 Cambridge Street, Burlington, Massachusetts 01803

DeepRock Manufacturing Co., Box 1, Opelika, Alabama 36801

Dempster Industries, Inc., 711 South 6th Street, Box 848, Beatrice, Nebraska 68310

(Destroilet) Marland Environmental Systems, Inc., 227 North Main Street, Walworth, Wisconsin 53184

Dometic Sales Corp., 2320 Industrial Parkway, Box 490, Elkhart, Indiana 46515

Duo-Matic Division, 450 West 169th Street, South Holland, Illinois 60473

Duo-Therm, La Grange, Indiana 46761

The Earth Stove, Box 70, Walpole, New Hampshire 03608

Eastern Environmental Controls, Inc., Box 475, Chestertown, Maryland 21620

Edmund Scientific Co., 1984 Edscorp Building, Barrington, New Jersey 08007

(Efel) Southport Stoves, Inc., 248 Tolland Street, East Hartford, Connecticut 06108

Emerson Electric Co., 8100 West Florissant Street, St. Louis, Missouri 63136

Energy Research & Development Corp., Town Line Road, Tomah, Wisconsin 54660

Enertech, Inc., Box 420, Norwich, Vermont 05055

Envirovac, 701 Lawton Avenue, Beloit, Wisconsin 53511

Fisher Stoves, River Road, Bow, New Hampshire 03301

Ford Sunglas, Ford Glass Division, 1 Parklane Boulevard, Dearborn, Michigan 48126

Franco-Belge Foundries of America, Inc., 70 Pine Street, New York, New York 10005

Friedrich Air Conditioning & Refrigeration, 4200 North Pan American Expressway, Box 1540, San Antonio, Texas 78295

Generac Corp., Box 8, Waukesha, Wisconsin 53187

General Electric Co., Heat Pumps, Appliance Park, Louisville, Kentucky 40225

General Electric Co., Solar Heating & Cooling-Marketing, Box 13601, Philadelphia, Pennsylvania 19101

Grumman Energy Systems, 4175 Veterans Memorial Highway, Ronkonkoma, New York 11779

H.C. Products Co., Box 68, Princeton, Illinois 61559

Heatilator Division, Vega Industries, Inc., West Saunders Street, Mount Pleasant, Iowa 52641

Heller-Aller Co., Perry & Oakwood Street, Napoleon, Ohio 43545

Honeywell, Inc., 2600 Ridgeway Road, Minneapolis, Minnesota 55413

(HS-Tarm) Tekton Corp., Conway, Massachusetts 01341

Hunter Olde Tyme Ceiling Fan Division, Robbins & Myers, Inc., Box 14775, Memphis, Tennessee 38114

Hydraform Products Corp., Box 2409, Rochester, New Hampshire 03867

Hydroheat Division, Ridgway Steel Fabricators, Inc., Box 382, Ridgway, Pennsylvania 15853

Independent Power Developers, Box 1467, Noxon, Montana 59853

Insulating Shade Company, Inc., Box 282, Branford, Connecticut 06405

Jacobs Wind Electric, Inc., Route 13, Box 722, Fort Myers, Florida 33908

Jacuzzi Bros., Inc., 11511 New Benton Highway, Little Rock, Arkansas 72203

Jet Aeration Co., 750 Alpha Drive, Cleveland, Ohio 44143

Johns-Manville, Ken-Caryl Ranch, Denver, Colorado 80217

(Jøtul) Kristia Associates, 343 Forest Avenue, Box 1118, Portland, Maine 04104

Kalwall, Solar Components Division, Box 237, Manchester, New Hampshire 03105

Kedco, Inc., 9016 Aviation Boulevard, Inglewood, California 90301

Kohler Co., Kohler, Wisconsin 53044

Lake Shore Industries, 2810 North Reynolds Boulevard, Toledo, Ohio 43615

The James Leffel & Co., 426 East Street, Springfield, Ohio 45501

Lennox Industries, Inc., 350 South 12th Avenue, Box 280, Marshalltown, Iowa 50158

Leslie-Locke, Ohio Street, Lodi, Ohio 44254

LOF Solar Energy Systems, Libbey-Owens-Ford Co., 1701 East Broadway, Toledo, Ohio 43605

Longwood Furnace Corp., Gallatin, Missouri 64640

The Majestic Co., 245 Erie Street, Huntington, Indiana 46750

Mansfield Sanitary, Inc., 150 First Street, Perryville, Ohio 44864

Marathon Heater Co., Box 165, RD #2, Marathon, New York 13803

Martin Industries, Building Products Division, Box 128, Florence, Alabama 35630

McCulloch Corp., 5400 Alla Road, Box 92180, Los Angeles, California 90009

Metalbestos Systems, 1820 East Fargo, Nampa, Indiana 83651

Microphor, Inc., 452 East Hill Road, Box 490, Willits, California 94590

(Morsø) Southport Stoves, Inc., 248 Tolland Street, East Hartford, Connecticut 06108

(Mullbänk) R.E.C. of U.S., Inc., 9800 West Bluemound Road, Milwaukee, Wisconsin 53226

Nashua Doubleheat Woodstoves, Heathdelle Sales Associates, Inc., RFD #4, Box 153, Laconia, New Hampshire 03246

Nayadic Sciences, Inc., R.D. #2, Clarks Summit, Pennsylvania 18411

Norcold, 1501 Michigan Street, Sidney, Ohio 45365

E.A. Nord Co., Everett, Washington 98206

(Nunsun) National Metalizing, Cranberry, New Jersey 08512

Olin Brass, East Alton, Illinois 62024

Onan, 1400 73rd Avenue, Minneapolis, Minnesota 55432

Oneida Heater Co., Box 148, Oneida, New Hampshire 13421

Owens-Corning Fiberglas Corp., Fiberglas Tower, Toledo, Ohio 43659

Owens-Illinois, Inc., Box 1035, Toledo, Ohio 43666

The Parlour Fan, Fasco Industries, Inc., Box 150, Fayetteville, North Carolina 28302

Pease Co., Ever-Strait Division, 2001 Troy Avenue, New Castle, Indiana 47362

Portland Stove Foundry, 57 Kennebec Street, Portland, Maine 04104

PPG Industries, Inc., One Gateway Center, Pittsburgh, Pennsylvania 15222

Preway, Inc., Wisconsin Rapids, Wisconsin 54494

PureCycle, 1668 Valtec Lane, Box 671, Boulder, Colorado 80306

Quench Water Purifier, Terraqua Products, Inc., 915 South Grand Street, San Pedro, California 90731

Real Gas and Electric Co., Box A, Guerneville, California 95446

Red Jacket Pumps Division, Wylain, Inc., Box 3888, Davenport, Iowa 52808

(Reflecto-Shield) Madico, Inc., 64 Industrial Parkway, Woburn, Massachusetts 01801

Revere Solar and Architectural Products, Inc., Box 151, Rome, New York 13440

Rheem, 7600 South Kedzie Avenue, Chicago, Illinois 60652

Riteway, Box 153, Harrisonburg, Virginia 22801

(Rohn Towers) Unarco-Rohn, 6718 West Plank Road, Box 2000, Peoria, Illinois 61601

Rolladen, Inc., 3930 North 29th Avenue, Hollywood, Florida 33020

S/A Energy Division, Crossroads Park Drive, Liverpool, New York 13088

(Scotchtint) 3M Company, Box 33121, St. Paul, Minnesota 55101

Sears, Roebuck & Co., Sears Tower, Chicago, Illinois 60684

Sencenbaugh Wind Electric Co., Box 11174, Palo Alto, California 94306

Sensor Technology, Inc., 21012 Lassen Street, Chatsworth, California 91311

Shenandoah Manufacturing Co., Inc., Box 839, Harrisonburg, Virginia 22801

Short Stoppers Electric, Rt. 4, Box 471B, Coos Bay, Oregon 97420

Simpson International Door, Simpson Timber Co., 900 Fourth Avenue, Seattle, Washington 98164

Small Hydroelectric Systems & Equipment, 15220 S.R. 530, Arlington, Washington 98223

(Solarcraft) State Industries, Inc., Ashland City, Tennessee 37015

Solar Energy Products, Inc., Drawer 1048, Gainesville, Florida 32602

Solarex Corp., 1335 Piccard Drive, Rockville, Maryland 20850

(Solaris) Thomason Solar Homes, Inc., 609 Cedar Avenue, Oxon Hill, Fort Washington, Maryland, Washington, D.C. 20022

Solaron, 300 Galleria Tower, 720 South Colorado Boulevard, Denver, Colorado 80222

Solar Power Corp., 20 Cabot Road, Woburn, Massachusetts 01801

(Sol-Ar-Tile) Architectural Research Corp., 13030 Wayne Road, Livonia, Michigan 48105

Sparco, c/o Enertech, Inc., Box 420, Norwich, Vermont 05055

Steelcraft Manufacturing Co., 9017 Blue Ash Road, Cincinnati, Ohio 45242

(Styrofoam TG) The Dow Chemical Co., Midland, Michigan 48640

(Sunpak Solar Collectors) Owens-Illinois, Inc., Box 1035, Toledo, Ohio 43666

(Sun Panel) LOF Solar Energy Systems, Libbey-Owens-Ford, 1701 East Broadway, Toledo, Ohio 43695

Sunworks Division, Enthone, Inc., Box 1004, New Haven, Connecticut 06508

Superior Fireplace Co., 4325 Artesia Avenue, Fullerton, California 92633

Teledyne Energy Systems, 110 West Timonium Road, Timonium, Maryland 21093

Tempwood, Mohawk Industries, Inc., Box 71, Adams, Massachusetts 01220

Thermograte Enterprises, Inc., 2785 North

Fairview Avenue, St. Paul, Minnesota 55113

Thetford Corp., Waste Treatment Products Division, Box 1285, Ann Arbor, Michigan 48106

Triangle Engineering Co., Drawer 38271, Houston, Texas 77088

(Tripolymer) C.P. Chemical Co., Inc., 25 Home Street, Yonkers, New York 10606

Unigen, Inc., 194 West Stone Street, Almont, Michigan 48003

Upland Stove Co., Inc., Box 87, Greene, New York 13778

U.S. Stove Co., Box 151, South Pittsburgh, Tennessee 37380

Vermont Castings, Inc., Prince Street, Randolph, Vermont 05060

Vermont DownDrafter, Vermont Woodstove Co., Box 1016, Bennington, Vermont 05201

Westinghouse Electric Corp., Solar Heating/Cooling Systems, 5205 Leesburg Pike, Falls Church, Virginia 22041

Winco Division, Dyna Technology, Inc., 7850 Metro Parkway, Minneapolis, Minnesota 55420

York Division, Borg-Warner Corp., Box 1592, York, Pennsylvania 17405

Yukon Industries, 229 Wycliff, St. Paul, Minnesota 55114

Zomeworks Corp., Box 712, Albuquerque, New Mexico 87103

INDEX

Note: Page numbers in italics indicate illustrative material and tables.

Wood
  to burn in wood stoves *(cont'd)*
    sources of, 133
    stacking, 134
  insulating value of, 62
  for multi-fuel furnaces, 137, 139, 140
  see also Fireplaces; Multi-fuel furnaces; Wood
    stoves
Wood-burning furnaces, 137–41, *137, 138, 139*
Woodlots, 133
Wood stoves, 1, 2, 9, 103, 114, 125–36, 145, 146
  airtight, 125–36
  for auxiliary heat, 5, 8, *82,* 101, 136, 145
  blowers, 130, 131, 132
  breaking in, 133
  cooking surfaces on, 127, 129, 130, 145
  costs of, 127, 128, 129, 130, 131, 132, 133
  creosote build-up, 130, 132, 133, 134
  downdrafters, 130–33, *131, 132*

efficiency of, 127, *128,* 132
Franklin, 124, 130
freestanding fireplaces and fireplace/stoves,
  122–25, *123, 125, 126,* 140
heat circulators, 130–33, *131, 132*
placement of, 129–30
as primary heat source, 8
shapes of, 127
stovepipe for, 130
wood to burn in, 130, 133–36
see also Fireplaces; Multi-fuel furnaces

Yellow Pages, 98, 169
York groundwater-to-air heat pumps, 109
Yukon Industries, 139

Zero-clearance fireplaces, 118–20, *118, 119*
Zomeworks Corporation, *79,* 80, 81, 83
Zoning codes, *see* Building and/or zoning codes